Writing Research Papers in the Social Sciences

James D. Lester
Austin Peay State University

James D. Lester, Jr.
Clayton State University

PEARSON
Longman

New York San Francisco Boston
London Toronto Sydney Tokyo Singapore Madrid
Mexico City Munich Paris Cape Town Hong Kong Montreal

Acquisitions Editor: Brandon Hight
Marketing Manager: Alexandra Smith
Production Manager: Denise Phillip
Project Coordination, Text Design, and Electronic Page Makeup: Electronic
    Publishing Services Inc., NYC
Cover Design Manager: John Callahan
Cover Designer: Maria Ilardi
Cover Illustration: © Images.com
Senior Manufacturing Buyer: Dennis J. Para
Printer and Binder: R.R. Donnelley and Sons
Cover Printer: Lehigh Press

For permission to use copyrighted material, grateful acknowledgment is made to the
copyright holders on pp. C-1–C-2, which are hereby made part of this copyright page.

Library of Congress Cataloging-in-Publication Data

Lester, James D.
    Writing research papers in the social sciences / James D. Lester, Sr., James D.
Lester, Jr.
        p. cm.
    Includes index.
    ISBN 0-321-26763-X
    1. Social sciences–Authorship–Handbooks, manuals, etc. 2. Social sciences–
Research–Methodology–Handbooks, manuals, etc. 3. English language–Rhetoric–
Handbooks, manuals, etc. 4. Report writing–Handbooks, manuals, etc. I. Lester,
James D. II. Title.
    PE1479.S62L47 2005
    808'.0663–dc22

                                                    2005029394

Copyright © 2006 by Pearson Education, Inc.

Please visit us at www.ablongman.com/lester

ISBN 0-321-26763-X

1 2 3 4 5 6 7 8 9 10 — DOC— 08 07 06 05

Contents

This complete research guide provides students and instructors with academic guidelines for writing and documenting research projects in the social sciences. The text supplies updates and directives for research papers written in APA style as well as electronic publishing.

Confirmation of Academic Styles

The Internet now plays, as it does with other aspects of our lives, a major role in research by our students and professional writers. This fact forces style guides like this one to keep pace. In the new publication manual of the *American Psychological Association*—the fifth edition—the staff "took aim at the moving target of electronic referencing and manuscript preparation" (Preface).

Publication Manual of the American Psychological Association. 5th ed. Washington: APA, 2001. Fifth Printing, 2002.

With the APA manual as a guide, *Writing Research Papers in the Social Sciences* emphasizes the role of field research while moving beyond the use of books and periodicals to stress the importance of computer technology and the Internet in modern research.

Help with Electronic Research and Presentation

Computers and the electronic revolution are so pervasive in research writing today that we cannot assign such work to a single chapter. Instead, every chapter of the text touches on the Internet's effect on topic searches, discovery of source material, gathering notes and drafting the paper, plagiarism and academic integrity, and, of course, documentation of the sources.

Writing Research Papers in the Social Sciences takes students step by step through the documentation of Internet sources. It also spends considerable space in helping students blend electronic citations into their writing. A checklist, "Evaluating Internet Sources," helps students gauge the quality of Internet articles.

Student Papers

Student writing examples show how real students research and draft papers on a wide range of topics. With documented manuscripts, they demonstrate different writing approaches for a research project in the social sciences.

Jamie Johnston "Prehistoric Wars: A Study in Social Hatred and Cruelty" (Theoretical essay)

Valerie Nesbitt-Hall "Arranged Marriages: The Revival is Online" (Empirical research)

Julie A. Strasshofer "The Effects of Communication Skills on Development of Interpersonal Relationships"(Research proposal)

Kaci Holz "Gender Communication: A Review of the Literature" (Literature review)

Expanded List of Sources by Disciplines

The Internet has also changed college libraries, so a list of books by discipline is insufficient. For each discipline, from Anthropology to Women's Studies, we refer students to the primary guides and indexes among the library's bound holdings and to the Internet sites that have gained solid academic acceptance, from *JSTOR* to *Educom* and *Medweb*.

The Writing Process

Writing Research Papers in the Social Sciences guides students through the necessary steps in a natural sequence.

Getting Started. We explain the reasons for writing a research paper and the ways to discover an academic topic.

Gathering Sources. We introduce field research and encourage students to conduct interviews, surveys, and other techniques for gathering empirical evidence in Chapter 3. Following that, we take them into the library to explain not only the printed materials but also electronic sources that can be accessed only through their identification number. Filtering the good Internet sources from the bad is a major theme of Chapter 5.

Plagiarism. Before students go any further, we discuss academic integrity in Chapter 6. We show what must be done when borrowing from sources and provide basic rules for avoiding plagiarism.

Critical Reading. We discuss at length the methods for finding sources that are reliable and worthy of paraphrase or quotation.

Getting Organized. Chapters 8 and 9 direct students in methods of organizing the paper and taking notes so the paper will meet the demands of academic form and style.

Blending the Sources. Chapter 10 is devoted to the most difficult task of all: drafting a manuscript that displays the student's voice while blending sources effectively into the narrative flow.

References. Chapter 11 presents the details for properly documenting sources and preparing the References page in APA style.

Research Formats. Chapters 12, 13, and 14 give specific directives for completing a theoretical essay, a report of an empirical study, and a review of literature respectively. Chapter 15 presents the details for creating electronic projects and documents.

Guidelines and Links. Appendix A is a glossary of the rules and techniques for preparing a manuscript. Appendix B, "A Listing of Reference Works for Your General Topic," gives a list of the best reference books in the library as well as excellent academic Internet sites. These lists are arranged alphabetically by discipline, from Anthropology and Art to Women's Studies and Writing.

Acknowledgments

The preface would not be complete without the recognition of many key people who served in the development of the first edition of *Writing Research Papers in the Social Sciences.*

We thank Linda Clark, a psychologist for Clayton County Schools in Georgia, who served as research assistant. For helping with the appendix of reference sources, we thank Sarah Dye, of Elgin College in Illinois. As you will see in the text and the ancillary material, we owe thanks to several students: Jamie Johnston, Valerie Nesbitt-Hall, Kaci Holz, and Julie A. Strasshofer.

For editorial assistance that kept us focused, we thank the Longman group headed by Joseph Opiela, vice president and publisher. Special thanks must go to Brandon Hight, acquisitions editor, and Denise Phillip, production manager. Finally, we want to recognize a great group of reviewers who offered penetrating and perceptive suggestions for this new edition: Catherine R. Baratta, Central Connecticut State University; Rebecca Brand, Villanova University; Tammy Conard-Salvo, Purdue University; Nancy J. Cooley, University of Maine; Joe Essid, University of Richmond; Marianna Footo Linz, Marshall University; Lisa Hazlett, University of South Dakota; Carolyn Hollman, Southern New Hampshire University; Mary Kiernan-Stern, George Mason University; Sherri B. Lantinga, Dordt College; Patricia Loesche, University of Washington; John D. Murray, Georgia Southern University; Elwin Myers, Texas A&M University—Corpus Christi; Carol J. Schuck, Ivy Tech State College–Central Indiana; Aimee Szilagyi, Middlesex County College; James B. Tuttle, Shepherd University; Thomas Waller, Tallahassee Community College; and Kristin Yonko, Delaware Technical and Community College.

As always, we are grateful for the support of our friends and peers. Most importantly, we acknowledge the support of our family. Martha, Mark, Debbie, Caleb, and Sarah have provided unending enthusiasm and encouragement.

James D. Lester, Sr.
jamesdlester@aol.com

James D. Lester, Jr.
jlester5@comcast.net

As a member of the academic community, you will be asked by instructors to write researched essays. The emphasis on research means quite simply that you must go beyond what you already know and think to find information from a variety of sources and incorporate the ideas and words of others in your manuscript. Thus, you will soon need to access the Internet, check out books from the library, and perhaps interview several people. You will absorb the words and opinions of experts and bring them to bear on your topic. You will become a facilitator, one who pulls together and makes sense of divergent views.

A research assignment may take various forms, such as these:

- "Write a paper that explores the former Berlin Wall as a symbol for the rise and fall of communism in the Soviet Union."
- "What are you curious about? Find a problem, question, or issue that piques your interest and that requires research."
- "Defend the contributions to American society of a famous but controversial person, such as Martin Luther King or Alexander Hamilton."
- "Conduct a survey of students and faculty on the problems of campus parking and discuss the implications of your findings."

These four examples merely touch the surface of possible assignments, but they demonstrate an important point: A research assignment may be open-ended or highly specific. Whatever kind of assignment you receive, you will need to follow a logical procedure for developing the paper. That is what *Writing Research Papers in the Social Sciences* is about. We designed it to carry you step by step to a finished research project.

Frequently-Asked Questions and Where to Find Answers

- Why do research at all?
  - Chapter 1 explains why we do research and report our findings.
- Need to find a research topic?
  - Chapter 2 tells how to find a topic that will interest you and your readers.
- Need to find information?
  - Chapters 3, 4, and 5 show you how to gather data through field research and laboratory testing, as well as to find information in the library and on the Internet.
- What about plagiarism and publishing on a Web site?
  - Chapter 6 addresses matters of integrity and honesty in reporting, especially in this electronic age when downloading the words of others is so easy.

- Which sources are reliable and worth citing?
  - Chapter 7 helps you judge sources so you know which to cite in your paper and which to dismiss.
- Time to get organized?
  - Chapter 8 helps you organize your notes and ideas for a focused paper.
- Need guidelines for taking notes?
  - Chapter 9 shows how to write effective notes that will transfer easily into your text.
- What about blending the sources and drafting the manuscript?
  - Chapter 10 gives your writing an academic style, one that blends sources effectively into your prose and encourages strength and purpose in your introduction, body, and conclusion.
- How do I list my references?
  - Chapter 11 presents the details for properly documenting sources and preparing the References page in APA style.
- What if I need to write a certain type of essay or focus on a specific area of study?
  - Chapters 12, 13, and 14 give specific directives for completing a theoretical essay, a report of an empirical study, and a review of literature respectively.
- What if I need to create a slide show for my findings or post my information on the Web?
  - Chapter 15 presents the details for creating electronic projects and documents.
- What about all the little details about formatting, numbering, ellipsis points, and so forth?
  - Appendix A provides a glossary of the rules and techniques for preparing a manuscript.
- Need a list of the best scholarly sources?
  - Appendix B, "Finding Sources for a Selected Discipline," gives you a list of the best reference books in the library as well as excellent academic Internet sites. These lists are arranged alphabetically by discipline, from Anthropology and Art to Women's Studies and Writing.

Writing Research Papers in the Social Sciences provides detailed, up-to-date information on the methods of scholarly research in APA style and writing from sources. We encourage you to write with the computer and conduct research on the Internet as well as in the field. Moreover, this text provides guidelines for publishing your paper in an electronic form, not merely on paper. We welcome thoughts and suggestions you may have on this text as you work through it. We wish you well!

James D. Lester, Sr.
jamesdlester@aol.com

James D. Lester, Jr.
jlester5@comcast.net

Writing from Research

At some point you will write a fully developed research report based on your investigations and reading. This text gives complete coverage of the process of report writing in the social sciences and the techniques for meeting the demands of form and style. Here are examples of such reports:

- A report based on interviews with minimum wage workers.
- A field report on a speed reading unit in a fifth-grade class to test reading comprehension.
- An observation of student drivers on campus parking lots, with a subsequent report.

These papers require investigation followed by a report on the nature of the project, the methods employed, the results of the study, and the implications to be drawn from the findings. Papers similar to these will appear on your assignment syllabus during your first two years of college, and the writing assignments will increase in frequency in upper-division courses. This text lessens the pressure by showing you how to conduct research in the field, in the library, and on the Internet. It also demonstrates the correct methods for designing the paper and documenting your reports.

Keep in mind that social science research is used in different ways, in different amounts, and for different purposes as instructors make demands on your talents of investigation into social issues and your ability to write reports. This text therefore introduces research as an engaging, sometimes exciting pursuit on several fronts—the lab, the field, the library, the Internet, the control group in a classroom, and so forth.

1a Why Do Research?

Instructors ask you to report on your investigations for several reasons:

Research teaches methods of discovery. It asks you to discover what you know about a topic and what others can teach you. Beyond reading articles and books, writing in the social sciences usually requires you to observe and experiment. The process tests your curiosity as you probe a complex subject to confirm a hypothesis, which is a theory requiring testing to prove its validity. For example, the hypothesis "A child's toy is determined by television commercials" requires an investigation of the literature as well as a survey of parents, your observation of children at a toy store, or your interview with a set of children (see pages 4–5 for more information about writing a hypothesis). You will learn to make a claim, research it carefully, and synthesize your ideas and discoveries with the knowledge and opinions of others.

Research teaches investigative skills. Your success will depend on your negotiating various sources of information taken from reference books in the library and computer databases to an observation of schoolchildren and interviews with their teachers. As you conduct research by observation, interviews, surveys, and laboratory experiments, you will gain experience in additional methods of investigation.

Research teaches critical thinking. As you examine the evidence on your subject, you will learn to discriminate between useful information and unfounded opinion, and between ill-conceived experiments and reliable evidence. Some sources, such as those on the Internet, may provide timely, reliable material, but they may also entice you with worthless and undocumented opinions.

Research teaches logic. Like a judge in the courtroom, you must make perceptive judgments about the issues surrounding a specific topic. Your discussion at the end of the report will be based on your findings and the insights you can offer. Your readers will rely on your logical response to your reading, observation, interviews, and testing.

Research teaches the basic ingredients of argument. You will be asked to discuss the implications of your findings. You should, in most cases, advance a hypothesis and then prove or disprove it. For example, if you argue that "nonverbal communication can reveal personality traits to an experienced psychologist," you will learn to anticipate challenges to your hypothesis and defend it with your evidence.

> Note: For help with making a claim and establishing a hypothesis, see 1d, pages 3–4.

Note: For help with making a claim and establishing a hypothesis, see 1d, pages 3–4.

1b   Learning to Write Citations for Your Sources

Research reports in the social sciences must follow certain conventions to give uniformity to articles written by millions of scholars; in like manner, the rules must govern your written assignments in psychology, sociology, education, political science, social work, and similar fields.

Governed by guidelines from the *American Psychological Association*, this format employs the *name and year system*, which asks you to provide the last name of your source followed immediately by the year, set within parentheses. Page numbers should be added if the citation includes a quotation.

Roberts (2004) found significant variations in timed responses by participants.

Details of the source are presented in a references list at the end of the paper. A reference entry looks like this:

Roberts, R. C. (2004). Timed responses of fifth graders to flash cards. *Education News, 15,* 14–19.

This system is explained fully in later chapters.

1c Learning the Variations in Form and Content

You may choose among three types of articles, or your instructor will specify one of these:

- The theoretical article.
- The report of empirical study.
- The review article.

Theoretical Article

The theoretical article draws on existing research to examine a theory. This type of paper is the one you will most likely write as a freshman or sophomore. You will trace the development of a theory, compare theories, or discuss the controversy surrounding a theory. Your analysis will examine the literature to arrive at the current thinking on topics such as autism, criminal behavior, dysfunctional families, and learning disorders. The theoretical article generally accomplishes four aims:

> Note: This type of paper, with an example, is discussed fully in Chapter 12, "Writing the Theoretical Essay," pages 163–174.

1. Identifies a problem or theory that has historical implications in the scientific community.
2. Traces the development and history of the theory.
3. Provides a systematic analysis of articles that explore the problem.
4. Arrives at a judgment and discussion of the prevailing theory.

Report of an Empirical Study

When you conduct field research and perform laboratory testing, you must report the details of your original research. The empirical report accomplishes four purposes:

1. Introduces the problem or hypothesis investigated and explains the purpose of the work.

2. Describes the method used to conduct the research, including the design, procedures, tools, subjects, and so forth.

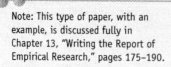

Note: This type of paper, with an example, is discussed fully in Chapter 13, "Writing the Report of Empirical Research," pages 175–190.

3. Reports the results and the basic findings with tables and charts as necessary.

4. Discusses, interprets, and explores the implications of the findings.

Review Article

You may be required to write a critical evaluation of a published article, an entire book, or a set of articles on a common topic. The purpose of the review is to examine the state of current research to determine whether additional work is in order. A review article accomplishes four goals:

1. Defines the problem to clarify the issue or hypothesis.
2. Summarizes the article or book under review.

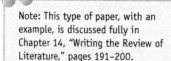

Note: This type of paper, with an example, is discussed fully in Chapter 14, "Writing the Review of Literature," pages 191–200.

3. Analyzes the state of research to discover strengths and possible weaknesses or inconsistencies.

4. Recommends additional research that might grow logically from the work under review.

1d Understanding the Scientific Terminology

Assignments in education, psychology, political science, and the other social sciences will usually require *analysis, definition, comparison,* or a search for *precedents* leading to a *proposal.* Your questions, theories, and hypotheses will motivate your work. Your experiments and testing will usually require a discussion of the *implications* of your findings. Therefore, you should understand the terms buried in the assignment, as explained here.

Theory and Hypothesis

Many scientific investigations begin with a theoretical question. This question is then stated as an assumption that serves as the hypothesis for the research project. The hypothesis is a prediction based on data that directs the research being done. Hence, a hypothesis is a prediction. It is the researcher's supposition or idea about the possible connection or relationship between variables.

> *Theoretical Question:* Do students who live on campus have higher GPAs?
> *Hypothesis:* Students who live on campus have higher GPAs.

This hypothesis is the researcher's idea and calls for research to prove or disprove the statement. In short, a hypothesis is a prediction about the outcome of the study. Briefly, a good research hypothesis has certain elements you can understand:

- It is a brief, clear declarative sentence.
- It often answers a question you are curious about.
- It usually offers an expected relationship, as shown above with students and their grade point averages.
- It implies that the statement can be tested for positive or negative results.

The driving force in social science writing is this system of assumptions that require research to prove or disprove various theories. Section 2e shows you how to frame a working theory or hypothesis and clarifies the differences in the basic forms.

Evaluation

To write a review article, you must evaluate the work in question with clear criteria of judgment. You then explain how the subject meets or fails to meet these criteria. For example, you may face one of these assignments:

- Evaluate the credibility of ACT scores in forecasting academic success.
- Evaluate a distance learning program for home-schooled children.
- Evaluate online therapy for persons with depression.
- Discuss the merits of medication for children with Attention Deficit Hyperactive Disorder (ADHD).

In many ways, every research paper is an evaluation. These few examples just scratch the surface of millions of topics.

Interpretation

To interpret, you must usually answer, "What does it mean?" You may be asked to examine a point of law, offer implications on test results, or interpret variations in scores. Questions often point toward interpretation:

What is Asperger's Syndrome?
What are the implications of anxiety in children?
What do these statistics on children and television violence tell us?
Can you explain your readings on dyslexia to others?

One student, writing about student success, found herself asking interpretive questions: Does joining a Greek letter organization increase the probability that a student will graduate? Does participation in a weekly study group improve student academic achievement in that course?

Definition

An extended definition shows that your subject fits into a selected and well-defined category. Note these examples:

Topic: Computers and Internet Addiction
You will need to define *addictive behavior* at the computer and discuss it from a psychological perspective.

Topic: Peer Pressure
You will need to define such terms as *school anxiety, self-esteem, personal responsibility*, and similar issues relevant to adolescents and teens.

Topic: Plagiarism as Criminal Misdemeanor
You will need to define the term *criminal misdemeanor* and prove that plagiarism fits the definition.

Topic: Political Theory
You will need to define such concepts as *the state, nationalism, political geography, nation building, consent of the governed*, and similar topics.

These examples demonstrate how vague and elusive our language can be. We know what *peer pressure* is in general, but your essay calls for a careful analysis of the terms *anxiety* and *self-esteem*.

A good definition usually includes three elements: the subject *(plagiarism)*; the class to which the subject belongs *(thievery)*; and its difference from others in this class *(theft of another's intellectual property)*. The argument might center on the legal term *misdemeanor*, which is a criminal act less serious than a felony.

Proposal

This type of argument says to the reader, "We should do something." It often has practical applications, as in these examples:

- We should examine and revise the reading curriculum for students in grades K–5 to reflect the influence of television, video games, and the Internet.
- We should cancel all drug testing of athletes because it presumes guilt and demeans the innocent.
- If mental health is important, access to mental health services by children in schools should be increased rather than decreased.

As shown by these examples, the proposal argument calls for action—a change in a program, a change in the law, or an alteration of accepted procedures. The writer must advance the proposal as the paper's hypothesis and must support it with reasons and evidence.

The proposal has three elements:

1. It should convince readers that a problem exists and is serious enough to merit action.

2. It must explain the consequences to convince the reader the proposal has urgency as well as validity.

3. It must address opposing positions on the issue.

Causal Argument

Unlike proposals that predict consequences, causal arguments show that a condition exists because of specific circumstances—that is, something has caused or created this situation, and we need to know why.

For example, one student asked this question: "Why do numerous students, like me, who otherwise score well on the ACT test, score poorly in the math section of the test and, consequently, enroll in developmental courses that offer no college credit?" This question produced a causal hypothesis (see page 18 for more details): The math section of the ACT examination imposes bias against otherwise bright students. The idea merited the student's investigation, so he gathered evidence from surveys, critical reading, and accumulated test results. Ultimately, he wrote passages on bias in the testing program and inadequate instruction in grade school and high school. He discovered specifics about the testing program.

Comparison and Analogy

A scientific argument often compares two subjects to discover differences, make a point, or defend a position. Investigating the behavior of rats in response to a stimulus is a standard assignment for psychology students. In educational research, students might compare a control group of fifth-graders with an experimental group. The stimulus is usually expressed in a hypothesis: "Overcrowding disrupts and destroys social harmony," or "A speed-reading component for fifth-graders will improve reading comprehension."

An analogy is a figurative comparison that allows the writer to draw parallels. For example, one student compared online matchmaking to the practice of prearranged marriages. When families arrange a marriage, they cautiously seek a good match in matters of nationality, economics, political alliances, and so forth. In comparison, argued this student, couples on the Internet seek a good match on similar grounds.

Precedence

Precedence refers to conventions or customs, usually established in the past. In judicial decisions, it is a standard established by previous cases, a *legal precedent*. If your subject is "performance assessment," you will be faced with the conflict between old testing methods and new theories and methods for evaluating student performance. For example, the SAT examination is well entrenched as a testing vehicle; it has precedence. Replacing it with a different measure would require careful research.

Implications

If you conduct any kind of test or observation, you will probably make field notes in a research journal and tabulate your results at regular intervals. At some point, you will be expected to explain your findings, arrive at conclusions, and discuss the implications of your scientific inquiry. Lab reports are elementary forms of this task. What did you discover, and what does it prove?

For example, in her paper "Arranged Marriages: The Revival Is Online," one student explored both the social and the psychological implications of online infidelity, the damage to self-esteem, and new demands on psychotherapy.

1e   Establishing a Schedule

The steps for research are fundamental. You will do well to follow them, even to the point of setting deadlines on the calendar for each step. You may wish to write dates when deadlines should be met.

Topic. Your topic, which usually requires the approval of the instructor, should address a problem, issue, or question. It may offer a theoretical question and present the hypothesis as the subject of research. See Chapter 2 for details.

Research. Reading articles and books will establish a basis for your research. Conducting field research and laboratory testing will provide the necessary evidence for reaching conclusions. See Chapters 3, 4, and 5 for details.

Organization. Instructors require different types of plans. For some, your research journal will indicate the direction of your work. Others might ask for a formal outline. In either case, see Chapter 6 for details about basic organizational models.

Writing. Write plenty of notes, keep accurate lab records, and collect photocopied and downloaded articles, all of which you should carefully label. Some notes will be summaries, others will call for carefully drawn quotations from the sources, and some will be personal responses. Chapters 9 and 10 discuss matters of scientific writing in detail.

Format. Proper manuscript design places your paper within the required conventions of the name and year system used in the social sciences. Chapters 11 and 12 provide the guidelines for in-text citations and the entries for the references page.

Revision and proofreading. At the end of the project, you should be conscientious about examining the manuscript and making all necessary corrections. With the aid of computers, you can check spelling and aspects of style. Appendix A offers tips on revision and editing.

Submitting the manuscript. Like all writers, at some point you must "publish" the paper, or release it to the audience, which might be your instructor, your classmates, or perhaps a larger group. Plan carefully to meet this final deadline. You may publish the paper in a variety of ways—on paper, on a disk, on a CD-ROM, or on your own Web site. Chapter 15 discusses methods for producing electronic projects.

2 Discovering Your Topic

This chapter explores six important steps for investigation of a topic in the social sciences:

- Relating your experiences to scholarly problems and academic disciplines.
- Speculating about a subject by using idea-generating techniques.
- Focusing the subject by consulting with others.
- Exploring the literature.
- Framing a working hypothesis.
- Drafting your research proposal.

Instructors usually assign research topics in the social sciences, but they sometimes allow students to select their own. In either case, your topic will call for a scholarly perspective, and you must follow the six steps listed above in pursuit of a paper worthy of submission.

2a Relating Personal Experience to Scholarly Problems

To clarify what we mean, let's examine how one student launched her project.

Valerie Nesbitt-Hall was assigned by her sociology instructor to research some aspect of the Internet that affects human behavior. Nesbitt-Hall began searching the literature and found a magazine cartoon of a young woman sitting at her computer while saying to a young man, "Sorry—I only have relationships over the Internet. I'm cybersexual." Although she laughed, Valerie knew she had discovered a topic to investigate with a question and a possible answer that would require her research:

> Does online romance affect human behavior?
>
> Human behavior is affected by online romance and matchmaking.

Personal interest often provides the groundwork for interesting research projects. For example, the topic "The Sufferings of Native Americans" could be improved to "Urban Sprawl in Morton County: The Bulldozing of Indian Burial

Grounds." The topic "Computer Games" could be refined to "Learned Dexterity with Video and Computer Games." This latter topic would require a definition of *learned dexterity* and an analysis of how video games promote it.

Remember, your instructor will expect discipline-specific topics such as these:

Education:	The Visually Impaired: Options for Classroom Participation
Political Science:	Conservative Republicans and the Religious Right
Sociology:	Parents Who Lie to Their Children
Psychology:	Identifying Grade-School Children with Dyslexia

You conduct the research by making inquiries into the issues, identifying variables, and examining data to solve a problem. When your topic addresses serious issues, you have a reason to:

- Examine with intellectual curiosity the evidence found in professional or peer-reviewed articles at the library and on the Internet.
- Conduct observations in the field and experiments in the laboratory.
- Share your investigation of the issues with the reader.

Write a meaningful conclusion that discusses the implications of the study rather than merely summarizes it. Consider using one of the following techniques:

1. Combine personal interests with an aspect of academic studies:

Personal interest:	My Grandmother
Academic subject:	Psychology
Possible topics:	"The Effects of Board Games on Memory Recovery in Stroke Patients"
	"The Effect of Regular Soap Opera Viewing on Mood in Nursing Home Patients"
	"Alzheimer's Disease: Effects on Grandchildren"

2. Consider social issues that affect you and your family:

Personal interest:	Elementary education of a child
Academic subjects:	Sociology and Education
Social issue:	The behavior of children in school
Possible topics:	"Attention Deficit Hyperactivity Disorder in the Elementary Classroom"
	"Should Schoolchildren Take Medicine to Treat Hyperactivity?"

3. Let your cultural background prompt you toward detailed research into your roots, traditional culture, and social background:

Ethnic background:	Native American
Academic subject:	Social work
Personal interest:	Survival of the tribes

You can also reach for good subjects by answering a question:

Is eating in the cafeteria or buying groceries a better budgeting tool?
Purchasing and cooking food has advantages over eating at the cafeteria.
Does joining a Greek letter organization increase the probability that a
student will graduate?
Participation in sororities and fraternities improve a student's chances
of graduation.
Does participation in a weekly study group improve student academic
achievement in a course?
Study groups that meet nightly or weekly improve a student's academic
achievement.

Granted, each statement answers the question, but investigation, research, and the production of proof are necessary to substantiate it. These elements are explored in depth here and in other chapters.

2b Speculating about a Subject by Using Idea-Generating Techniques

At some point you will need to contemplate the issues and generate ideas worthy of investigation. Ideas can be generated in the following ways:

Free Writing

To free write, focus on a topic and write whatever comes to mind. Do not worry about grammar, style, or penmanship, but keep writing nonstop for a page or so to develop phrases, comparisons, personal anecdotes, and specific thoughts that help focus issues of concern. Below, a student writes on violence for a political science project:

The savagery of the recent hazing incident at Glenbrook North High
School demonstrates that humans, both men and women, love a good fight.
People want power over others, even in infancy. Just look at how siblings
fight. And I read one time that twins inside the womb actually fight for
supremacy, and one fetus might even devour or absorb the other one.
Weird, but I guess it's true. And we fight vicariously, too, watching boxing
and wrestling, cheering at fights during a hockey game, and on and on. So
personally, I think human beings have always been blood thirsty and power
hungry. The French philosopher Rousseau might claim a "noble savage"
once existed, but personally I think we've always hated each other.

This free writing sets the path for this writer's investigation into the role of war in human history. He has found a topic for exploration.

Listing Key Words

Keep a list of fundamental terms you see in your readings. These can help focus the direction of your research. James Johnston built this list of terms:

prehistoric wars	early weapons	noble savages
remains of early victims	early massacres	slaves
sacrificial victims	human nature	power
limited resources	religious sacrifices	honor

These key words can help in writing the rough outline, as explained below.

Outlining Key Words

Writing a rough outline early in the research project might help you see if the topic has enough substance for the length required. At this point, try to recognize the hierarchy of major and minor issues.

Prehistoric wars
    Evidence of early brutality
            Mutilated skeletons
    Evidence of early weapons
            Clubs, bows, slings, maces, and so on
            Walled fortresses for defense
    Speculations on reasons for war
            Resources
            Slaves
            Revenge
            Religion
Human nature and war
        Quest for power
        Biological urge to conquer

This initial ranking of ideas grew in length and depth during Johnston's research (see pages 166–174 for his paper).

Clustering

Another method for discovering the hierarchy of your primary topics and subtopics is to cluster ideas around a central subject. The cluster of related topics can generate a multitude of interconnected ideas. Here's an example by James Johnston:

Narrowing by Comparison

Comparison limits a discussion to specific differences. Any two works, any two persons, any two groups may serve as the basis for a comparative study. One writer expressed a comparison in this way:

> Ultimately, the key questions about the cause of war, whether ancient or current, centers on one's choice between biology and culture. On the one side, society as a whole wants to preserve its culture, in peace if possible. Yet the biological history of men and women suggests that we love a good fight.

That comparative choice could become the capstone of the student's conclusion.

Asking Questions

Stretch your imagination with questions.

1. General questions examine terminology, issues, causes, and other matters. For example, having read a section of Henry Thoreau's essay "Civil Disobedience" for a sociology class, one writer asked:

> What is "civil disobedience"?
>
> Is dissent legal? Is it moral? Is it patriotic?
>
> Is dissent a liberal activity? Is it conservative?
>
> Should the government encourage or stifle dissent?
>
> Is passive resistance effective?

Answering these questions pointed the student to a central issue or argument:

Civil Disobedience: Shaping Our Nation by Confronting Unjust Laws

2. Rhetorical questions are based on the various modes of writing. One student in a sociology class framed these questions about state-sanctioned gambling and its effect on the social fabric of the state:

Comparison:	How does a state lottery compare with horse racing?
Definition:	What is a lottery in legal terms? in social terms? in religious terms?
Cause/Effect:	What are the consequences of a state lottery on funding for education, highways, prisons, and social programs?
Process:	How are winnings distributed? Does money pass from the rich to the poor or from the poor to the rich?
Classification:	What types of lotteries exist, and which are available in this state?
Evaluation:	What is the value of a lottery to the average citizen? What are the disadvantages?

3. Academic disciplines across the curriculum provide questions:

Psychology:	What is the effect of gambling on the mental attitude of the college athlete who knows huge sums hang in the balance on his or her performance?
Sociology:	What compulsion in human nature prompts people to gamble on athletic competitions?
Education:	What percentage of the lottery money actually goes into education?

4. Explore the basic elements of a subject with journalistic questions: Who? What? Where? When? Why? and How? For example:

Who?	Athletes
What?	Illegal drugs
When?	During off-season training and also on game day
Where?	Training rooms and elsewhere
Why?	To enhance performance
How?	Through pills and injections

The questions can prompt a writer to examine team pressure as a cause for drug usage by athletes.

2c   Focusing the Subject by Consulting with Others

Interviews

You may need to consult with your instructor, published experts, and other people with experience. Ask for ideas and reactions to your subject. For

Exploring Ideas with Others

- Consult with your instructor.
- Discuss your topic with three or four classmates.
- Listen to the concerns of others.
- Conduct a formal interview (see pages 26–28).
- Join a discussion group.
- Take careful notes.
- Adjust your research accordingly.

example, Valerie Nesbitt-Hall knew a couple who married after initially meeting in a chat room on the Internet. She requested an interview and got it (see pages 26–28 for the interview and pages 179–185 for her use of the interview in the finished paper). The techniques for interviewing are discussed in greater detail in Section 3a, pages 26–32.

Discussion Groups

What are other people saying about your subject? A discussion group of your peers can provide valuable insight into potential issues, problems, and sources. With a round-table discussion, you can ask questions to focus your work. You might also be challenged to focus on key issues you have overlooked. You might use the computer to share ideas and messages with other scholars interested in your subject. Somebody may answer a question or point to an interesting aspect that had not occurred to you.

With discussion groups, you have choices:

- A round-table discussion group at a study room in the library or dormitory.
- Classroom e-mail groups that participate in online discussions.
- Online courses that feature a discussion room for forums that require student participation.
- MUD and MOO discussion groups, or multi-user domains that work over the Internet rather than via e-mail.
- Online chatting with one or more participants in real time, even with audio and video, in some cases.

For example, your instructor may set up an informal classroom discussion list and expect you to participate by e-mail with her and your fellow students. You can also find many discussion groups on the Internet, but the manner in which you use them is vital to your academic success. Rather than chat, solicit ideas and get responses to your questions about your research.

CHECKLIST

Narrowing a General Subject to a Scholarly Topic

Unlike a general subject, a scholarly topic should:

- Examine one narrowed issue, as in Valerie Nesbitt-Hall's focus on Internet matching services as a way to arrange a date and even a marriage.
- Address knowledgeable readers and carry them to another plateau of knowledge.
- Have a serious purpose that demands analysis of the issues, argues from a position, and explains complex details.
- Investigate the subject by reviewing the literature, examining data, conducting empirical research, surveys, and interviews, and directly observing or collecting data in the field.
- Meet the expectations of the instructor and conform to the course requirements.

2d Exploring the Literature

Electronic databases now provide excellent, up-to-date information on most scholarly topics. Some can be found on the Internet, but many of the best databases are accessed through your library. Books on your topic can be identified by means of the library's electronic book catalog. Here are three suggestions:

1. Go to the reliable databases available through your library, such as Info-Trac (general), PsychLIT (psychology), PUBMED (health), ERIC (education), PAIS (political science), and others. These are monitored sites filtered by editorial boards and peer review. You can reach them from remote locations at home or the dorm room by connecting electronically to your library. See Chapter 4 for details on ways to access library resources.
2. Look for articles on the Internet that first appeared in a printed version. In many cases, the original print version was examined by an editorial board.
3. Look for Internet articles with reputable sponsors, especially universities, museums, or professional organizations. Chapter 3 discusses the pros and cons of Internet searching. You can also look at the Web site accompanying this book (http://www.ablongman.com/lester) for tips and examples on evaluating Internet sources.

Topic selection goes beyond choosing a general category such as "single mothers." It includes finding a research-provoking issue or question such as "The foster parent program seems to have replaced the orphanage system.

Has it been effective?" Then frame a subject you wish to explore—for example, "The foster parent program has failed the children just as the orphanage system of another age failed the children." Take a stand, make a claim, and begin your investigation to provide credence for your position.

2e Framing a Working Theory or Hypothesis

The hypothesis is an assumption that requires a review of the literature, careful testing in the lab, and/or a review of existing or new data to support its validity. You should expand your topic into a scholarly proposal to support and defend in your paper. However, be sure to consult with your instructor concerning the scope of your project. Here are several types of claims. Keep in mind that they go by different names and have different applications in specific disciplines.

The Variable Hypothesis:

Children with autism display various cognitive strengths and

weaknesses.

The researcher must provide evidence to show that children with autism can concentrate for long periods of time; excel in music, math, mechanics, and science; display long-term memory; be creative; and demonstrate many other positive traits. Some variables are dependent only on the independent variable.

The Conditional Hypothesis:

Behaviors of self-abuse, such as overeating, head banging, self-

mutilation, bulimia, and anorexia, can be reduced by counseling,

monitoring, diet therapy, and medication.

Certain conditions must be met. The control will depend on the patient's ability to respond adequately to the tasks to prove the hypothesis valid. Examining one item—for example, bulimia—should suffice for an undergraduate study. Note: A study of this type may require field research that involves one or more human subjects.

The Statistical Hypothesis:

Class size has no effect on the number of laboratory experiments

designed and demonstrated in class.

This type of examination is also known as a *null hypothesis.* The null hypothesis states that there is no difference between two conditions beyond chance differences. If a statistically significant difference is found, the null hypothesis is rejected.

The Causal Hypothesis:

> A child's choice of toy is determined by television commercials.

In psychology, the search is for a relationship. How does one thing affect another? Thus, a causal hypothesis assumes the mutual occurrence of two factors and asserts that one is responsible for the other. The student who is a parent could conduct observational research to support or oppose the supposition. A review of the literature would certainly serve the writer.

In effect, your work will include an examination of the prevailing literature as well as some type of field research, such as a survey of an elementary classroom or a survey of senior citizens at a retirement community. Everything is subject to examination, even the number of times you blink while reading this text.

A theory can be a prevailing idea or the conventional wisdom that exists in the academic community, yet it too is subject to review and analysis. For example, the SAT and ACT examinations, theoretically, are effective measuring tools for predicting student success in college. The relationship is now undergoing careful scrutiny that suggests the subjective theory is flawed by objective evidence. In another case, subjective theories for treating adolescent substance abuse vary greatly from state to state and agency to agency because of objective evidence. Here is one student's subjective theory that requires objective evidence:

> Chat rooms and online matching services are like prearranged marriages of the past. They enable people to meet only after a prearranged engagement by e-mail.

The writer will defend this subjective theory by citing evidence from interviews and the literature.

You might develop an argument with a *because* clause, as based on your reading:

> Hyperactive children need medication because ADHD is a medical disorder, not a behavioral problem.

The subjective theory that children benefit from medication is supported by evidence in the literature, which argues for a medical solution rather than behavioral modification. This writer must defend the theory by citing evidence and addressing any unstated assumptions—for example, that medication alone will solve the problem.

Sometimes the theory will serve as the hypothesis for a paper:

> Discrimination against young women in the classroom, known as "shortchanging," harms the women academically, socially, and psychologically.

Here the student will probably cite literature on shortchanging.

2f   Drafting a Research Proposal

A research proposal in APA style comes in two forms:

1. A short paragraph to describe the project for yourself and to inform your instructor of your project, or
2. A formal, multi-page report that provides background information, your rationale for conducting the study, a review of the literature, your methods, and the possible implications of the work.

In addition to the examples here, you can find a fully developed research proposal on pages 21–23.

The Short Proposal

A short proposal identifies four essential ingredients of your work:

- The specific topic
- The purpose of the paper (explain, analyze, argue)
- The intended audience (general or specialized)
- Your stance as the writer (informer or advocate)
- The preliminary theory or hypothesis

For example, here is Valerie Nesbitt-Hall 's short initial proposal:

This study will examine computer matchmaking as a viable alternative to traditional methods for initiating a friendship. The Internet provides an opportunity for people to meet, chat, reveal themselves at their own pace, and find, perhaps, a friend, lover, or even a spouse. Thus, computer matchmaking has social and psychological implications that can be explored in the literature of both psychologists and sociologists. In many ways, computer matchmaking is similar to the arranged marriages of past generations. Such arrangements are now considered old-fashioned or a product of foreign culture, but consider this hypothesis: The Internet, especially its online dating services and chat rooms, has brought arranged marriages into the twenty-first century. People are able to meet in a remote manner without immediate intimacy. Those persons who maintain an anonymous distance until a true romance blossoms are anticipating, in essence, a carefully arranged date that might become a marriage. This study will therefore examine the social and psychological implications for those persons seeking a match in cyberspace.

This writer has identified the basic nature of her project and can now search for evidence in the literature.

The Long Proposal

Some instructors may assign the long proposal, which includes some or all of the following elements:

1. A *cover page* with the title of the project, your name, and the person or agency to which you are submitting the proposal:

Arranged Marriage 1

Running Head: ARRANGED MARRIAGES: THE REVIVAL IS ONLINE

Arranged Marriages: The Revival Is Online

Valerie Nesbitt-Hall

Austin Peay State University

2. A preliminary *abstract* in 50 to 100 words.

Arranged Marriages 2

Abstract

Arranged marriages are considered old-fashioned or a product of some foreign cultures, but consider that the Internet, especially its online dating services and chat rooms, has brought arranged marriages into the twenty-first century. The Internet provides an opportunity for people to meet, chat, reveal themselves at their own pace, and find, perhaps, a friend, lover, or even a spouse. Thus, computer matchmaking has social and psychological implications that have been explored by psychologists and sociologists. The social implications affect the roles of both men and women in the workplace and in marital relations. The psychological implications involve online infidelity, cybersexual addiction, and damage to self-esteem; yet those dangers are balanced against success stories. Those persons who maintain an anonymous distance until a true romance blossoms are anticipating, in essence, a carefully arranged date that might become a marriage.

3. A *purpose statement* with the *rationale* for your project. In essence, this is your identification of the audience that your work will address, and the role you will play as investigator and advocate.

> This project was suggested by Dr. Lee Ling to fulfill the writing
> project for English 2100 and also to serve the University Committee on
> Computers, which has launched a project on student Internet
> awareness. This paper, if approved, would become part of the
> committee's Student Booklet on Internet Protocol.

4. A *statement of qualification* that explains your experience and perhaps
   the special qualities you bring to the project. Nesbitt-Hall included this
   comment in her proposal:

> I bring first-hand experience to this study. I have explored the
> Internet like many other students. I joined a service, entered my
> profile, and began looking at photographs and profiles. It was exciting
> at first, but then I became bored; it seemed that everything and
> everybody blended into a fog of indifference. Then, when some jerk
> sent a vulgar message, I withdrew my profile and username. I'll just
> remain old-fashioned and start my dates with a soda at the student
> center.

If you have no experience with the subject, you can omit the statement
of qualification.

5. A *review of the literature,* which will survey the articles and books you
   examined in your preliminary work.

> Limited research is being done in the area of online romance. My
> search of the literature produced a surprisingly short list of journal
> articles. Maheu (1999) discussed methods of helping clients, even to
> the point of counseling in cyberspace itself, which would establish
> professional relationships online. Schneider and Weiss (2001) described
> it but offered little interpersonal insight. Cooper (2002) has published
> an excellent collection of articles in his guidebook for clinicians, and
> he has argued that online dating has the potential to lower the
> nation's divorce rate. Kass (2003) identified the "distanced nearness"
> of a chat room that encourages self-revelation while maintaining
> personal boundaries" (cited in Rasdan, 2003, p. 71). Epstein (2003)
> argued that many arranged marriages, by parents or by cyberspace,
> have produced enduring love because of rational deliberation
> performed before moments of passionate impulse. In addition,

Schneider and Weiss (2001) have listed some of the advantages to online romance: It links people who are miles apart; impressions are made by words, not looks; there is time to contemplate a message; there is time to compose a well-written response; and messages can be reviewed and revised before transmission (p. 66).

6. A *description of your research methods* is usually part of your proposal, which includes the design of the *materials* you will need, your *timetable,* and, where applicable, your *budget.* These elements are required in a proposal but omitted in the research paper. Consult with your instructor concerning the scope of your project. Here is Nesbitt-Hall's description:

> This paper will examine online dating as a forum for arranged dates and arranged marriages. The Method section will explore the methods used by Match.com and other dating services as a testing board for people with similar interests to form communication lines that might last one minute or one year. The Subjects section will examine the people who participate, from the modest person to one who is aggressive, and from high-profile people like Rush Limbaugh to those with low profiles and quiet lifestyles. The Procedures section will examine the process so common to the services: to bring two compatible people together on the Web. There they can e-mail each other, participate in instant messaging (IM) chats, send attachments of favorite songs or personal photographs, and, eventually, exchange real names, phone numbers, and addresses. The various services provide not only lists of available people but also personality tests, detailed profiles of subjects, and even nightclubs with calling cards for patrons to share with others whom they find interesting. The Results section will explore online romance as productive for some people, as a haven for the lurking voyeur, and as potential disaster for the gullible and careless. The Case Study will provide a success story for online dating. The Discussion section will explore the social and psychological implications for men and women, especially those addicted to cyberspace.

CHECKLIST

Explaining Your Purpose in the Research Proposal

- Explain and define the topic. Use *explanation* to review and itemize factual data.
- Analyze the specific issues or variables. Use *analysis* to classify parts of the subject and to investigate each in depth.
- Persuade the reader with the weight of the evidence. Use *persuasion* to question the general attitudes about a problem and then to affirm new theories, advance a solution, recommend a course of action, or—in the least—invite the reader into an intellectual dialogue.

YOUR RESEARCH PROJECT

1. Ask questions about a possible subject, using the list on pages 14-15, and write answers that might serve as your hypothesis. Submit your list and answers to your instructor.

2. Look around your campus or community for subjects. Talk with your classmates and even your instructor about campus issues. Focus on your hometown community in search of a problem or social concern such as drug abuse, school busing, overcrowded classrooms, or road rage. If you are a parent, consider issues related to children, such as safe, adequate childcare. After you have a subject of interest, apply the techniques described on pages 12-15, such as clustering, free writing, or listing key words. Submit your topic, narrowed to a specific problem or hypothesis, to your instructor.

3. To determine if sufficient sources are available and to narrow the subject even further, visit the Internet, investigate the library's databases (e.g., InfoTrac), and dip into the electronic book catalog at your library. Keep printouts of interesting articles or book titles. Submit a copy of one article to your instructor.

4. Write a brief research proposal and submit it to your instructor (see pages 19-20).

Gathering Data by Field Research and Laboratory Testing

Research in the social sciences is often empirical, which means the researcher gathers data in practical and pragmatic ways to test a hypothesis. Let us consider the following hypothesis:

Overpopulation causes stress, which results in abnormal behavior.

That seems to be a reasonable proposition, but the scientific community wants supportive data and considers it a statistical hypothesis (see page 18). Data can be collected in a laboratory or in the field. For example, in the laboratory, the scientific researcher often uses rats. A control group of 12 rats might be placed in one cage and left without stimulus during the test period. An experimental group of 12 rats, placed in a cage, is stimulated. Each day, 12 additional rats are added to the cage and observed day after day for changes in behavior. This experiment continues until the rats react in negative or hostile ways, attacking each other for a number of reasons—food, space, or sex, to name three. Meanwhile, the control group lives in relative peace and harmony. The eventual report will describe the design of the study, chart the results, and discuss the implications of the findings.

The same hypothesis could be tested by field research, which means going outside the laboratory. For example, the researcher could observe classroom students with a control group and an experimental group. The latter is stimulated by overpopulation, the results are tabulated, and the findings are reported. Thirty-five students in a classroom, compared with fifteen, may result in stress for many of the crowded students, affecting their grades and their overall classroom behaviors.

Such reports have great value for educators who might reduce class size, for corporate managers who use cubicles to give employees their own space, and for traffic engineers who attempt to spread out the flow of automobiles.

In like manner, you will be called on to conduct research. You might find yourself observing student behavior at a parking lot or surveying a selected group with a questionnaire. This type of research is not beyond the realm of first-year and second-year students, and you should consider it an important element of your educational development.

Evidence for your study should come from reputable sources. Broad references to issues in society might include how the topic has been viewed on a television talk show or in weekly magazines; however, this type of information is not a source worth citing in a research project. Additionally, personal communication is not worthy of reference in an empirical study.

Beyond the library, source information can be found in a variety of places. Therefore, converse with people in person, by letter, or via e-mail. If time permits, conduct interviews or use a questionnaire. Watch television specials, visit the courthouse archives, and conduct research by observation under the guidance of an instructor (see page 39). Build a table, graph, or chart with the evidence collected, and make it part of your study. Maintain all of your field notes, interview transcripts, survey data, and so forth because your instructor may ask to see them or you may wish to place them in an appendix at the end of your paper.

Strict guidelines exist for the design of scientific reports in APA style, so you should follow the appropriate model as described on pages 3–8. For example, the report of empirical research requires four parts:

1. Introduction of the problem with the hypothesis
2. Your methods, tools, and subjects
3. The results of the study
4. A discussion of the implications

In addition, you should be objective while conducting the research. All writers get deeply involved in their subject, but they must couple that involvement with the skill of detachment. What are the facts? What conclusions do they support? Conduct the research, document the results, and then discuss their implications.

For example, student Gena Messersmith (see her letter on page 29) had strong personal feelings about her daughter's condition as she researched Attention Deficit Hyperactivity Disorder; hence, Messersmith forced herself to remain objective. As a safeguard, allow your instructor to review your methods and apparatus before launching the study.

3a Investigating Local Sources

Interviewing Knowledgeable People

Talk to people who have experience with your subject. Personal interviews can elicit valuable in-depth information. They provide information few others have. Look to organizations for experienced persons. For example, if writing on the history of the local school system, you might contact the county historian, a senior citizen's organization, or a retired teacher or two. If convenient, post a notice soliciting help:

I am writing a study on the history of the local school system in
1950s. Wanted: People who have knowledge of the schools during that
decade.

Try establishing e-mail conferences with knowledgeable people. Another
way to accomplish this task is to request information from a discussion group.
Try using the discussion board if you are in an online class. For accuracy, save
files or record the discussions and interviews with a tape recorder (with written permission of the person interviewed, of course). Information worthy of
documentation should come from credible sources, but for sociology and some
other disciplines it might be necessary to include information from an interview, e-mail, or other personal correspondence. Do not include personal correspondence as an entry on your References page (see pages 75–76 for details).

Through research and personal interviews with M. S. Thornbright, the county
historian, the precise location of various schools was identified. Schools were
segregated at this time, and differences in facilities and locations were noted.
The reality of equal but separate schools at the time of the Brown vs. Board of
Education decision in 1954 is reflected in the history of this community.

Be prepared for the interview. Know your interviewee's professional
background and have a set of pertinent questions, with follow-ups. Keep the
interview focused on the principal issue. Subjects may wander to tangential
ideas, so always bring them back to the central subject with an appropriate
question. Maintain an ethical demeanor that honors with accuracy the statements of the subject. See also guidelines in the Checklist on page 32.

Student Valerie Nesbitt-Hall researched the role of computer matching
services and chat rooms in promoting online romance. Because she knew two
people who had met online and eventually married, she decided to request
an interview—online, of course. These were her questions and, in brief form,
the responses of the subjects—Steven of Scotland and Jennifer of the United
States. (See Nesbitt-Hall's paper on pages 178–185):

1. When did you first meet online?
   Answer: *September of 1996.*
2. What prompted you to try an online matching service?
   Answer: *We didn't really try online matching services. We chatted in a
   chat room, became friends there, and met in person later.*
3. Who initiated the first contact?
   Answer: *Stephen initiated the first online chat.*

4. How long into the relationship did you correspond by e-mail before one of you gave an address and/or phone number? Who did it first, Steve or Jennifer?

    Answer: *We chatted and corresponded by e-mail for nine months before Jennifer shared her phone number.*

5. How long into the relationship did you go before sharing photographs?

    Answer: *At nine months we began to share written correspondence and photographs.*

6. Who initiated the first meeting in person? Where did you meet? How long were you into the relationship before you met in person?

    Answer: *Stephen first requested the meeting, and Jennifer flew from the States to Glasgow, Scotland. This was about a year into the relationship.*

7. How much time elapsed between your first online discovery of each other and your marriage?

    Answer: *One and a half years after our first chat, we were married.*

8. Did you feel that online romance enabled you to prearrange things and protect your privacy before meeting in person?

    Answer: *Yes. We were cautious and at times reluctant to continue, but we kept coming back to each other, online, until we knew the other well enough to trust in the relationship. Once we got offline into what we might call real-time dating, the love blossomed quickly.*

9. When you finally met in person, did you feel that you really knew the other person spiritually? emotionally? intellectually?

    Answer: *Yes.*

10. Not to put you on the spot, but do you feel as a couple that the relationship has been excellent to this point?

    Answer: *Yes, super.*

11. Has the difference in nationalities been a problem?

    Answer: *Yes, but only in relation to sorting out immigration matters. Also, Jennifer's parents were concerned that she was going to another country to see someone she had never met.*

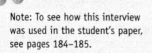

Note: To see how this interview was used in the student's paper, see pages 184–185.

12. Finally, would you recommend online matching services or chat rooms to others who are seeking mates?

    Answer: *Yes, in the right circumstances. We were lucky; others might not be.*

Writing Letters and Corresponding by E-Mail

Correspondence provides a written record for research. As you would in an interview, ask pointed questions so correspondents will respond directly to your central issues. Tell the person who you are, what you are attempting to do, and why you have chosen to write this particular person or set of persons. If germane, explain why you have chosen this topic and what qualifies you to write about it.

Gena Messersmith

12 Morningside Road

Clarksville, TN 37040

Ms. Rachel G. Warren, Principal

Glenview Elementary School

Clarksville, TN 37040

Dear Ms. Warren:

I am a college student conducting research into methods for handling hyperactive children in the public school setting. I am surveying each elementary school principal in Montgomery County. I have contacted the central office also, but I wished to have perspectives from those of you on the front lines. I have a child with ADHD, so I have a personal as well as a scholarly reason for this research. I could ask specific questions on policy, but I have gotten that from the central office. What I would like from you is a brief paragraph that describes your policy and procedure when one of your teachers reports a child with hyperactive behavior. In particular, do you endorse the use of medication for managing that child's behavior? Names will be confidential, for an assigned code will be used for each subject to ensure confidentiality and anonymity.

I have enclosed a self-addressed, stamped envelope for your convenience. You may e-mail me at messersmithg@apsu.edu.

Sincerely,

Gena Messersmith

This letter makes a fairly specific request for a minimum amount of information. It does not require an expansive reply. From the response, a generalization or specific example can be used, but the data should not be cited as a reference.

Basic policies were gathered from local elementary school principals. A common procedure is the principal counsels first with the school nurse and second with the parents. Seventy percent of the principals polled encouraged the use of medication. Some noted reasons for encouraging medication included its calming effect upon the child, the resulting benefits to the learning atmosphere of the classroom, and so on.

Note: If Messersmith decided to build a table or graph from the principals' replies, she would need to document the survey as shown on page 30.

Reading Personal Papers

Search out letters, diaries, manuscripts, family histories, and other personal materials that might contribute to your study. The city library may house private collections, and the city librarian can usually help you contact the county historian and other private citizens who have important documents. Obviously, handling private papers must be done with the utmost decorum and care. Again, provide an in-text citation to the source:

R. C. Joplin (2003) shared with me her grandfather's notebooks, unpublished, which contained numerous references to the old Dunbar High School along with several photographs. Several drawings by Joseph Joplin, not to scale, provided clues to life at a segregated school.

Note: Every reference or source needs a bibliography note except for personal communications.

Joplin, J. (1924). *Notes on my life.* Unpublished manuscript.

Attending Lectures and Public Addresses

Watch bulletin boards and the newspaper for a featured speaker who might visit your campus. When you attend, take careful notes and, if you can, request a copy of the lecture or speech. Remember, too, that many lectures, reproduced on video, are available in the library or in departmental files. Provide an in-text citation to the source and make a bibliography entry on the reference page. The in-text citation might read like this:

One psychologist reminded attorneys that the most prevalent reaction of children who are physically and sexually abused is a retreat into silence, a withdrawal so deep that memory can be erased (Lockerby, 2004).

The reference entry would look like this:

Lockerby, R. W. (2004, January). *Sounds of silence from abused children.* Paper presented to the meeting of the Sumner County Bar Association, Gallatin, TN.

Investigating Government Documents

Documents are available at four levels of government: city, county, state, and federal. As a constituent, you are entitled to examine many kinds of records on file at various agencies. If your topic demands it, you may contact the mayor's office, attend and take notes at a city council assembly, or search out printed documents.

Local government

Visit the courthouse or county clerk's office for facts on elections, marriages, births, and deaths. These archives include wills, tax rolls, military assignments,

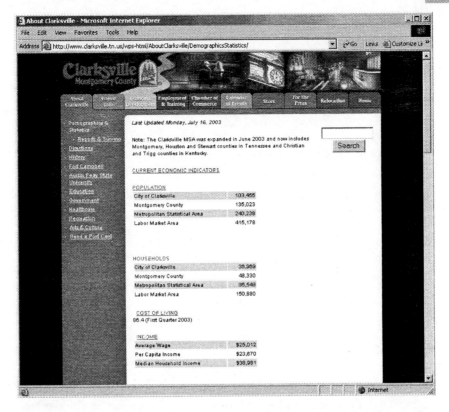

FIGURE 3.1 Population and Demographics: Clarksville/Montgomery County, Tennessee

deeds to property, and much more. Therefore, a trip to the local courthouse can be rewarding, helping you trace the social history of the land and its people. Figure 3.1 shows the type of information readily available to a student conducting research on a city's population and demographics.

State government

Telephone a state office that relates to your research, such as Consumer Affairs (general information), the Public Service Commission (which regulates public utilities such as the telephone company), or the Department of Human Services (which administers social and welfare services). The agencies may vary by name in your state. Remember, too, that the state's archival storehouse makes its records available for public review.

Federal government

Your United States senator or representative can send you booklets printed by the Government Printing Office, usually without cost. A list of these documents appears in a monthly catalog issued by the Superintendent of Documents, *Monthly Catalog of United States Government Publications*, Washington, DC 20402, available with an excellent search engine at

---

CHECKLIST

Interviews, Letters, Private Papers, Courthouse Documents

- Set your appointments in advance.
- Consult with experienced persons. If possible, talk to several people in order to weigh different opinions. Telephone and e-mail interviews are acceptable.
- Be courteous and on time for interviews.
- Be prepared with a set of focused, pertinent questions for initiating and conducting the interview.
- Handle private and public papers with great care.
- For accuracy, record interviews with a tape recorder (with permission of the person interviewed, of course).
- Get written permission before citing a person by name or quoting his or her exact words.
- Send helpful people a copy of your report along with a thank-you note.

---

http://www.access.gpo.gov/. In addition, you can gain access to the National Archives Building in Washington, D.C., or to one of the regional branches in Atlanta, Boston, Chicago, Denver, Fort Worth, Kansas City, Los Angeles, New York, Philadelphia, or Seattle. These archives contain court records and government documents that you can review in two books: *Guide to the National Archives of the United States* and *Select List of Publications of the National Archives and Record Service* (see http://www.archives.gov/). You can borrow some documents on microfilm if you consult the *Catalog of National Archives Microfilm Publications*.

The researcher should also make a bibliography entry to record the source of this table.

Clarksville/Montgomery County Economic Development Council. (2003).

 Population and demographics: Clarksville/Montgomery County,

 Tennessee. Retrieved January 16, 2004, from www.clarksville.tn.us

3b   Examining Audiovisual Materials, Television, and Radio

Important data can be found in audiovisual materials: films, filmstrips, music, phonograph recordings, slides, audiocassettes, and videocassettes. You will find these sources both on and off campus. Consult such guides as

Using Media Sources

- Watch closely the opening and closing credits to capture the necessary data for your bibliography entry. The format is explained on page 155.
- Your citations may refer to a performer, director, or narrator, depending on the focus of your study.
- As with the live interview, be scrupulously accurate in taking notes. It's best to write direct quotations because paraphrases of television commentary can unintentionally be distorted and biased.
- Plan your review of a media presentation, even to the point of preparing a set of criteria to help with your judgment or preparing a list of questions for which you want answers.

Educators Guide (film, filmstrips, and tapes), *Media Review Digest* (nonprint materials), *Video Source Book* (video catalog), *The Film File*, or *International Index to Recorded Poetry*. Television, with its many channels, such as the History Channel, offers invaluable data. With DVD or VCR, you can record a program for detailed examination. Again, write bibliography entries for any materials that contribute to your paper.

Fleischer, A. (2003, June 1). *Taking on the press* [Interview]. Atlanta: CNN.

3c Conducting a Survey

Surveys can produce current, first-hand data that you can tabulate and analyze. Use a formal survey only when you are experienced with tests and measurements as well as with statistical analysis or when your instructor will help you with the instrument. Be advised that most schools have a Human Subjects Committee that sets guidelines, draws up consent forms, and requires confidentiality or anonymity of participants for information gathering that might be intrusive. An informal survey gathered in the hallways of campus buildings lacks credibility in the research paper. Here are a few guidelines.

Developing a Questionnaire

Ask yourself these questions as you begin developing a questionnaire. Sample answers are provided.

What hypothesis are you examining?

Parental attitudes toward medication for ADHD.

Teacher attitudes toward medication for students with ADHD.

Why are you doing the evaluation?

> To learn teachers' ideas and beliefs about the value of medication as an effective means for working with ADHD students.

What do you hope to accomplish?

> To find information about the strengths and weaknesses among educators regarding the effectiveness of medication for students with ADHD.

Can you get the information you need from existing sources, which would make the survey unnecessary?

> No. This survey has not been performed previously, and it is applicable to the school system, parents, and students.

How can you clarify your objective?

> Using a Likert Scale or a yes/no questionnaire, decipher the ways that teachers feel medication is beneficial for students with ADHD.

What are you measuring? Select from this list:
Attitude
Knowledge
Skills
Goals and aspirations
Behavior
Perceptions

> This survey will measure teachers' attitudes and knowledge about the effectiveness of medication for ADHD.

Note: A sample can be statistically similar to a complete population if each participant represents the whole population in terms of age, sex, race, education, income, residence, and other factors. You might pull names from a hat, select every tenth person, or carefully select from groups by sex, race, and classification as freshman, sophomore, junior, senior, graduate student.

What is the population to be surveyed? Can you test a random sample rather than the entire population?

> The questionnaire will seek responses from teachers for grades K to 5 at four local elementary schools.

What method will you use to collect the data?
Mail
Telephone
E-mail
Personal interview

Personal distribution
Internet Web site (see pages 37–38)

The survey will be personally distributed.

Will the collection be anonymous or confidential? Anonymous surveys do not ask for names of respondents, yet an e-mail survey may violate such anonymity. Confidential surveys include the names of respondents, but individual responses may not be shared and the confidentiality may not be violated. Destroy all identifying data after your report is completed.

The survey will be confidential and anonymous; all records will be

erased from the computers.

Will you need approval before administering the questionnaire? Your instructor's approval might be sufficient, but consult your college catalog for regulations on protection of subjects who participate in evaluation and research.

I have approval from my professor and dean, approval from the

university committee, and approval from the school system

because the purpose of the survey is to determine the attitudes of

teachers concerning the effectiveness of medication of ADHD.

Program evaluation and the findings are intended for internal use.

Designing the Questionnaire
Giving directions to participants

Include these items:

A brief explanation of the questionnaire's purpose
Instructions on completing the survey
Directions on submitting the questionnaire (e.g., mail, e-mail, submit button, and so on)
Conditions of confidentiality

Wording the questions

Avoid slang, culture-specific, and technical words. Avoid words with connotations of bias that might influence the respondent. Avoid the word *and* to ensure that you ask only one question. Avoid the word *not* in questions requiring a yes or no answer. Keep multiple choice questions distinct and exclusive. Keep the questionnaire short and simple. Only ask questions whose answers are important to your research.

Writing a cover letter

Make a connection with the respondent. Introduce yourself and explain the importance of the survey. If the respondent will benefit from your research, tell them how so that he or she will take whatever time is needed to complete the survey. The cover letter should include these items:

The purpose of the study

The sponsor (such as the dean of admissions)

Reasons why the response is important

A promise of confidentiality explaining that responses will be anonymous and used in data analysis, not kept as individual records. Reassure the respondents of the data transfer security measures you have put into place

The deadline for returning the questionnaire

Informed consent, which is typically represented by the return of the form

Writing the questionnaire

Place the easiest and least controversial questions at the beginning of the survey. Try to arrange questions on the same subject matter together. Do not ask leading questions or make assumptions. Do not ask questions that require long, written answers, but do invite a brief commentary on the issues by the respondent. Include a comment section where respondents can personalize or explain their answers. Offer these options where appropriate: don't know, not applicable, none, other. Be consistent in the design. If the yes option is listed before the no option the first time, always show it that way.

Conducting a pilot study to test your design

Early in your work, test your questionnaire with a small group of students to get input on the language used, the clarity of the questions, and the potential for recovering pertinent data. A pilot is your test run to see if everything works before you build the complete version.

Designing the questions

The most frequently used question types are multiple choice, ratings, scales (agree/disagree, excellent/poor), and short-answer questions that allow either numeric or written answers. Examples are:

Multiple Choice:

Which television news program do you primarily watch?

1. CNN
2. ABC
3. CBS
4. NBC
5. FOX
6. Other

Rating Scales:

In terms of importance to you, please rate the university's electronic enrollment process. The scale is from 1, not important or valuable, to 5, very important and valuable.

Ease of access	1	2	3	4	5
Ease of navigation	1	2	3	4	5
Accuracy in listing course choices	1	2	3	4	5
Availability of courses with options	1	2	3	4	5

Agreement Scales:

These usually appear as agree/disagree or always/never. Note: Always include the "no opinion" option.

Are you satisfied with the university's electronic enrollment system? The scale is from 1, very dissatisfied, to 5, very satisfied.

1   2   3   4   5   no opinion

Questions Requiring Short Written Answers:

If you could do one thing to improve the university's enrollment system, what would it be?

Short-answer Questions:

Did you find the electronic enrollment system easy to use?   Yes No
Did you build your course schedule successfully?   Yes No

Writing Online Surveys

Internet surveys offer the possibility of collecting data in a short time from a large population, and the tabulation of results can be electronically tabulated. You create the questionnaire, place it online, recruit subjects, and let a software program, such as Microsoft Access, build a database. Your analysis of the data can begin within days.

Web-based data collection can be flexible, allowing randomization of question order and various skip patterns. In addition, gathering data online offers a relative degree of privacy and makes it easier for respondents to admit to their behavior, such as cheating on examinations, alcoholism, or unprotected sex.

To create a questionnaire for the Internet, use a Web page application such as Microsoft FrontPage or Macromedia DreamWeaver. You will need to read and follow the advice given in the tutorials about forms and hypertext buttons.

To send the forms, you can submit the questionnaire to members of a discussion group or send e-mail messages to a selected list of possible respondents whom you then direct to the Web site for the survey.

To collect the data from an Internet survey, you have three choices:

1. Have the completed survey sent directly to you via e-mail if it is brief.

2. Have the completed survey sent to a file controlled by software such as Microsoft Excel.

3. Have the completed survey sent to a database controlled by software such as Microsoft Access.

Note: For more information on these programs, go to the Web site at http://www.ablongman.com/lester.

Ethical guidelines require researchers to allow subjects to skip questions they do not wish to answer. Ask your respondents to answer each question, but include a response option for each item that allows the respondent to skip the item. Note this example:

Which type of graduation speaker do you prefer?

Politician
Professional or academic person
Successful graduate of the school
Other; please specify:
Skip this question

Your online questionnaire should include an option for withdrawal from the survey. If the respondent withdraws, discard all data from that subject.

For confidentiality, you should reassure respondents that you will not attempt to capture information they do not voluntarily provide. In addition, you might indicate you will save the e-mail addresses in a separate file from the responses so individual responses cannot be linked to a specific e-mail address. Also, remember that in most cases you may only guarantee confidentiality, not total anonymity.

Label your survey in the bibliography entry:

Electronic enrollment survey. (2004). Unpublished raw data. Knoxville: University of Tennessee.

CHECKLIST

Conducting a Survey

- Keep the questionnaire short, clear, and focused on your topic.
- Write unbiased questions. Let your professor review the instrument before you use it.
- Ask subjects for a quick response to a scale (Choose A, B, or C), to rank responses (first choice, second choice, and so on), or to fill blanks.
- Arrange for an easy return of the questionnaire, even to the point of providing a self-addressed, stamped envelope.
- Retain e-mail responses until the project is complete, and then erase them from the computer.
- Provide a sample questionnaire and your tabulations in an appendix.
- Tabulate the results objectively. Even negative results that deny your hypothesis have value.

Unlike interview questions that elicit a response from one person or a couple, the questionnaire gathers multiple responses from many people, from twenty-five to several thousand. It should be designed for ease of tabulation, with results you can arrange in graphs and charts. If you want to build a table or graph from the results, see pages A-9 to A-10 for examples and instructions.

3d Conducting Experiments, Tests, and Observations

Empirical research, within and outside a laboratory, can determine why and how things exist, function, or interact. Your paper will explain your methods and findings in response to a hypothesis (see pages 18–23). An experiment thereby becomes primary evidence for your paper. Several methods can be used to collect data. We have discussed interviews (pages 26–28) and questionnaires (pages 33–37). Listed below are a few other methods. Consult with your instructor at all times with regard to your work and its design.

Observation

Observation is field research that occurs generally outside the lab in the field, which might be a child care center, a movie theater, a parking lot, or the counter of a fast food restaurant. The field is anywhere you can observe, count, and record behavior, patterns, and systems. It might include observing the thumb-sucking habits of infants, the eating disorders of fourteen-year-old girls, the self-discipline practiced by children on a playground, or students searching for a parking place on campus lots. We seldom notice the careful study conducted by retail merchandisers who want to know our buying habits or the analysis by a basketball coach on the shot selections by members of his team. Finding patterns in human behavior is the goal, and gathering data is a way of life for marketing firms, television networks, politicians—and, especially, behavioral researchers.

Most experiments and observations begin with a hypothesis (see pages 18-19), which is a statement assumed to be true for the purpose of investigation. Here is an example:

Academic success in the elementary grades increases with extra-curricular activities, such as band, choir, athletics, yearbook, and art.

The hypothesis might be "The more active the student happens to be in extracurricular activities, the more teachers can expect success in the student's academic performance." However, two other words come into play: *variable* and *indicator.* Things subject to change are variables that must be indicated in some manner.

Variable	**Indicator**
Extracurricular activity	Participation in sports, band, choir, and so forth
Academic success	Grade point average

This researcher will study and observe the grade point average in correlation with the students' activities.

The study might be further advanced by the use of control and experimental groups. Thus, one set of students would be the control group and receive no stimulus, while the experimental group would be stimulated to participate actively in three or more extracurricular activities. The findings from scientific observation would eventually be the subject of the student's report.

In some situations, the researcher can begin observation without a hypothesis and let the results lead to conclusions.

Laboratory Experiments

If you collect your primary data in the laboratory, you must carefully design the equipment to meet the demands of the study. Your methods for recording information must be regimented to the point that another researcher could follow your steps and obtain identical results. Laboratory experiments are used extensively in the social sciences as well as the physical sciences and engineering fields. Your instructor will assign, design, and supervise your lab work.

Field Experiments

You might be asked to investigate a subject outside the laboratory but with controls for measuring the data.

- Observation and interviewing, as discussed earlier, are two types of field research.
- Ethnographies are studies of societies by anthropologists, such as a study to recreate the social climate of the Cherokee Indians in North Carolina or Georgia before the forced march to Oklahoma.
- Case studies usually involve participant observation to describe people in special social settings, such as a study of six families, each with a child diagnosed with autism.
- Action research investigates a specific problem that is localized, such as observing the behavior of smokers outside a classroom building, counting the number of drivers without seat belts locked, or keeping a diary or notebook on oral responses to a question.
- Documentary research requires you to read the literature and draw conclusions, not perform empirical research; for example, you would read documents written by the parents of children with autism.

3e Structuring Your Scientific Report

Generally, a report on an experiment or observation follows a format involving four distinct parts: introduction, method, results, discussion. Understanding these elements will help you design your final report.

Introduction to explain the design of your experiment:

- Present the point of the study.
- State the hypothesis and how it relates to the problem.
- Provide the theoretical implications of the study.
- Explain the manner in which this study relates to previously published work.

Method to describe what you did and how you conducted the study:

- Describe the subjects who participated, whether human or animal.
- Describe the equipment and how you used it.
- Summarize the procedure in execution of each stage of your work.

Results to report your findings:

- Summarize the data you collected.
- Provide the necessary statistical treatment of the findings with tables, graphs, and charts.
- Include findings that conflict with your hypothesis.

Discussion that explains the implications of your work:

- Evaluate the data and its relevance to the hypothesis.
- Interpret the findings as necessary.
- Discuss the implications of the findings.
- Qualify the results and limit them to your specific study.
- Make inferences from the results.

CHECKLIST

Conducting an Experiment or Observation

- Explain the purpose of your work.
- Express a clear hypothesis.
- Select the proper design for the study: lab experiment, observation, or the collection of raw data in the field.
- Include a review of the literature, if appropriate.
- Keep careful records and accurate data.
- Do not allow your expectations to influence your interpretation of the results.
- Negative or unexpected results have merit; present them in that light.
- Maintain respect for human and animal subjects. In that regard, you may find it necessary to get approval for your research from a governing board. Read your college's rules and regulations on any research that requires testing humans or animals.

Note: Consult the Lester Web site (http://www.ablongman.com/lester) for additional information, examples, and links to sites that discuss in greater detail the matters of experiment and observation.

Your experiment and the writing of the report will require the attention of your instructor. Seek his or her advice often. This model can also be used for a fully developed proposal.

YOUR RESEARCH PROJECT

1. Select an event involving human behavior and observe it for one week. Record your field notes in a double-entry format by using the left side of the page to record and the right side of the page to comment and reflect on what you observe. Afterward, write a brief paragraph discussing your findings and submit it to your instructor.

Record:	Response:
Day 1 10-minute session at the parking lot—three cars negotiating the lanes and two sitting, waiting for a slot to open.	Some drivers are restless and rush around in hopes of finding a parking space. Others seem resigned to a long wait.
Day 2 10-minute session at the parking lot—six cars rushing up and down the lanes and two cars sitting quietly at the end of two lanes.	I saw a hint of road rage as one student lost an opening to a car in front and began banging on the steering wheel.
Day 3 10-minute session at the parking lot—interviewed one of the students who parked and waited quietly for a slot.	I asked, "How long do you usually have to wait?" She said, "Sometimes 10 minutes, sometimes 30, but one eventually opens. I can study while I wait."

2. Look carefully for subjects in which research outside the library will contribute to your report. Determine the kind of field research that will serve your needs: correspondence? local records? the news media? a questionnaire? an observation? an experiment?

3. Write a preliminary questionnaire that will survey members of your class about their jobs and the number of hours worked that might be devoted to their studies. Work closely with your instructor to design an instrument that will affect your research and your findings. Submit your questionnaire to your instructor. Most instructors want to examine and approve any questionnaire you will submit to others and to approve the design of your experiment or observation.

4. Follow university guidelines for working with human subjects.

4 Gathering Data in the Library

The library should be a center of your research, whether you access it electronically from your dorm room or go there in person. The library houses the academic books and periodicals, so it is essential to most research in the social sciences.

Why is the library a better resource than the Internet? Scholarship, that's why! The articles you access through the library are, in the main, written by scholars and published in books or journals only after careful review by a board of like-minded scholars.

Also, most of your library's databases can only be accessed with your academic identification. By logging on at the library from any computer in almost any place, you can download scholarly articles to your computer, print files, and read articles and books online. However, you also need to visit the library in person for access to journals and articles that are unavailable through electronic media and to browse the stacks for other helpful resources.

4a Launching the Search

Your research strategy in the library should include four steps, with adjustments for your individual needs.

1. Conduct a preliminary search for relevant sources. Scan the reference section of your library for its electronic sources as well as an abundance of printed indexes, abstracts, bibliographies, and reference books. Search the library's electronic book catalog and dip into the electronic networks, such as Silverplatter, for access to thousands of academic articles. This preliminary work will serve several purposes:

   - It shows the availability of source materials with diverse opinions.
   - It provides a beginning set of reference citations, abstracts, and full-text articles.
   - It defines and restricts your subject.
   - It gives you an overview of the subject by showing how others have researched it.

   Your preliminary search should include a tour of the entire library if orientation classes have not given you an overview.

2. Refine the topic and evaluate the sources. Narrow your topic to a manageable idea. With a refined topic, you can spend valuable time reading abstracts, articles, and pertinent sections of books to build a mix of journal articles and books that can accompany your Internet articles and field research.

3. Search the literature. First, consult Appendix B of this book, "A Listing of Reference Works for Your General Topic" (pages A-24–A-36), which gives you several appropriate electronic and printed sources for disciplines in the social sciences. It sends students in education to ERIC (online), *Current Index to Journals in Education,* and Edweb (online), and it sends students in psychology to *Psychological Abstracts,* PsycINFO, and PsycREF. Second, search the library's electronic book catalog (see pages 46–49) for books on your topic. Third, examine the library's electronic databases, such as InfoTrac and Silverplatter (see pages 49–51) for general information on your topic. Fourth, let the library's electronic databases search databases in your field, such as PsycINFO or ERIC. Fifth, consult the printed texts in the library's reference room.

4. Read and take notes. As you examine books, articles, essays, reviews, computer printouts, and government documents, write complete notes so you can transcribe them or paste them into your text, taking care to avoid plagiarism and to document the source accurately. Don't delay the writing task until you face a huge, intimidating pile of printouts, research notes, and photocopies.

4b Developing a Working Bibliography

Preserve your notes, printouts, photocopies, and downloaded files with full publication information and the URLs of Internet materials. Your final manuscript will require a bibliography page listing all your sources, so now is the time to accumulate the data in an organized fashion.

If you want to be fully organized—and your instructor may require this—maintain a working bibliography. This list of your sources may be kept in a notebook or, more efficiently, in a computer file. Either way, producing a set of bibliography entries has three purposes:

1. It locates articles and books for note-taking purposes.
2. It provides names, dates, and page numbers for your in-text citations, as in this example:

> Milner (2003) and Hasler (2004) have noted that good mental
> health can be stabilized by proper and effective diet.

3. It provides information for the final reference page (see Chapter 11). If you keep your entries current within a computer file, you can easily insert

them into your References page at the end of your manuscript. Each working bibliography entry should contain the following information—with variations, of course—for books, periodicals, government documents, and Internet sources:

- Author's name
- Title of the work
- Publication information
- The URL for Internet sources

For now but not for the final References page, add (1) the call number for books you must find in the stacks, and (2) a personal note describing the source's contribution to your work.

Working Bibliography Entry for a Book

HV881.T67 1997

Toth, J. (1997). *Orphans of the living: Stories of America's children in foster care.* New York: Simon & Schuster.

Books, Level 3

Case studies here can serve as examples for my paper.

Working Bibliography Entry for a Journal Article

McKay, J. S. (2003). Caretakers bias in the study of young children. *Journal of the American Academy of Child and Adolescent Psychiatry, 42,* 1267–1295.

The foster parents tell biased reasons for conditions of the children under their care. I can use this source.

Working Bibliography Entry for an Abstract Found on an Academic Database

Lancaster, M. K. (2001). *The transracial adoption debate in the United States.* Paper presented at the Annual National Conference of the National Association of African American Studies and the National Association of Hispanic and Latino Studies, Houston, TX. Abstract retrieved June 5, 2004, from ERIC database.

This paper addressed the issue of white couples adopting black children, which is seen as a divisive issue because a child's racial identity might be affected.

Working Bibliography Entry for a Magazine Article

Hayes, D. (2004, January 22). Trend toward private fostering of

teenagers expected to shatter myth. *Community Care, 23,* 12.

About one in ten children is
privately fostered with the
teenager's friends, the parent's
friends, or a relative, all
without proper monitoring.

Note: Choose magazines and Internet sites for their academic value and the articles for scholarly wisdom. Critical review of sources is vital.

Working Bibliography Entry for an Internet Article

Foster parenting in Kansas. (2003, October 21). Bill of rights for foster

children. Retrieved June 5, 2004, from

http://www.accesskandas.org/fostercare/FC_Bill_of_Rights.html

Kansas has a Bill of Rights for foster
children that features ten
articles of inherent rights, such
as the right to an education
and the right to loving care.

Note: Consult the index for the form of other sources (e.g., anthology, lecture, or map). Then, turn to the appropriate pages for examples.

4c   Finding Books on Your Topic

Your library's electronic book catalog will give you call numbers and descriptions of the books housed in the library as well as links to books stored in the library's network of academic sources on the Internet.

Using Your Library's Electronic Book Catalog

The computerized catalog of your school's library and its holdings probably has a special name, such as LIBNET, FELIX, ACORN, UTSEARCH, and so forth. In theory, it lists by subject, author, and title every book in the library and those books it can access online. Begin your research at the catalog by using a key word search to a subject, such as "foster children." The monitor will show a list of books, and you can click the hyperlinks to gather more information. The entries look something like these:

A guidebook for raising foster children / Susan McNair Blatt; foreword by
 Sherwood Boehlert.
By Blatt, Susan McNair, 1945, 2000.
Orphans of the living: Stories of America's children in foster care / Jen-
 nifer Toth.
By Toth, Jennifer. 1997.

The next procedure is to click on one, such as the Toth book, and get full details with call number and availability. You can print the information and use it to find the book in the stacks and to supply your working bibliography.

Using the Library's Bibliographies

A bibliography is a list of books and articles pertaining to a specific subject. The electronic book catalog will locate bibliographies of your discipline. Here are a few examples:

> *Education:* *A Guide to Reference and Information Sources,* by Lois J. Buttlar
>
> *Sociology:* *A Guide to Reference and Information Sources,* by Stephen H. Aby
>
> *Psychology:* *A Guide to Reference and Information Sources,* by Pam M. Baxter
>
> *Political Science: Illustrated Search Strategy an Sources: With an Introduction to Legal Research for Undergraduates,* by Roger C. Lowery and Sue A. Cody

The electronic catalog will also search for bibliographies devoted to specific topics. For instance, one student entered *bibliographies + social work with the aged.* The catalog quickly provided this source:

> *Gerontological Social Work: An Annotated Bibliography,* edited by Iris A. Parham.

If you leave the computer terminal and walk to the library's Reference Room, you can examine printed references. For example, the printed version of the *Bibliographic Index* helped one political science student find a bibliographic list hidden on pages 247–264 of a text:

> Prehistoric War
>
> LeBlanc, Steven A. Constant Battles: The Myth of the Peaceful, Noble Savage. New York: St. Martins, 2003 p 247–264.

If it fits your research, make a bibliography entry, like this one:

> LeBlanc, S. A. (2003). *Constant battles: The myth of the peaceful, noble savage.* New York: St. Martins, 2003.

The Reference Room is also a place to search the trade bibliographies, which can help you in three ways:

- Discover sources not listed in other bibliographies or in the card catalog.
- Locate facts of publication, such as place and date.
- Determine if a book is in print.

Search this work for your topic:

Subject Guide to Books in Print (New York: Bowker, 1957–date).

Note: Online, the *Subject Guide to Books in Print* may appear as *Books in Print*.

Use a key word or the subject classifications to find a current book on your topic. You may also consult the following trade bibliographies, which you might find online or in printed versions:

Books in Print lists by author and title all books currently in print.
Publishers' Weekly offers current publication data on new books and new editions.
Paperbound Books in Print locates all paperback books on one topic.
Cumulative Book Index provides complete publication data on books.
Library of Congress Catalog: Books, Subject provides a ready-made bibliography to books on hundreds of subjects.
Ulrich's International Periodicals Directory helps you locate current periodicals, both domestic and foreign, and to order photocopies of articles.

Searching for bibliographies in encyclopedias

Specialized encyclopedias can help your preliminary research, giving this type of list:

Baker Encyclopedia of Psychology and Counseling
The Corsini Encyclopedia of Psychology and Behavioral Science
Encyclopedia of Psychology

Select one, scan an article, and look especially at the end of the article for a bibliography. It might point you to additional sources, like this one in *Encyclopedia of Psychology.*

Further References

Clarke, E., & Dewhurst, K. *An illustrated history of brain function.*
Clarke, E., & O'Malley, C. D. *The human brain and spinal cord.*
Ferrier, D. *The functions of the brain.*
Finger, S., & Stein, D. G. *Brain damage and recovery: Research and clinical perspectives.*
McHenry, L. C., Jr. *Garrison's history of neurology.*

Two other sources for finding subject-specific encyclopedias are:

Note: Select one or two items that fit your topic to search for full publication data.

ARBA Guide to Subject Encyclopedias and Dictionaries, edited by Susan C. Awe
Oxford Reference Online (available as a library database)

*Examining the bibliographies at the end of books
and journal articles*

When you go into the stacks, look for bibliographies at the end of books.
Jot down titles on cards or photocopy the list for reference. Look also for bibliographies at the end of relevant articles in scholarly journals. For example,
students of social work depend on the bibliographies in issues of *Social Work
Research and Abstracts,* and students in women's studies courses can examine the bibliographies in *Women's Studies Abstracts.* In addition, the journals
themselves provide subject indexes to their own contents. For example, if
your subject is "Adoption," you will discover that a majority of your sources
are located in a few key journals. In this case, going straight to the annual
index of one of those journals is a useful short-cut.

4d   Finding Scholarly Articles

An index furnishes the exact page number(s) to specific sections of books
and to individual articles. It often provides
an abstract of the article and, in many
instances, the full text. Thus, at the library's
computer terminals, you might download
several scholarly articles without going into
the stacks at all.

> Note: Popular magazines and
> newspapers generate ideas that
> may show a need for the study,
> but your research project should
> be based on academic articles.

Searching Electronic Databases to Periodicals

The library network gives you access to electronic databases that focus
on the disciplines of the social sciences. These and others might be available
to you:

CIAO	Political science, sociology, and international studies
Criminology	Sociology and criminal justice
CQ Weekly	Articles and documents on the U.S. Congress
ERIC	Education and mass communication
GPO	Government publications on all subjects
InfoTrac	All subjects
JSTOR	Social sciences
Lexis-Nexis Academic	News, business, law, medicine, reference
MMY	Reviews of psychological research in mental measurements
ProjectMUSE	Social sciences, arts, humanities
PsycINFO	Psychology, medicine, education, social work
ViVa	Women's studies

These will introduce you to academic articles worthy of your time.

Using the H. W. Wilson Indexes

For many years, the Wilson Company of Minneapolis has provided excellent indexes to periodical literature. The tradition continues, and the indexing firm stays current by providing its indexes online as well as in printed versions. The company indexes topics that send you to articles in a wide variety of periodicals in many disciplines.

Social Sciences Index

The *Social Sciences Index* (online or in print) should be one of your primary sources. It indexes journal articles for 263 periodicals in all disciplines of the social sciences.

Education Index

Consult this index for articles in education, physical education, and related fields.

Readers' Guide to Periodical Literature

The *Readers' Guide to Periodical Literature* (online or in print) indexes important reading for the early stages of research in magazines such as *Aging, Psychology Today, Gender and Sexuality, Atlantic Monthly, Current Sociology, Foreign Policy,* and many others. Select articles worthy of your academic review.

Searching for an Index to Abstracts

An abstract is a brief description of an article, usually written by the author. An index to abstracts can accelerate your work by allowing you to read a summary before you assume the task of locating and reading the entire work. You may find abstracts at the electronic book catalog by entering the key word *abstracts,* which will produce a list similar to this:

Abstracts of current studies
Dissertation abstracts international
Social work abstracts
Psychological abstracts

By clicking on one, such as "psychology abstracts," you will be directed to a searchable database, such as PyscINFO, which will produce the type of entry shown in Figure 4.1.

Searching for Abstracts of Dissertations

You may also wish to examine the abstracts to the dissertations of graduate students in *Dissertation Abstracts International (DAI),* which you can access online through your library's electronic book catalog under *ProQuest Digital Dissertation.* You may also find *DAI* in the Reference Room as a printed version. For example, searching with the key words "foster children" might produce several citations, each similar to this one:

> Record 1 of 34 in PsycINFO 1999-2001/01
> AN: 2000-15373-006
> DT: Journal-Article
> TI: Evaluating an electronic monitoring system for people who wander.
> AU: Altus,-Deborah-E; **Mathews,-R.-Mark**; Xaverius,-Pamela-K; Engelman,-Kimberely-K; Nolan,-Beth-A-D
> SO: American-Journal-of-Alzheimer's Disease. 2000 Mar-Apr; Vol 15(2): 121-125
> PB: US: Prime National Publishing Corp.
> IS: 0182-5207
> PY: 2000
> AB: Wandering away from home, or elopement, is a behavior that places persons with dementia at risk of serious injury and may lead family caregivers to place their loved ones in institutions or to severely restrict their independence. This study evaluated the Mobile Locator, an electronic device designed to help caregivers quickly locate a person who has eloped. This 6 month pilot study included case studies of 7 users and an opinion survey of family caregivers, professional caregivers, and search and rescue workers. The survey results showed that respondents were positively impressed by the device, only identifying cost as a potential drawback. Case studies revealed that the equipment was easy to use, effective, and helpful to caregivers' peace of mind. These results suggest that the Mobile Locator is a valuable tool deserving of further study. (PsycINFO Database Record © 2000 APA, all rights reserved)

FIGURE 4.1 Sample entry from PsycINFO
(1) AN = accession number; (2) DT = document type; (3) TI = title of the article; (4) AU = author;
(5) SO = source; (6) PB = publisher; (7) IS = ISSN number; (8) PY = publication year;
(9) AB = abstract of the article.

Foster children and the effects of multiple placements on their behavior and academic performance by Cathey, Katrese Nicole CALIFORNIA STATE UNIVERSITY, LONG BEACH, 2003

Undergraduates seldom consult dissertations, but you might find one that directly affects your research.

4e   Searching for a Biography

When your academic research involves the life of a person, you will find biographies in books and articles, in print as well electronic versions. A digital search at the library will quickly yield multiple sources, such as these:

Biography Reference Bank
Current Biography: 1940–Present

Current Biography Illustrated
Wilson Biographies Plus Illustrated

Just be certain that you get an academic biography, not a fast-paced magazine article.

4f Searching for Articles in the Newspaper Indexes

For many years, searching for newspaper articles was difficult, if not impossible. There were no indexes capable of doing the task. Now the electronic networks enable you to find newspaper articles from across the nation. On the library's list of databases, click on Lexis-Nexis Academic; this provides a search engine to articles in hundreds of newspapers. For example, a search for articles on "foster children" produced 125 articles in such diverse newspapers as *The Baltimore Sun, Palm Beach Post,* and *The Herald* of Rock Hill, South Carolina. If Lexis-Nexis Academic is not available, type "newspapers" at the electronic book catalog. You can also go straight to the Internet at Newspapers.com. However, be selective in researching a newspaper to find quality in certain sections, such as an editorial page, prospective section, or academic review of books.

4g Searching the Indexes to Pamphlet Files

Librarians routinely clip items of interest from newspapers, bulletins, pamphlets, and miscellaneous materials and file them alphabetically by subject in loose-leaf folders.

Vertical File Index is a regular stop during preliminary investigation. Sometimes called the *vertical file,* it will have clippings on many topics, such as:

"Abuse of the Elderly in Nursing Homes"
"Home Schooling"
"Everything Doesn't Cause Depression"
"Medicare and Mental Health Services"

The *Vertical File Index* gives a description of each entry, the price, and the information for ordering the pamphlet. Check at your library's electronic card catalog to see if your librarians have created an online index to local pamphlets.

The CQ Researcher, online and in print, features many pamphlets devoted to such topics as "Adolescents and Youth" that focuses on drinking on campus, drug testing, underage drinking, employment, pregnancy, and so forth. It examines each topic in depth, gives background information, shows a chronology of important events or processes, expresses an outlook, and provides an annotated bibliography. In one place you have material worthy of quotation and paraphrase as well as a list of additional sources. Each issue also contains annotated bibliographies to point you toward other sources. Here's an example of an annotated bibliography from a list of sources on Internet Plagiarism as provided by *CQ Researcher*.

Kellogg, Alex P., "Students Plagiarize Online Less Than Many

Think, a New Study Finds," *The Chronicle of Higher Education,*

Feb. 15, 2002, p. 44.

Social Issues Resources Series (SIRS), online or in print, collects articles on special topics and reprints them as one unit on a special subject, such as abortion, or prayer in schools. *SIRS* yields 10 or 12 articles in one booklet. Its information is similar to that shown above for *The CQ Researcher.* The correct citation form to articles found in *SIRS* or *CQ Researcher* is shown above.

4h   Searching for Government Documents

All branches of the government publish massive amounts of material. Many documents have great value for researchers, so investigate the following source if your topic is one that government agencies might have investigated. On your library's network, go to GPO on Silverplatter. On the Internet, go to GPOAccess. This database will direct you to the files of the Government Printing Office. The database list includes *Congressional Bills, Congressional Record, Economic Indicators, Public Laws,* the *U. S. Constitution,* and much more. A key word search will yield an entry similar to that shown in Figure 4.2.

Record 5 of 366 in GPO on SilverPlatter 1976-2000/10
1 — AN: 99053103
2 — SU: Y 4.AG 4:S.HRG.106-444
3 — CA: United States. Congress. Senate. Special Committee on Aging.
4 — TI: Nursing home residents: short-changed by staff shortages : forum before the Special Committee on Aging, United States Senate, One Hundred Sixth Congress, first session, Washington, DC, November 3,1999.
5 — SO: Washington: U.S. G.P.O. For sale by the U.S. G.P.O., Supt. of Docs. Congressional Sales Office, 1999 [i.e. 2000].
6 — SE: United States. Congress. Senate. S. hrg.; 106-444.
7 — IT: 1009-B-01 1009-C-01 (MF)

FIGURE 4.2 From GPO on Silverplatter
(1) AN = accession number; (2) SU = document number; (3) CA = corporate author; (4) TI = title; (5) SO = source; (6) SE = series; (7) IT = GPO item number

A reference entry for the source above, a Senate hearing, should look like this:

U.S. Senate. Special Committee on Aging. (1999). "Nursing home
residents: Short-changed by staff shortages." Washington, DC:
U.S. Government Printing Office.

Here are other works that index government documents:

Monthly Catalog of the United States Government Publications is the printed version of GPO.

Public Affairs Information Service Bulletin (PAIS), online and in print. This work indexes articles and documents published by miscellaneous organizations. It's a good place to start because of its excellent index.

Congressional Record, online and in print. This daily publication provides Senate and House bills, documents, and committee reports.

Public Papers of the Presidents of the United States, online and in print. This work is the publication of the executive branch, including not only the president but also all members of the president's cabinet and various agencies.

The US. Code, online and in print. The Supreme Court regularly publishes decisions, codes, and other rulings, as do appellate and district courts. State courts also publish rulings and court results on a regular basis.

Note: See page 158 for correct methods of writing reference citations for government documents.

CQ Weekly, online and in print. This database tracks the activities of the U. S. Congress.

4i Searching for Essays within Books

Some essays get lost in collections and anthologies. You can find such essays, listed by subject, on this database at your library:

Essay and General Literature Index on Silverplatter

The print version is:

Essay and General Literature Index, 1900-1933. New York: H. W. Wilson, 1934. Supplements, 1934-date.

This reference work helps you find essays hidden in anthologies. It indexes material of both a biographical and a critical nature. It helped a student in political science find this essay buried on pages 46-65 of a book edited by R. A. Sherrill.

King, Martin Luther, 1929-1968

Note: Your electronic book catalog will give you the call number to Sherrill's book.

Raboteau, A. J. Martin Luther King and the tradition of black religious protest. (*In* Religion and the life of the nation; ed. by R. A. Sherrill, p. 46-65).

The Library Search

When you start your research on a topic, you will need to switch back and forth from the computer terminals to the library stacks of books and periodicals and also to the printed bibliographies and indexes, given the resources of your library. Start, perhaps, with the sources on this list.

To find books:
> The library's electronic book catalog with a key word, author's name, or title
> The library's electronic catalog with the key words "bibliographies + your discipline," which might be, for example, health, genetics, or psychology.

To find periodical articles:
> The library's electronic database with a key word
> The library's electronic database with the key words "indexes + your discipline"
> The printed indexes, like *Social Sciences Index,* at the library's reference room

To find an abstract:
> The library's electronic database with the key words "abstracts + your discipline"

To find biographies in books and periodicals:
> The library's electronic database with key word "biography"
> *Biography Index,* online or in print

To find newspaper articles
> The library's electronic database, Lexis-Nexis Academic Online, go to http://www.newspapers.com

To find pamphlet files:
> The library's network to *SIRS* and *CQ Researcher*
> Ask your librarian for local files

To find government documents:
> The library's network to GPO on Silverplatter, online as GPOAccess

To find essays within books:
> *Essay and General Literature Index,* online or in print

To find microforms:
> The library's electronic database to ERIC

4j   Using Microforms

Online sources are gradually replacing microforms, but your library may have magazines and newspapers converted to a small, single sheet of film called a *microfiche* (flat sheet of film) or *microfilm* (a roll). Your library will specify in the cardex files (the list of periodicals) how journals and magazines are housed, whether in bound, printed volumes or microforms. Use a microfilm reader, usually located near the microfilm files, to browse the articles. Should you need a printed copy of a microfilmed article, the library will supply coin-operated machines, or the clerks will copy it for you.

Your library may also house guides to special microform holdings, which carry such titles as *American Culture, 1493–1806: A Guide to the Microfilm Collection,* or perhaps *American Social Work Periodicals, 1800–1850: A Guide to the Microfilm Collection.* Every library has its own peculiar holdings of microfilm and microfiche materials; the librarian can help you.

YOUR RESEARCH PROJECT

1. If you have not done so with an orientation group, take the time to tour your school's main library. Identify its sections and the types of information that are available. Chat with a librarian, especially at the reference room. Stroll through the stacks of books, and visit the periodicals section. Find the journals, pick up a bound volume of *Journal of Sociology,* open it, and notice how it contains 12 issues of one year's publications. Look at one article to note the language, style, and format of a scholarly publication. Write a paragraph for submission to your instructor in which you describe the difference between a journal article and a magazine article.

2. At the library, sit down at a computer terminal and investigate its options. Make up a topic for the moment—perhaps child abuse, orphans, teenage pregnancy, or home schooling—and search for books or articles at the terminal. Try to find an abstract or a full-text article to print at the terminal. Submit a copy of the abstract or the full-text article to your instructor.

3. Go to the reference desk and ask the librarian for a specialized bibliography on your topic—that is, say something like this, substituting your topic: "Do you have a specialized bibliography on global warming?" Write a report for your instructor on what bibliographies you find.

4. Locate the library's holdings of *The CQ Researcher.* Page through the booklets or scan through the Internet files (http://www.cqpress.com) to note how they provide several penetrating articles on a common topic.

In the index to *The CQ Researcher,* you can see if your chosen topic is treated in a special issue. Find one article of interest in *The CQ Researcher,* copy it, and submit it to your instructor.

5. To test the resources of the library, search for information about the day you were born. Don't limit yourself to major events of the day; seek also hometown news and political events. The popular culture of the decade will be evident in the advertisements; note what people were buying and the prices they paid. Write a report on this special day and submit it to your instructor.

5 Finding and Filtering Internet Sources

The Internet is now a major source of research information, and we know that many students start their research on the World Wide Web. That's okay. You may start your research on the Web, but don't you dare stop there! Let's address immediately the good, the bad, and the ugly with respect to Internet sources.

First, the ugly: You can buy a canned research paper and submit it as your own. However, just because you buy a research paper does not mean you own it and can put your name on it. You always have the obligation of identifying the source, and the author or publisher retains rights to the content, whether in printed form or an electronic format. Also ugly, and also considered plagiarism, is downloading Internet material into your paper without citation and documentation, thereby making it appear to be your own work. For a full discussion of plagiarism, see pages 81–93.

Second, the bad: You will find articles that are not worthy of citation in your research paper. You must filter unsubstantiated personal opinion pieces. These will pop up on your browser list and may be nothing more than a home page. You must also filter commercial sites that disguise their sales pitch with informative articles. In other cases you will encounter advocacy pages that are biased in favor of the group's position on the environment, gun control, abortion, and so forth. See also the Checklist, page 62, "Evaluating Internet Sources."

Third, the good: The Internet, if you know where to look, is loaded with absolutely marvelous material that was unattainable just a few years ago. It offers instant access to millions of computer files relating to almost every subject, including articles, illustrations, sound and video clips, and raw data. Much of it meets basic academic standards, yet you should keep in mind that the best academic material is available only through databases at your college library, such as InfoTrac and PsycINFO. That is, you can rest assured that scholarly articles found through the library's Web are far more reliable than those you might find by general access through Google or Yahoo! Also, a significant number of journal articles are now available as PDF files, which are reproductions of the original pages (see page 71 for more details).

This chapter will help you with two tasks:

1. To become efficient searchers for academic information on the Web.

2. To become accomplished at evaluating and filtering the complex web of Internet sites.

5a Beginning an Internet Search

To trace the good and the bad of Internet research, let's follow the trail of one student, Sherri James, who decided, because she is a competitive swimmer, to investigate the use of drugs for enhancing one's performance in the pool—not that she wanted to try drugs but to educate herself and produce a research paper at the same time. Remember, you may select topics that affect you personally.

Probably the first thing most students do, like Sherri James, is visit a favorite browser, such as one of these:

About.com	http://home.about.com/index.htm
AltaVista	http://altavista.digital.com/
AOL Netfind	http://www.aol.com/netfind
Excite	http://www.excite.com
Google	http://www.google.com/
Hotbot	http://www.hotbot.com

CHECKLIST

Using Online Rather Than Print Versions

Online versions of articles offer advantages, but they also present problems. On the plus side, you can view them almost instantly on the monitor rather than searching, threading, and viewing microfilm or microfiche. You can save or print an abstract or article without the hassle of photocopying, and you can even download material to your computer and, where appropriate, insert it in your paper. However, keep these drawbacks in mind:

- The text may differ from the original printed version and may even be a digest. Therefore, cite the Internet source to avoid giving the appearance of citing from the printed version. There are often major differences between the same article in *USA Today* and in *USA Today DeskTopNews*. In APA style, cite the correct version on your References page.

- Online abstracts may not accurately represent the full article. In fact, some abstracts are not written by the author at all but by an editorial staff member. Therefore, resist the urge to quote from the abstract and write a paraphrase of it—or, better, find the full text and cite from it (see also pages 127–128).

- You may need to subscribe, at a modest cost, to some sites. A company has the right to make demands before giving the general population access to its material.

Infoseek   http://infoseek.com
InferenceFind   http://www.inference.com
Lycos   http://www.lycos.com
Magellan   http://www.magellan.com
Webcrawler   http://webcrawler.com
Yahoo!   http://www.yahoo.com

At the search window, Sherri James typed "fitness and drugs" as she began her search for psychological information on athletes who willingly jeopardize their careers by using steroids and blood doping. She wanted to examine this theory: "Athletes who use illegal substances damage themselves psychologically as well as physically." At first, James was directed to Beachbody.com, healthandfitness.com, and trulyhuge.com. Notice that all three sites are commercial sites (.com). Also, they each want to sell something—Power 90 supplements, a carb-electrolyte drink, or cybernetics nutritional products and instructional videos. One site, which shall remain anonymous, advertised steroids for sale, such as Epogen and Erythropoietin. For Sherri James, these Internet locations offered no information, except to suggest this note that she jotted into her research journal:

> With supplements, drugs, and even steroids readily available on Web sites, it's no wonder so many athletes get caught in the quick-fix bodybuilding trap.

Next, Sherri James found two swimming articles: "Three Steps to Swimming Success" and "Beat Fatigue in Long Meets." These were written by Rick Curl, a noted swim coach who has trained Olympic champions. Curl advocated three elements in training: in-pool workouts, out-of-pool training, and nutrition. For nutrition, the articles encouraged swimmers to "refuel their muscles with a sports drink containing plenty of carbohydrates." And guess what? The articles were promoting and selling two sports drinks. Sherri James noticed that the site, Powering Muscles, is sponsored by PacificHealth Laboratories, the makers of Accelerade sports drink and Eudurox Recovery drink. This site, too, was a .com site. Thus, Sherri James wrote a note to position the good instruction from the swim coach within the context of the site:

> Despite promoting two commercial supplements for swimmers, successful swim coach Rick Curl goes beyond pitching the nutritional products to offer valuable advice on in-pool techniques as well as out-of-pool aerobic training, stretching, and calisthenics.

At this point, Sherri James decided to try a browser's directory. In Yahoo! she found hyperlinks to:

Business and Economy
Computer and Internet
News and Media

Entertainment
Recreation and Sports

She clicked on the last one and found another list, which contained what she was looking for—a hyperlink to Drugs in Sports. There she found 13 links, among them:

Doping and Sports—Offers collective expert assessment from the CNRS.

Drugs in Sport—Provides information on performance-enhancing drugs in sport, the latest articles on the subject, reports, resources, and useful Web sites.

Findlaw: Drug Use in Sports—Includes a story archive and background information on testing, prevention, policies, and commonly used drugs.

NCAA Drug Testing—Contains information on the association's drug testing policy.

PlayClean—Promotes anti-doping policies and preventing youth drug use through sports, from the Office of National Drug Control Policy.

Sherri had now found site domains other than commercial ones, such as .org, .gov, .net, and .edu. At NCAA.org, she was able to print out the NCAA Drug Testing Program and use portions of the rules in her paper. Here is one of her notes:

The NCAA clearly forbids blood doping. It says, "The practice of blood doping (the intravenous injection of whole blood, packed red blood cells or blood substitutes) is prohibited and any evidence confirming use will be cause for action consistent with that taken for a positive drug test" (Bylaw 31.1.3.1.1). Thus, the athlete who thinks he or she will gain a psychological or physiological advantage runs the risk of banishment from all games, and that's when the permanent psychological damage occurs.

At Playclean, Sherri found a link to http://www.whitehousedrugpolicy.gov and an article entitled "Women and Drugs" by the Office of National Drug Control Policy. She was now finding material worthy of notetaking:

A study by scientists at Columbia University has found the signals and situations of risk are different for girls and that "girls and young women are more vulnerable to abuse and addiction: they get hooked faster and suffer the consequences sooner than boys and young men" ("Women and Drugs").

Sherri James had begun to find her way to better sources on the Internet, but she still needed to examine the academic databases by logging on at her college library (see pages 49–57) and by doing field research, such as interviewing fellow athletes or conducting a survey by means of a questionnaire (see pages 33–42).

Evaluating Internet Sources

1. Prefer the .edu and .org sites. Usually, these are domains developed by an educational institution, such as Ohio State University, or by a professional organization, such as the American Sociological Society.

2. The .gov (government) and .mil (military) sites usually have reliable materials. The .com (commercial) sites are suspect for several reasons:

   • They may sell advertising space.

   • They often charge for access to their files.

   • They can be Internet service provider (ISP) sites, which people pay to use and to post their material. Although some ISP sites might have good information, they are usually no more reliable than vanity presses or want ads.

3. Look for the professional affiliation of the writer, which you will find in the opening credits or an e-mail address. Go in search of the writer's home page. Type the writer's name at a search engine to see how many results are listed. Also, type the writer's name at Amazon.com for a list of his or her books. If you find no information on the writer, you must rely on a sponsored Web site—that is, if the site is not sponsored by an organization or institution, you should probably abandon the source and look elsewhere.

4. Look for a bibliography accompanying the article, which will indicate the scholarly nature of the work.

5. Usenet discussion groups offer valuable information at times, but some discussions lack sound, fundamental reasoning or evidence to support the opinions.

6. Treat e-mail messages as mail, not scholarly articles. A similar rule applies to chat.

7. Check whether or not the site offers links to professional or commercial sites. Links to educational sites serve as a modern bibliography to additional reliable sources. Links to commercial sites are often attempts to sell you something.

8. Learn to distinguish among the different types of Web sites, such as advocacy pages, personal home pages, informational pages, and business and marketing pages. This site provides evaluation techniques: http://www.science.widener.edu/~withers/webeval.htm.

9. Your skills in critical thinking can usually determine the validity of a site. For more help in critical thinking, see page 2.

5b Reading an Internet Address

In the library, you employ a call number to find a book. On the Internet, you employ a uniform resource locator (URL), like this one: http://www.georgetown.edu/ library_catalogues.html.

- The *protocol* (http://) transmits data.
- The *server* (www, for World Wide Web) is the global Internet service that connects the multitude of computers and the Internet files.
- The *domain* (georgetown.edu) names the organization feeding information into the server with a *suffix* to label the type of organization: .com (commercial), .edu (educational), .gov (government), .mil (military), .net (network organization), or .org (organization).
- The *directory/file* (library_catalogues) finds one of the server's directories and then a specific file.
- The *hypertext markup language* (html) names the computer language used to write the file.

Often, knowing just the protocol and the server domain will get you to a home site from which you can search deeper for files. The URL http://lcweb.loc.gov/homepage takes you to the Library of Congress (see Figure 5.1), where you can examine a specific directory, such as Thomas: Congress at Work (see Figure 5.2). In Thomas, you have access to legislation of both the House and the Senate, with links to many other sites and a search engine for finding specific information.

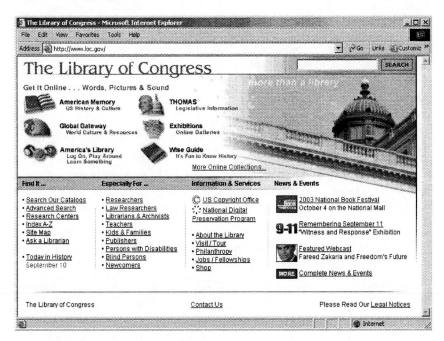

FIGURE 5.1 The home page for the Library of Congress

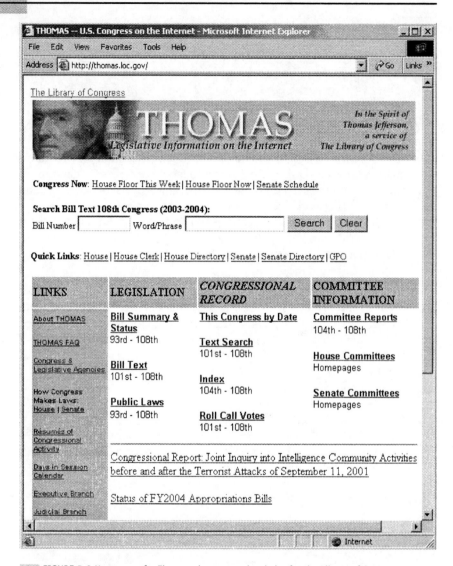

FIGURE 5.2 Home page for Thomas, the congressional site for the Library of Congress

You can search the current Congress for the text of bills. At the Thomas search engine, enter a word or phrase, such as "student financial aid," and the site will take you to a list of resolutions, bills, and acts, like the five listed here:

1. Responsible Student Financial Assistance Assurance Act of 2003 (Introduced in House) [H.R.696.IH]
2. Hazing Prohibition Act of 2003 (Introduced in House) [H.R.1207.IH]

3. To express the support and commitment of the U.S. House of Representatives for the troops serving to protect and defend the United States of America by encouraging actions to extend . . . (Introduced in House) [H.RES.158.IH]

4. To express the sense of the House of Representatives that the maximum Pell Grant should be increased to $5,800. (Introduced in House) [HRES.144.I]

5. Educational Excellence for All Learners Act of 2003 (Introduced in Senate) [S.8.IS]

At this point, you have the option of reading the House bills, the resolution, or the Senate bill by clicking on the underlined links. The House bill on hazing and loss of financial aid is shown in Figure 5.3. In effect, you will have moved rather quickly from the home page of the Library of Congress to a specific piece of legislation you might wish to use in your paper.

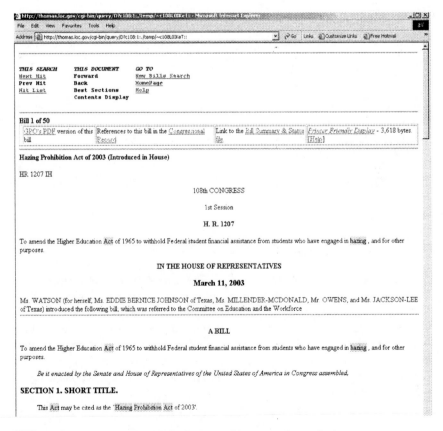

FIGURE 5.3 H.R. 1207.I, a bill in the House of Representatives on hazing

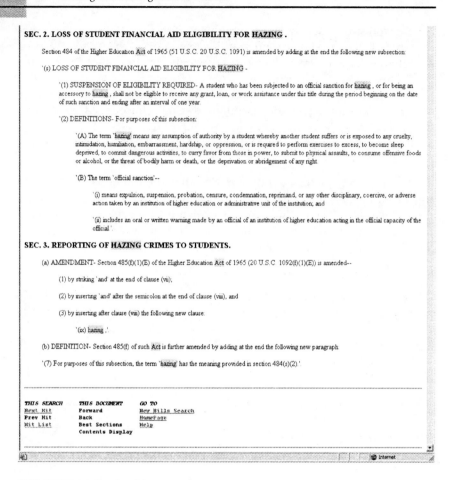

SEC. 2. LOSS OF STUDENT FINANCIAL AID ELIGIBILITY FOR HAZING .

Section 484 of the Higher Education Act of 1965 (51 U.S.C. 20 U.S.C. 1091) is amended by adding at the end the following new subsection:

'(s) LOSS OF STUDENT FINANCIAL AID ELIGIBILITY FOR HAZING -

'(1) SUSPENSION OF ELIGIBILITY REQUIRED- A student who has been subjected to an official sanction for hazing , or for being an accessory to hazing , shall not be eligible to receive any grant, loan, or work assistance under this title during the period beginning on the date of such sanction and ending after an interval of one year.

'(2) DEFINITIONS- For purposes of this subsection:

'(A) The term 'hazing' means any assumption of authority by a student whereby another student suffers or is exposed to any cruelty, intimidation, humiliation, embarrassment, hardship, or oppression, or is required to perform exercises to excess, to become sleep deprived, to commit dangerous activities, to curry favor from those in power, to submit to physical assaults, to consume offensive foods or alcohol, or the threat of bodily harm or death, or the deprivation or abridgement of any right.

'(B) The term 'official sanction'--

'(i) means expulsion, suspension, probation, censure, condemnation, reprimand, or any other disciplinary, coercive, or adverse action taken by an institution of higher education or administrative unit of the institution; and

'(ii) includes an oral or written warning made by an official of an institution of higher education acting in the official capacity of the official '.

SEC. 3. REPORTING OF HAZING CRIMES TO STUDENTS.

(a) AMENDMENT- Section 485(f)(1)(E) of the Higher Education Act of 1965 (20 U.S.C. 1092(f)(1)(E)) is amended--

(1) by striking 'and' at the end of clause (vii);

(2) by inserting 'and' after the semicolon at the end of clause (viii); and

(3) by inserting after clause (viii) the following new clause:

'(ix) hazing ,'.

(b) DEFINITION- Section 485(f) of such Act is further amended by adding at the end the following new paragraph:

'(7) For purposes of this subsection, the term 'hazing' has the meaning provided in section 484(s)(2).'.

THIS SEARCH	THIS DOCUMENT	GO TO
Next Hit	Forward	New Bills Search
Prev Hit	Back	HomePage
Hit List	Best Sections	Help
	Contents Display	

FIGURE 5.3 (*Continued from page 65*)

5c   Using a Search Engine

By this point, you probably have a favorite search engine and know how to use it. So this section merely lists the types of search engines and the way they perform. Keep in mind that they change often, and more are added each year while others disappear. Also, search with more than one browser because one cannot catalog even half the sites available. In addition, we cannot stress enough the importance of using the educational search engines listed on pages 68–69; with those, you can have confidence that the articles have a scholarly basis, not a commercial one.

Subject Directory Search Engines

These search engines are compiled and indexed by individuals to guide you to general areas that are then subdivided to specific categories. Your key words control the results listed.

About.com	http://home.about.com/index.htm
Go.network	http://go.com
Lycos	http://www.lycos.com
Yahoo!	http://www.yahoo.com

Yahoo! is an edited site with plenty of directories and subdirectories. Figure 5.4 shows the opening page from Yahoo!. You can make a key word search or click on one of the categories, such as Society and Culture, to go deeper into the Web directories and, eventually, the articles.

Robot-Driven Search Engines

Another set of engines respond to a key word by electronically scanning millions of Web pages. Your key words control the size of the results listed.

AltaVista	http://altavista.digital.com
AOL Netfind	http://www.aol.com/netfind
AskJeeves	http://www.askjeeves.com
Excite	http://www.excite.com
Google	http://www.google.com
Hotbot	http://www.hotbot.com
Infoseek	http://infoseek.com
InferenceFind	http://www.inference.com
Magellan	http://www.magellan.com
NorthernLight	http://www.northernlight.com
Webcrawler	http://webcrawler.com

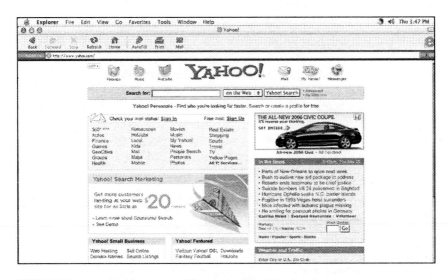

FIGURE 5.4 Opening home page of the search engine Yahoo!

Metasearch Engines

A metasearch examines your topic in several of the search engines listed above. Thus, you need not search each engine separately. For example, when you enter a query at the Mamma.com Web site, the engine simultaneously queries about ten of the major search engines, such as Yahoo!, Webcrawler, and Magellan. It then provides you with a short, relevant set of results. You get fewer results than you might at one of the major search engines. For example, the request for "chocolate + children" produced 342,718 results on AltaVista but only 50 on Mamma.com. The claim is that a metasearch engine gives you the most relevant sites because it selects the first few listings from each of the other search engines under the theory that each engine puts the most relevant sites at the top of its list; however, some commercial sites are able to buy their way to the top. Here are four metasearch engines:

Dogpile	http://dogpile.com
Mamma.com	http://mamma.com
Metacrawler.com	http://metacrawler.com
Metafind.com	http://metafind.com

Specialized Search Engines

Other search engines specialize in one area, such as WWWomen (women's studies), TribalVoice (Native American Studies), and Bizweb (business studies). In addition, many Web sites, such as the Library of Congress and New York Times Online, have search engines just for themselves. Even the sites for local newspapers have search engines to their own archives (see page 73).

To discover any specialized search engine, go to one of the major sites, such as AltaVista, and ask, "Where can I find a search engine on women's studies?" The computer will name specialized search engines:

Cybergrrl—Resources and programming for women online.

Diotima—Materials for the study of women and gender in the ancient world.

Femina—A comprehensive, searchable directory of links to female-friendly sites and information on the World Wide Web.

ViVa—A bibliography of women's history in historical and women's studies journals.

Educational Search Engines

Educational search engines provide subject indexes to the various disciplines (humanities or sciences) and to subtopics under those headings (history, literature, biochemistry, and so on). Try several because they will take you to academic material, not commercial sites with advertising banners popping up all over the screen.

Argus Clearinghouse	http://www.clearinghouse.net
English Server	http://eserver.org

Internet Public Library	http://ipl.sils.umich.edu
Knowledge Source (SIRS)	http://www.sirs.com
Library of Congress Subject	http://lcweb.loc.gov/global/
Planet Earth	http://www.nosc.mil/ planetearth/info.html
SavvySearch	http://www.cs.colostate.edu/ ~dreiling/smartform.html
SearcheBOOKS	http://www.searchebooks.com
SearchEDU	http://www.searchedu.com
SearchGOV	http://www.searchgov.com
SearchMIL	http://www.searchmil.com
Voice of the Shuttle	http://humanitas.ucsb.edu/

We return now to Sherri James and her investigations. She entered the phrase "blood doping" at the SearchEDU Web site, which produced an article along with links to five additional sites worthy of her investigation.

Performance-Enhancing Drugs and Athletics

Jennifer Wolff

This group of computer links deals with the use of performance enhancing drugs and practices in the sporting arena. They primarily focus on the use of steroids and blood doping. There are many reasons why this kind of drug use is prohibited in athletics, besides just the physical harm they cause. Performance-enhancing drugs violate the basic premise of athletics—fair competition. At times athletes may feel that using steroids, for example, is necessary to do because many of their competitors are doing it, and thus the athletes are coerced into taking drugs to be on an equal level. Blood doping has received the same negative attention, as it is commonly used among distance runners and cyclists to build up oxygen in their blood. Athletics are becoming more of a competition of drugs, rather than of athletes. These links will help to define what steroids, blood doping, and other performance enhancers are, and how they affect the body. There is a link to NCAA which deals with drug testing, as well as one to the Canadian Center for Ethics in Sport. These two organizations talk about the ethics surrounding performance-enhancing drug use, and what is being done to put an end to it among athletes.

Blood Doping: Is It Really Worth It?—http://is.tc.cc.tx.us/~mstorey/beckham.html

This extensively detailed article shows how blood doping is used among athletes, and the effects it brings about.

OSU Student Health Services: Steroid Abuse—http://studenthealth.oregonstate.edu/brochures/steroid-abuse.php

This page gives a definition as to what steroids are, their risks, and how they work.

Use of Anabolic/Androgenic Steroids by Athletes—http://www.medstudents.com.br/sport/sport2.htm

This gives a more detailed description of steroids and its muscular effects—a more medical approach to understanding how steroids enhance the body.

Canadian Centre for Ethics in Sport—http://www.cces.ca

This is part of the home page for the Canadian Centre for Ethics in Sports. This page states why this organization believes drugs should not be allowed in sport.

NCAA Drug Testing—http://www1.ncaa.org/membership/ed_outreach/health-safety/drug_testing/index.html

This is part of NCAA's home page, which focuses solely on its drug testing procedures for intercollegiate athletics.

HINT: Most Web programs include a Bookmark or Favorites tool, used to save addresses for quick access. When you find a file you want to access later, create a bookmark so you can revisit it with just a click of the mouse.

Note: If you are working at a university computer laboratory, do not add bookmarks to the hard drive. Instead, save the bookmarks to your computer disk by using Save As in the File menu.

For example, in Netscape, simply click on Bookmarks, then click on Add Bookmark. This automatically adds the URL to the list of bookmarks. In Microsoft Internet Explorer, use the button bar marked Favorites to create bookmarks.

5d Searching for Articles in Online Journals and Magazines

The Internet can help you find articles in online journals and magazines. However, do not forget that the best source for academic journals is your library's database collection.

Online Journals

You can find online journals in three ways.

1. Access your favorite search engine and do a keyword search for "journals" plus the name of your subject. For example, one student accessed AltaVista and ran a keyword search for "journals + fitness." The search produced links to 20 online journals devoted to fitness, such as Health Page, Excite Health, and Physical Education. Another student's search for "women's studies + journals" produced a list of relevant journals, including Feminist Collections, Resources for Feminist Research, and Differences. By accessing one of these links, you can examine abstracts and articles.

2. Access a search engine's subject directory. In Yahoo!, for example, one student selected Social Science from the key word directory, clicked on Sociology, clicked on Journals, and accessed links to several online journals, such as Edge: The E-Journal of Intercultural Relations and Sociological Research Online.

3. If you already know the name of a journal, go to your favorite search engine to make a key word query—for example, "Psycholoquy," a social science journal.

Many online periodicals offer key word searches to their articles. In addition, they often provide full-text articles you may download; however, some online journals charge a fee or require you to join the association before they permit you access.

Online Magazines

Several directories exist for discovering articles in magazines:

NewsDirectory.Com   http://www.newsdirectory.com/new/

This search engine directs you to magazine home pages where you can begin your free search in that magazine's archives. Under "current events," for example, it will send you to *Atlantic Monthly* at theatlantic.com, *Harper's* at Harpers.org, and *Newsweek* at Newsweek.com.

Electric Library   http://www3.elibrary.com

This site has a good search engine, but it requires membership (which is free for one month). Remember to cancel your membership after research is finished or charges will accrue.

Pathfinder   http://pathfinder.com

This site gives you free access to *Time* magazine; it has a good search engine to thousands of archival articles.

ZD Net   http://www.zdnet.com

This search engine provides excellent access to industry-oriented articles in banking, electronics, computers, management, and so on. It offers two weeks of free access before charges begin to accrue.

Another way to access online magazines is through a search engine's directory. For example, one student accessed AltaVista, clicked on Health and Fitness in the directory on the home page, clicked on Publications, then Magazines. The result was a list of 40 magazines devoted to various aspects of health and fitness, such as *Healthology* and *The Black Health Net.*

5e   Searching for Articles in Newspapers and Media Sources

To find almost any newspaper in the United States, even local weeklies, consult:

http://www.newspapers.com

This site takes you to the Internet sites for over 800 newspapers. In most cases, the online newspaper has its own internal search engine that enables you to examine articles from its archives. Figure 5.5 shows the opening page of the online site for a local newspaper in Larchmont Village, California. Notice especially the hyperlink at the upper left, "Archives," a feature that enables you to find articles from past issues.

Most major news organizations maintain Internet sites. Consult one of these:

The Chronicle of Higher Education   http://www.chronicle.com

This site requires a paid subscription, so access it through your library at no cost.

CNN Interactive   http://www.cnn.com

CNN maintains a good search engine and takes you quickly without cost to transcripts of its broadcasts. It's a good source for research in current events.

C-SPAN Online   http://www.c-span.org

This site focuses on public affairs and offers both a directory and a search engine for research in public affairs, government, and political science.

Fox News   http://www.foxnews.com

This site provides articles from its own network and also from news services, such as Reuters and the Associated Press.

London Times   http://www.the-times.co.uk/news/ pages/Times/frontpage.html

The *Times* provides directories and indexes, but not a search engine, so improve your search for articles in the *Times* with searchuk.com.

National Public Radio Online   http://www.npr.org

NPR provides audio articles via RealPlayer or other audio engines. Be prepared to take careful notes.

Larchmont Chronicle

Hancock Park • Windsor Square • Fremont Place • Park LaBrea • Larchmont Village • Miracle Mile

August 2005

- ▷ Home
- ▷ Archives
- ▷ News Alert!
- ▷ Calendar
- ▷ Local Links
- ▷ Homeowners' Associations
- ▷ Demographics
- ▷ Advertising
- ▷ About us
- ▷ Contact Info

Site design

Greater Wilshire Election
Challenges to Greater Wilshire election reviewed. Voter fraud among complaints filed.

Miracle Mile Safety Summit
State and city officials headline Safety Summit

Robin Kramer
Political know-how propels Robin Kramer to top post as chief of staff for Mayor Antonio Villaraigosa

Lisa McRee
Stay-at-home mom on California road

Jamie Chalfont
Congress awards local teen with national Gold Medal Award

Larchmont Charter school
Reality television show gives school makeover

GALLERY GUIDE
Cars in Los Angeles, China and earth 2031

Gardens
Cool off with refreshing backyard water fountains

Larchmont Chronicle
5421/2 Larchmont Boulevard
Los Angeles, CA 90004

Editor & Publisher: Jane Gilman

FIGURE 5.5 The home page for the *Larchmont Chronicle*

The *New York Times* on the Web   http://www.nytimes.com

You can read recent articles for free. However, if you search the 365-day archive, be prepared with your credit card. Articles cost $2.50. After purchase, they appear on the monitor for printing or downloading.

USA Today DeskTopNews   http://www.usatoday.com

This site has a fast search engine and provides information about current events.

U.S. News Online   http://www.usnews.com

This magazine site has a fast search engine and provides free, in-depth articles on current political and social issues.

Wall Street Journal   http://www.wsj.com

This business-oriented site has excellent information, but it requires a subscription.

The Washington Times   http://www.washingtontimes.com/

Look here for up-to-the-minute political news.

The CQ Weekly   http://library.cq.com

This magazine, formerly named *The Congressional Quarterly Weekly*, keeps tabs on congressional activities in Washington.

To find other newspapers and online media, search for "newspapers" on Yahoo! or AltaVista. Your college library may also provide Lexis-Nexis, which will search news sources for you.

5f   Accessing E-Books

One of the best sources of full-text, online books is the Online Books Page at the University of Pennsylvania:

http://digital.library.upenn.edu/books/

This site indexes books by author, title, and subject. Its search engine will take you quickly to a set of electronic books listed by subject, as shown here:
Psychology (including Parapsychology and the Occult)

- *Psychology and Industrial Efficiency* by Hugo Münsterberg (HTML at York)
- *Psychoanalysis and Civilization* by Paul Rosenfels (HTML at the English Server)
- *History of Psychology: A Sketch and an Interpretation* by James Mark Baldwin (HTML at York)
- *Classics in Psychology, 1855–1914: Historical Essays* by Robert H. Wozniak (HTML and PDF at thoemmes.com)
- *The Romance of American Psychology: Political Culture in the Age of Experts* (Berkeley: University of California Press, 1995) by Ellen Herman (HTML at UC Press)
- *Freud and His Critics* (Berkeley: University of California Press, 1993) by Paul A. Robinson (HTML at UC Press)
- *Preachers of the Italian Ghetto* (Berkeley: University of California Press, 1992), ed. by David B. Ruderman (HTML at UC Press)
- *Thoughts on Man, His Nature, Productions, and Discoveries* by William Godwin (HTML at UV Press)

- *Psychology, or, A View of the Human Soul* by Friedrich August Rauch (page images at MOA)
- *Psychology, or, Elements of a New System of Mental Philosophy, On the Basis of Consciousness and Common Sense* by Samuel Simon Schmucker (page images at MOA)
- *Text-Book of Intellectual Philosophy, for Schools and Colleges* by James Tift Champlin (page images at MOA)
- *The Principles of Psychology* by William James (illustrated HTML at York)
- *Psychology, Phenomenology, and Chinese Philosophy*, ed. by Vincent Shen, Vincent Knowles, and Tran Van Doan (HTML at crvp.org)

5g Using Listserv, Usenet, and Chat Groups

E-mail discussion groups have legitimacy for the exchange of academic ideas when everybody in the group has the same purpose, project, or course. Chat rooms seldom have academic value. Let's look at each briefly.

E-Mail News Groups

The word *Listserv* is used to describe discussion groups that correspond via e-mail about a specific educational or technical subject. For example, your sociology instructor might ask everybody in the class to join a *listserv* group on gay marriage issues. To participate, you must have an e-mail address and subscribe to the list as arranged by your instructor.

In like manner, online courses, which have grown in popularity, usually have a discussion area where students are expected to participate by responding to general questions for the group or corresponding with each other about assignments, issues, and other topics. On the Blackboard system, for example, online students have a Discussion Board with any number of Forums where they may participate or where they are required to participate.

Liszt   http://www.liszt.com

Search Liszt's main directory of more than 90,000 mailing lists. Also you may click on a topic, such as Computers (250 lists), Health (271 lists), Humanities (254 lists), and many others.

Tile.Net   http://www.tile.net/

This site provides access to lists, Usenet newsgroups, and other sites.

At some point you may wish to join a list. Each site explains the procedure for subscribing and participating via e-mail in a discussion. However, you are advised to use extreme caution if you visit the Usenet groups via the commercial search engines. Student Sherri James visited the Yahoo! site for listserv groups in swimming and fitness, but she abandoned the search because the groups, by their titles, seemed obscene—for example, See Girls in their Speedos.

A few additional aspects of listserv and Usenet are FAQ, lurking, and moderated and unmoderated lists.

- *FAQ* (frequently asked questions) sections provide answers to questions new members often have.
- *Lurking* is watching messages on the list without participating.
- *A moderated list* has an editor who screens messages that go out.
- *Unmoderated lists* have an automatic process that distributes any message that comes through.

Real-Time Chatting

Usenet and Chat groups use Internet sites with immediate messaging rather than e-mail. To access Usenet, go to dogpile.com or metacrawler.com and click the People & Chat button before launching your search. Typing "fitness" might take you, under a fictional name, to a reasonable discussion, but probably not. Another way to find discussion groups is through a key word search for "List of online chat groups" at one of the search engines. If you want a commercial site that requires a monthly fee, try Usenet.com. However, you cannot cite from these anonymous sources, so they are best avoided for your academic work.

5h Examining Library Holdings via Internet Access

Most major libraries now offer access to their library catalog via the Web, which means you can search their collections for books, videos, dissertations, audiotapes, special collections, and other items from any Web-linked computer. However, you must open an account and use your identification to log in, just as you do on site at your college library. You may sometimes order books through interlibrary loan online. Additionally, some libraries now post full-text documents, downloadable bibliographies, databases, and links to other sites.

If you need identification of all books on a topic, as copyrighted and housed in Washington, D.C., consult:

Library of Congress   http://www.loc.gov

This site allows you to search by word, phrase, name, title, series, and number. It provides special features, such as an American Memory Home Page, full-text legislative information, and exhibitions, such as the various drafts of Lincoln's Gettysburg Address.

For an Internet overview of online libraries, their holdings, and addresses, consult:

LIBCAT   http://www.metronet.lib.mn.us/lc/lc1.html

This site gives you easy access to almost 3,000 online library catalogs.

LIBWEB   http://sunsite.berkeley.edu/libweb

This site takes you to home pages of academic, public, and state libraries. You will be prompted for a public-access login name, so follow the directions for entering and exiting the programs.

Another kind of online library is:

Carl UnCover   http://www.carl.org./uncover/

This site provides a key word search of 17,000 journals by author, title, or subject. Copies of the articles will be faxed, usually within the hour, for a small fee.

5i   Finding an Internet Bibliography

You can quickly build a bibliography on the Internet in two ways: by using a search engine or by visiting an online bookstore.

Search Engine

At a search engine on the Internet, such as AltaVista, enter a descriptive phrase, such as "Child Abuse Bibliographies." You will get a list of bibliographies, and you can click the mouse on one of them, such as:

Child Abuse
Child Abuse. Child Abuse Articles. Child Abuse Reports.
http://www.childwelfare.com/kinds/pr01.htm

Clicking with the mouse on the hypertext address will carry you to a list:

Child Abuse Articles
Child Abuse Reports
Child Sexual Abuse
Substance Abuse

Clicking on the first item will produce a set of hypertext links to articles you might find helpful, such as this one:

"Suffer the children: How government fails its most vulnerable citizens—abused and neglected kids," by David Stoesz and Howard Jacob Karger (*The Washington Monthly,* 1996).

Online Bookstore

Use the search engines of Amazon.com and BarnesandNoble.com to gain a list of books currently available. In most cases, the books on the list will be available in your library. For example, one student searched BarnesandNoble.com for books on "Fad Dieting." She received the list as shown in Figure 5.6, which formed the beginning of a complete bibliography.

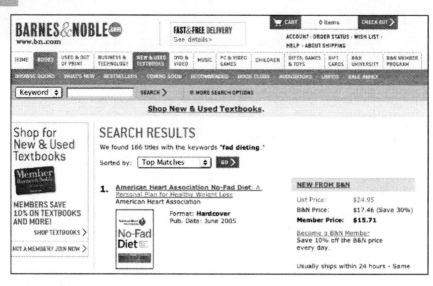

FIGURE 5.6 A page from the Barnes & Noble Internet site listing books on the topic "fad dieting"

5j   Conducting Archival Research on the Internet

The Internet makes possible all kinds of research in library and museum archives. You may have an interest in this type of work. If so, consider several ways to approach the study.

Go to the Library

Go physically into a library and ask about the archival material housed there, or use the library's electronic catalog. Most libraries have special collections. The Stanford University Library, for example, offers links to antiquarian books, old manuscripts, and other archives. It also provides ways to find material by subject, by title, and by collection number. It carries the researcher to a link, such as London (Jack) Papers, 1897–1916 (m0077) [html]. Clicking here takes the researcher to file descriptions and the files. These can be accessed by Internet if the researcher has the proper credentials for entering and using the Stanford collection.

Go to an Edited Search Engine

An edited search engine, such as Yahoo!, may give you results quickly. For example, requesting "Native American literature + archives" produced such links as:

American Native Press Archives
Native American History Archive

Native Americans and the Environment
Indigenous Peoples' Literature
Sayings of Chief Joseph

One or more of these collections might open the door to an interesting topic and enlightening research.

Go to a Metasearch Engine

A metasearch engine such as Dogpile.com offers a way to reach archival material. Make a keyword request, such as "native American literature + archives." Dogpile will list such sites as Reference Works and Research Material for Native American Studies, which is located at www.stanford.edu. There, the Native American Studies Collections offers several valuable lists:

Native American Studies Encyclopedias and Handbooks
Native American Studies Bibliographies
Native American Studies Periodical Indexes
Native American Biography Resources
Native American Studies Statistical Resources
Links to other Native American sites on the Internet
Links to Usenet discussion groups related to Native Americans

Thus, the researcher obtains a wealth of archival information to examine.

Use Search Engine Directories

Use the directory and subdirectories of a search engine and let it take you deeper and deeper into the files. Remember, this tracing goes quickly. Here are examples of links at several engines:

Excite Guide: Lifestyle: Cultures and Groups: Native Americans: Literature
Lycos: Entertainment: Books: Literature: Native American Literature
AltaVista: Society: History: Indigenous People: Native Americans: Art

The latter site, for example, carried one researcher to the Red Earth Museum in Oklahoma City (see Figure 5.7).

Go to Newspaper Archives

Use www.newspapers.com to locate a newspaper of interest, and then use the newspaper's search engine to explore its archive of articles.

YOUR RESEARCH PROJECT

1. Conduct a search of your topic at Metacrawler or one of the major search engines. After finding a list of sources, print it and submit it to the instructor. Next, click on one of the sites found on Metacrawler, print it, and submit it also to the professor.

FIGURE 5.7 The home page of the Red Earth Museum, where a student might find archival information on Native Americans

2. Go to www.google.com and click on Groups. In the search box, ask for "psychology." The emerging list will show many newsgroup sites. Print a copy of the newsgroups shown on the first page and submit it to your instructor.

3. *Voice of the Shuttle* is a large and powerful search engine for educational information. Enter this URL http://vos.ucsb.edu/ and search for your topic. If unsuccessful, try one of the other educational search engines listed on pages 68–69. Submit to your instructor a relevant article that you find here.

4. When you find an Internet article directly devoted to your subject, evaluate it as described on page 62. Write an answer to this question: "Does this site have merit?" Submit your answer to your instructor. Later, apply the same test to other Internet articles as you find them.

5. As with library sources, begin making bibliography entries and writing notes for promising Internet sources. Begin building a computer file of promising sources, develop a folder of printouts from the Internet, and save pertinent information you will need later for your bibliography entries (see pages 44–46 for more information on a working bibliography, and see pages 155–160 for examples of the bibliography for Internet sources). Be prepared to submit your working bibliography and preliminary notes to the instructor for evaluation.

6 Avoiding Plagiarism by Integrating Sources

You probably know that turning in someone else's research paper or lab notes as your own work is plagiarism of the worst kind. But do you really understand plagiarism? Are you comfortable that you understand when to document (cite) sources and when not to? Do you know what criteria to use? Most problems related to plagiarism arise in college writing because students lack clear and confident answers to these questions, and not because students want to cheat the system. In this chapter we define plagiarism, explore the ethical and community standards for researched writing in an academic environment, and give you examples of the worst and best of citations.

Although it provides information at the touch of a finger, the Internet creates a concern because it makes it easy for a student to download material and paste it into a paper. This borrowing is not a problem *unless* you fail to acknowledge the source with an in-text citation and a bibliography entry at the back of the paper.

Let's look at it this way: Intellectual property has value just like the cash drawer at a local fast food restaurant, but words are not hard currency, and they cannot be confined to a cash box. In fact, ideas and theories must be shared if they are to multiply and grow. What's more, the law gives students limited rights to copy from sources. Nevertheless, the word *plagiarism* raises a red flag so the purpose of this chapter is to make you comfortable with and knowledgeable about the ethics of research, especially with respect to these matters:

- Using sources to enhance your credibility.
- Using sources to place your work in its proper context.
- Honoring property rights.
- Avoiding plagiarism.
- Sharing credit and honoring it in collaborative projects.
- Honoring and crediting sources in online classrooms.
- Seeking permission to publish material on your Web site.

6a Using Sources to Enhance Your Credibility

Citing a source in your papers signals something special and positive to your readers—you have researched the topic, explored the literature about it, and know how to cite the sources in your paper. You need to share the literature, not hide it within your prose. Notice how the student in this next passage provides a clear citation to the source:

> Should we consider optimism as an emotional issue like depression? According to O'Malley and Bowman (2003), optimism is an emotion that can be examined the same as depression. Also, Watkins (2004) confirmed optimism as "an emotional high that few people can sustain without periods of doubt and depression. However, studies show that depression had few moments of optimism" (pp. 1274–1275). Thus, this paper will explore the issues and define optimism in a scientific manner.

The two citations give clear evidence of the writer's investigation into the subject, and they enhance the student's image as a researcher.

6b Placing Sources in a Proper Context

Your sources will reflect all kinds of special interests, even biases, so you must position them within your paper as *reliable* sources. If you must use a biased or questionable source, tell your readers up front. For example, if you are writing about cigarette advertising, you will find different opinions in a farmer's magazine, a health and fitness magazine, a journal article in the library, and a trade journal sponsored by a tobacco company. You owe it to your reader to scrutinize sources for:

- Special interests that might color the report.
- Personal ideas and experiences with no researched data as support.
- Lack of credentials.
- A Web site with no sponsor listed.
- Opinionated speculation, especially that found in commercial articles.
- Trade magazines that promote special interests.
- Extremely liberal or extremely conservative positions.

Student Wanda Wilson, in researching sibling rivalry, positioned a personal account with a careful description of the source, as shown in this note.

> Sibling rivalry has affected almost every family with two or more children, and it's a condition that extends into future years after the children have married and moved to different parts of the country. In a personal interview (2004) with a middle child who is now a married adult, the woman expressed her personal bias: "The downside of sibling rivalry is that getting involved in it means someone usually ends up

unhappy: me." She compensated by replacing her tendency toward sibling rivalry to "remember there's only one person I need to persuade that I'm a fabulous parent and person: myself." This personal response corresponds to findings by various authorities.

Note: Personal communications cannot be cited in the bibliography. See page 155 for details.

Thus, the personal account from an interview can complement the scholarly articles to be found in journals and books.

6c Honoring Property Rights

If you invent a new piece of equipment or a child's toy, you can get a patent that protects your invention. You own it. If you own a company, you can register a symbol that serves as a trademark for the products produced. You own the trademark. In like manner, if you write the computer program for a video game, you own the program. Others must seek your permission before they can reproduce it and sell it.

The principle behind copyright law is relatively simple. Copyright begins at the time a creative work is recorded in some tangible form—a written document, a drawing, a tape recording. It does not depend on a legal registration with the copyright office or patent office in Washington, D.C., although most completed works are registered. The moment you create something original, that expression is your intellectual property. You have a vested interest in any profits made from the distribution of your work. For this reason, inventors, designers, engineers, writers, and other creative professionals guard their works and do not want them used without compensation. For example, music companies wish to stop you from downloading music onto your private computer without payment.

A scholarly article in a scientific journal does not have a market value like a piece of music, but the writers of journal articles nevertheless deserve recognition that we must provide with in-text citations and bibliography entries. As a student, you don't have to pay money to use copyrighted material in your research paper under a doctrine of *fair use* as described in the U.S. Code, which says:

> The fair use of a copyrighted work . . . for purposes such as criticism, comment, news reporting, teaching (including multiple copies for classroom use), scholarship, or research is not an infringement of copyright.

Note: If you decide to *publish* your research paper on a Web site, then new considerations come into play (see 6g, "Seeking Permission to Publish Material on Your Web Site").

Thus, as long as you borrow for educational purposes and give the source proper recognition, you are acting legally. See Section 6d for more details about proper documentation.

6d Avoiding Plagiarism

First, develop personal notes and laboratory records with your own findings and ideas on a topic. Discover how you feel about the issue or experiment. Then, rather than copy sources one after another onto your pages of text, try to express your own ideas while synthesizing the ideas of the authorities by using *summary, paraphrase,* or *direct quotation,* which are explained fully on pages 121–126. Rethink and reconsider ideas gathered by your reading, make meaningful connections, and when you refer to the ideas or exact words of a source—as you inevitably will—give the other writer full credit.

Major violations, which can bring failure in the course or expulsion from school, are:

- The use of another student's work.
- The purchase of a canned research paper.
- Copying whole passages into a paper without documentation.
- Copying a key, well-worded phrase into a paper without documentation.
- Putting specific ideas of others into your own words without documentation.

Each of these instances reflects a deliberate attempt on the part of the writer to deceive.

A closely related error that is not technically plagiarism is knowingly fabricating information. You may not make up fictitious information and pass it off as documented fact. Some news reporters have lost their jobs because of fabrication.

In addition, carelessness might plunge you into plagiarism. For example:

- The writer fails to enclose quoted material within quotation marks, yet he or she provides an in-text citation with name and page number.
- The writer's paraphrase never quite becomes paraphrase; too much of the original is left intact—but again, the writer provides a full citation to name and page.

In these situations, instructors might step in and help the beginning researcher, or a peer reviewer might suggest revision, for these problems can mar an otherwise fine piece of research.

What's more, double standards exist. Magazine writers and newspaper reporters often present quotations and paraphrases with little or no academic documentation. However, as an academic writer, you must document fully all borrowed ideas and words.

The academic citation—name, year, page number, and bibliography entry—establishes three things that confirm your reliability and credibility:

1. A clear trail for other researchers to follow if they want to consult the source.
2. Information for other researchers who might need to replicate (reproduce) the project.
3. The timeliness of the material.

CHECKLIST

Documenting Your Sources

- Let the reader know when you begin borrowing from a source by introducing the quotation or paraphrase with the last name of the authority and the year of publication within parentheses: Johnston (2004). . . .
- Enclose within quotation marks all quoted materials—keywords, phrases, and sentences—and supply the page number for quoted matter except that drawn from unpaged Internet sources.
- Set quotations of 40 or more words in an indented double-spaced block; cite the relevant page numbers after the last period.
- Make certain that paraphrased material is rewritten into your own style and language. The simple rearrangement of sentence patterns is unacceptable. You are not required to list page numbers for paraphrases.
- Write a bibliography entry on the References page for every source cited in the paper, including sources that appear only in content footnotes, tables, illustrations, or an appendix. Do not make an entry on the References page for e-mail documents and other data not recoverable by others.

> Note: Do not document the source if an intelligent person would and should know the information, given the context of both writer and audience. However, when in doubt, cite!

When you provide the academic citation, you make it clear *who* you have read, *how* you used the material in your paper, and *where* others can find it.

> Hicks (2004) argued in his essay, "A Lesson for the Future," that "young people's ability to think about the future is not very well developed and their images tend to be pessimistic" (p. 435).

6e   Borrowing from a Source Correctly

Given copies of two abstracts and the opening section of a full article, let's look first at the original documents, a PDF file and two abstracts, and then examine how the students borrowed from the three sources.

From Steaming Mad to Staying Cool: A Constructive Approach to Anger Control

Eva L. Feindler and Karen E. Starr

Teaching children and adolescents to recognize how they feel when they are angry and what pushes their buttons enables them to make better choices about how they express their anger. They learn that staying cool gives them the power to create more positive outcomes for potentially negative encounters. Through self-assessment and role-plays, they learn to negotiate conflict constructively and to apply what they have learned in real-life situations.

Anger—and its expression—makes us uncomfortable. When children or adolescents get angry, they are often told, "Stop! Don't be angry!" or "No, you don't mean it." Because of the oft-occurring link between anger and aggressive behavior, we seek to prevent aggression by invalidating the emotion preceding it. But anger is a naturally occurring emotion. We can be irritated, annoyed, or enraged, and each of these feelings can be legitimate, given a particular situation. The problem arises when we don't know what to do with our anger—when we express it inappropriately, hurting other people and creative negative experiences.

In Anger Control Training (ACT) (Feindler & Ecton, 1990; Feindler & and Gutman, 1994; Feindler, 1995), we teach children and adolescents about the emotion of anger. We help them to understand the experience of being angry—to recognize the feeling, both cognitively and physically; to learn what sets them off, what pushes their buttons or "triggers" their anger; and finally, how best to express their anger in a particular situation.

Children are surprised to learn that their anger is okay. Most of the adults in their lives have told them it is not all right to be angry, so it is very empowering for them to feel that their anger is a legitimate emotion. They key component of this realization, however, is that they must then make the cognitive shift to understand how they can and should express it and how a prosocial response to anger expression can help them solve interpersonal problems and negotiate conflict constructively.

The ACT Anger Management Protocol

ACT focuses on the three hypothesized components of the anger experience; physiological responses, cognitive processes, and behavioral responses (Novaco, 1979).

Physiological Responses

From the physiological aspect, we help adolescents to identify their experience of anger. Are they "boiling mad," "getting steamed," or feeling "stone cold?" We help them to label the various intensities of their emotion and to recognize the early physical warning signs, such as tensed muscles, a flushed feeling, or a quickened heart rate. During this component of the training, we validate the experience of anger as a normal and frequently occurring emotion that has an intensity range that is under their control. To help them reduce the accumulated physiological tension and to increase their capacity to think through the interpersonal event in a more rational fashion, we teach them arousal management skills, such as deep breathing, imagery, and relaxation.

We then teach them to recognize what "pushes their buttons." The adolescents are asked to identify and track common triggers of their anger by using a self-monitoring assessment called the Hassle Log. This is simply a checklist that describes the interpersonal provocations that happen in their daily lives. It includes items such as the day, the time, and the location of the . . .

Full Text: COPYRIGHT 2003 Pro-Ed
Personality & Social Psychology Bulletin, April 2003 v29 i4 p545(11)

Conflict over emotional expression: implications for interpersonal communication.

Myriam Mongrain; Lisa C. Vettese.
Author's Abstract: COPYRIGHT 2003 Sage Publications, Inc.

The current study examined the role of conflict over emotional expression for subjective and interpersonal functioning. The Ambivalence Over the Expression of Emotion Questionnaire (AEQ) was administered to female students who were videotaped while engaging in a conflict-resolution and feedback task with their boyfriends. External ratings showed ambivalent women to be less positive in their verbal statements and to be more constricted in their nonverbal expressions. When mood and other personality constructs were controlled for, ambivalence entailed greater overt submissiveness. Ambivalent women also displayed lower congruence between their verbal and nonverbal communication, irrespective of depression and other personality variables. These data suggest that conflict over emotional expression entails less congruent communication, less positivity in close relationships, and a subordinate stance for the ambivalent individual.

Keywords: ambivalence over emotional expression; verbal communication; nonverbal communication
Article A99187187
Women and Language, Fall 2002 v25 i2 p61(1)

Gender differences in adolescents' behavior during conflict resolution tasks with best friends." (Abstracts). (Brief Article)

Full Text: COPYRIGHT 2002 George Mason University

Black, K. A. "Gender differences in adolescents' behavior during conflict resolution tasks with best friends." Adolescence 35.139 (2000): 499–512.

This study examined gender differences in adolescents' behavior during conflict resolution tasks with their best friends. It also examined gender differences in adolescents' descriptions of those friendships. Thirty-nine adolescents were videotaped while discussing unresolved problems with their best friends. In addition, adolescents completed the Friendship Questionnaire (Furman and Adler, 1982). The results indicated that there were significant gender differences. On the conflict resolution tasks, females were rated lower in withdrawal and higher in communication skills and support-validation than were males. On the Friendship Questionnaire, males rated their relationships with best friends higher in conflict than did females. Methodological considerations are discussed.

Article A88183470

STUDENT VERSION A (a case of rank plagiarism that steals the exact wording of the sources)

The ability of a person to interrelate with others in personal, as opposed to public, relationships has been a very important aspect of societal structures. There is a concern that the breakdown of the American family has lead to a breakdown of the American society leading to crime, violence, and a decay in moral values, for teaching children and adolescents to recognize how they feel when they are angry and what pushes their buttons will enable them to make better choices about ways to express their anger. The children can learn that staying cool will give them the power to create more positive outcomes for their conflicts with other children. Young women, especially, are often ambivalent in their emotional expression and failed to be positive in their close relationships. Also, young women demonstrate more withdrawal than young men during a test of their conflict resolution in conversations with their best friends.

This passage reads well, and the unsuspecting reader will probably think so also. However, the writer has borrowed the entire passage from the three sources, so it is plagiarism of the first order. The writer implies to the reader that these sentences are an original creation when, actually, everything after the first sentence is borrowed without any recognition of the sources.

STUDENT VERSION B (plagiarism that paraphrases and summarizes improperly and that provides a vague citation)

The ability of a person to interrelate with others in personal, as opposed to public, relationships has been a very important aspect of societal structures. There is a concern that the breakdown American family has lead to a breakdown of the American s leading to crime, violence, and decay in moral values. We nee teach children how to identify their anger, recognize it, control make wise decisions when they finally do express their anger. By staying cool they can avoid the down side of anger. In particular, young women have problems with their emotional outbursts, and they displayed more withdrawal when faced with anger-producing conflicts (Mongrain, Feindler, & Black, 2003).

This version is less than acceptable. It merely summarizes the three sources without identifying the precise authors, and the in-text citation at the end of the passage appears to be one source when in fact it should cite three separate articles with the correct identification of all authors. The next version handles these matters effectively.

STUDENT VERSION C (an acceptable version with proper citations to the sources)

Experts have begun examining the gender implications of anger with studies of young women and young men who must make choices at a moment of irritation and frustration. Black (2002) found major deviations in females and men in withdrawal patterns. Mongrain and Vettese (2003) found women to be less positive and even subordinate when faced with moments of anger. Feindler and Starr (2003) offer this synopsis:

Anger—and its expression—makes us uncomfortable. When children or adolescents get angry, they are often told, "Stop! Don't be angry!" or "No, you don't mean it." Because of the occurring link between anger and aggressive behavior, we seek to prevent aggression by invalidating the emotion preceding it. But anger is a naturally occurring emotion. We can be irritated, annoyed, or enraged, and each of these feelings can be legitimate, given a particular situation. The problem arises when we don't know what to do with our anger—when we express it inappropriately, hurting other people and creating negative experiences. (p. 158)

With these words, Feindler and Starr have made a vital point: Anger is a natural emotion, and trying to stop our anger may cause more harm than good.

Required Instances for Citing a Source

1. An original idea derived from a source, whether quoted or paraphrased. This next sentence requires an in-text citation and quotation marks around a key phrase.

> Genetic engineering is a social as well as a biological issue, for a child's body shape and intellectual ability are predetermined, which raised for one source "memories of Nazi attempts in eugenics" (Riddell, 2004, p. 19).

2. Your summary of original ideas by a source.

> Genetic engineering is a social as well as a biological issue. It has been described (Rosenthal, 2003) as the rearrangement of the genetic structure in animals or in plants, which is a technique that takes a section of DNA and reattaches it to another section.

3. Factual information that is not common knowledge.

> Genetic engineering has its risks: a nonpathogenic organism might be converted into a pathogenic one or an undesirable trait might develop as a result of a mistake (Madigan, 2004).

4. Any exact wording copied from a source.

> Woodward (2003) asserted that genetic engineering is "a high stakes moral rumble that involves billions of dollars and affects the future" (p. 68).

Student Version C represents a satisfactory handling of the source material. The sources are acknowledged at the outset of the borrowing, one passage is quoted as a block, and a page citation closes the material. Let's suppose, however, that the writer does not wish to quote the entire passage. Student Version D shows a paraphrased version.

STUDENT VERSION D (an acceptable version with several citations to a set of paraphrases)

> Experts have begun examining the gender implications of anger with studies of young women and young men who must make choices at a moment of irritation and frustration. Black (2002) found major deviations in females and men in withdrawal patterns. Mongrain and Vettese (2003) found women to be less positive and even subordinate when faced with moments of indignation and negative outbursts intended to hurt and diminish others. Feindler and Starr (2003) have pointed out that anger causes discomfort to others because it suggests belligerent conduct, so youngsters are cautioned about controlling their outbursts. However, Feindler and Starr insisted that anger is a natural reaction to high emotion and is, in many cases, appropriate. Thus, a learning curve would help children identify appropriate passion and avoid tantrums that hurt others. Feindler and Starr have made a vital point: Anger is a natural emotion and trying to stop our anger may cause more harm than good.

This version also represents a satisfactory handling of the source material. In this case, no direct quotation is employed, the authors are acknowledged and credited, and the essential commentaries by the sources are paraphrased in the student's own language.

In truth, the rules are simple: Anything borrowed must be cited by author and year, and any directly quoted matter must be cited by a page number to the article, book, or PDF file, but not to standard Internet sites that fail to provide original pagination.

6f Honoring and Crediting Sources in Online Classrooms

A rapidly growing trend in education is the Web-based course or online course via e-mail. In general, you should follow the fair use doctrine of printed sources (see page 83)—that is, give proper credit and reproduce only limited portions of the original.

What you send back and forth with classmates and the instructor(s) has little privacy and even less protection. Rules are gradually emerging for electronic communication. In the meantime, abide by a few commonsense principles:

1. Credit sources in your online communications just as you would in a printed research paper, with some variations. Include these items:

- The author, creator, or Webmaster of the site.
- The date of publication on the Web.
- The title of the electronic article.
- The sponsoring journal, conference, or organization.
- The date you retrieved the article.
- The address (URL).

2. Download to your file only graphic images and the text from sites that specifically offer users the right to download them.
3. Non-free graphic images and text, especially an entire Web site, may be mentioned in your text, even paraphrased and quoted in a limited manner, but not downloaded into your file. Instead, provide hyperlinks or URL addresses. In that way, your reader can find the material and count it as a supplement to your text.
4. Seek permission if you download substantive blocks of material. See Section 6g if you wish to publish your work on the Web.
5. If in doubt, consult by e-mail with your instructor, the moderator of a listserv, or the author of an Internet site.

6g Seeking Permission to Publish Material on Your Web Site

If you have your own home page and Web site, you might wish to publish your paper online. However, the moment you do so, you are *publishing* the work and putting it into the public domain. That act carries responsibilities. In particular, the fair use doctrine of the U.S. Code pertains to the personal educational purposes of your usage. When you load onto the Internet borrowed images, text, music, or artwork, you are making that intellectual property available to everybody all over the world.

Short quotations, a few graphics, and a small quantity of illustrations to support your argument may be examples of fair use if you cite the sources carefully. However, permission is needed if the amount you borrow is substantial. The borrowing cannot affect the market for the original work, and you cannot misrepresent it in any way. The courts are still refining the law. For example, would your use of three *Doonesbury* comic strips be substantial? Yes, if you reproduce them in full. Would it affect the market for the comic strip? Probably not; such usage is hardly copyright infringement. Follow these guidelines:

- Seek permission for copyrighted material that you publish within your Web article. Most authors will grant you free permission. The problem is tracking down the copyright holder.
- If you make the attempt to get permission, and if your motive for using the material is *not for profit,* it's unlikely you will have any problem with the copyright owner. The owner would have to prove that your use of the image or text caused him or her financial harm.

- You may publish without permission works that are in the public domain, such as a section of a speech by the President from the White House or William James's 1890 book *The Principles of Psychology*.
- Document any and all sources you feature on your Web site.
- You may need permission to provide hypertext links to other sites. Some sites do not want their address clogged by inquiring visitors. However, right now the Internet rules on access are being freely interpreted.
- Be prepared for other persons to visit your Web site and even borrow from it. Decide beforehand how you will handle requests for use of your work, especially if it includes your creative efforts in research, design, and composition.

YOUR RESEARCH PROJECT

1. Submit a passage to your instructor that borrows from three sources. Thus, you must begin to maintain a systematic scrutiny of what you borrow and how you cite it. Remember that direct quotation reflects the voices of your sources and that paraphrase maintains your voice. Just be certain, with paraphrase, that you don't borrow the exact wording of the original. Remember, you need the source's last name, the year, and a page number if you quote directly.

2. Submit to your instructor a photocopied or scanned page that describes your college's attitude about plagiarism. This assignment requires you to look at your college bulletin and the student handbook. Do these publications say anything about plagiarism? Do they address the matter of copyright protection? What penalties might be imposed?

3. Write a paragraph that features a block quotation of more than 40 words and submit it to your instructor. Remember, introduce the block with a colon, indent it 5 spaces, and provide a page number outside the final period within parentheses: (p. 567).

4. If you think you might publish your paper on the Web, and if it contains substantial borrowing from a source, such as five or six tables from an article in the *Journal of Sociology,* begin now to seek permission for reproducing the material. In your letter or e-mail, give your name, school, the subject of your research paper, the material you want to borrow, and how you will use it. You might copy or attach the page(s) of your paper in which the material appears.

A paper in the social sciences that features the APA style usually does more than merely cite literature. It features information from reading, testing, surveying, and observation. Usually you combine the evidence, such as the literature on teenage binge drinking and your personal survey administered to a set of first-year college students. Thus, you test the validity of your hypothesis at all stages of your research, drawing ideas from printed sources, from your field research, and from your work in the laboratory.

- Printed sources should be scholarly books and up-to-date journal articles. These works, peer-reviewed before publication, provide authenticity. Less reliable are articles from magazines, newspapers, and trade books.
- Internet sources should be sites sponsored by professional organizations; these can be identified by the domain tags .edu, .gov, and .org. Your library provides the academic pipeline to Internet articles of academic value (see especially pages 62–63 for details).
- Laboratory testing produces research journals, logs, tables, graphs, and charts that can be transferred to the Results section of your report.
- Field research produces the tabulated results of surveys, the data from interviews, and the notes and records drawn from observation of experimental groups and sites.

7a   Drawing Ideas from the Sources

After you find sources relevant to your subject, you should begin your critical reading. Pause often in your reading to contemplate what is being said. Reread some passages, remembering that you are looking for ideas and quotations for your research. If the material is on a computer screen, print a hard copy so you can make marginal notes. React to the material by doing something more than reading—circle a word, highlight a phrase, make a note in the margin, or write notes in your notebook. Consider these preliminary techniques:

- Highlight certain words and phrases of the discipline. For example, articles on the safety of automobile air bags feature a common set of words, such as *air bag technology, deployment force, belted occupants, deactivate,* and so forth. Some writers even make vocabulary lists of the appropriate language. If you feel unsure about the meaning of a word, consult a dictionary or visit the computer's thesaurus. For example, you might replace *deactivate* with a synonym such as *disengage, disable,* or *switch off.*

- Highlight selected sentences you might quote directly or paraphrase. Especially look for sentences that establish the argument, shift it to another level, or provide convincing conclusions.
- Highlight illustrations, graphs, and charts to illustrate your ideas. Find ways to copy them and download them. Remember to keep citation information.
- Highlight comments that seem questionable to you or arguments that appear unsupported. Circle the item and frame a question or rebuttal in the margin, as explained next.

7b Writing Marginal Notes

To help you interpret, evaluate, define, and question a piece of writing, you should make notations on margins, on separate sheets of paper, on sticky notes, on the margins of your own books and articles, and on photocopied materials and computer printouts. Do not write in library books.

- Ask questions that challenge the writer and the meaning of the passage— for example: Is this true in this circumstance? Is this true in all situations? Why use this term? What does the writer really mean? Most articles make an argument, so you may question the content of the passage:
    Does this essay have a main idea—a theory, a central assertion, a proposal or proposition?
    Where is the evidence for this statement?
    Did this event actually cause the second event?
    What is the connection between the variables?
    What are the writer's premises?
    Isn't this an exaggeration?
    Has this writer researched the subject deeply?
    Is the writer displaying bias?
    Is the writer being humorous or serious?

- Paraphrase to give complex ideas your clarification, interpretation, and evaluation. Paraphrasing prevents excessive quotations. Also, it should reveal what you believe and how you feel about the issues. You can record these ideas in the margins or in separate notes in your research journal. Placing your thoughts in the margin puts the idea in proximity to words you might eventually quote or paraphrase. Here is an example of a passage that has been highlighted and annotated to show how critical reading can mean examining passages with meticulous care— underlining important words and phrases, circling words to be defined, and making marginal notes.

From *The Lessons of Terror*
Caleb Carr

Long before the deliberate military targeting of civilians as a method of affecting the political behavior of nations and leaders came to be called *terrorism,* the tactic had a host of other names. From the time of the Roman republic to the late eighteenth century, for example, the phrase that was most often used was *destructive war.* The Romans themselves often used the phrase *punitive war;* although strictly speaking punitive expeditions and raids were only a part of destructive war. For while many Roman military campaigns were indeed undertaken as punishment for treachery or rebellion, other destructive actions sprang out of the simple desire to impress newly conquered peoples with the fearsome might of Rome, and thereby (or so it was hoped) undercut any support for indigenous leaders. In addition, there was a pressing need to allow the famous Roman legions, who were infamously underpaid, to plunder and rape as a reward for their almost inhuman steadiness in the heat of battle. The example of Rome incorporates nearly every possible permutation of warfare against civilians: in this as in so many things, antiquity's greatest state provided a remarkably complete set of precedents for many later Western republics and empires.

The Romans knew only one way to fight—with relentless yet disciplined ferocity—but they eventually devised several ways to deal with the peace that ensued. The first and most successful was inclusive in nature: the peoples of conquered provinces could, if they agreed to abide by Roman authority and law, aspire to become citizens of the republic (and later the empire). Indeed, some new subjects, particularly merchants and other civic leaders, could achieve the status quite quickly. Even slaves could aspire to citizenship, for early on the Romans had devised a remarkable system of manumission, providing multiple avenues by which slaves could escape the hopelessness of unending bondage (and the tendency toward rebellion that hopelessness often breeds) by attempting to earn, buy, or be granted first freedom and then actual citizenship. Freedmen played an important part in Roman history (more than one emperor was saved by a loyal freedman); and on the whole, these complementary policies—granting citizenship to conquered peoples and offering slaves the hope of manumission—may safely be called the central domestic foundation on which the near millennium of Roman hegemony rested.

7c Discovering the Writer's Intentions

Writers have different agendas, so you benefit with critical reading and analysis to uncover each writer's intentions:

Inquiry
Negotiation
Persuasion
Evidence
Assertion
Inference
Implication

Inquiry is an exploratory approach to a problem in which the writer examines the issues as a truth-seeking adventure.

> This writer has gathered and examined the options available for providing on-campus psychological services for students.

Negotiation attempts to resolve a conflict by inventing answers that offer a mediated solution.

> In search of psychological services, this writer has studied the positions of faculty members and staff, on-campus students, commuting students, and local health care professionals.

Persuasion strives to convince the reader a position is valid, factual, and worthy of the reader's full and thoughtful approval.

> Providing on-campus psychological services offers the best solution for meeting the immediate needs of students.

Note: Discover quickly which position the writer is using—inquiry, negotiation, or persuasion. Then introduce that mood into your notes:
Harrison (2004) inquired, questioned, examined
Harrison (2004) explored, discussed, balanced
Harrison (2004) argued, disputed, persuaded

Other writers offer evidence, make assertions, draw inferences, and discuss the implications.

Evidence is a writer's proof in the form of facts, data, charts, surveys, and support from experts on the topic. It forms the basis for assertions and inferences.

Average grades for graduating seniors at Gastovia High School
have changed from 2.3 in 1995 to 2.9 in 2004.

Assertion makes a statement, claim, declaration, affirmation, or denial.
Writers make assertions backed by evidence, but they sometimes make claims
without adequate proof.

Grade inflation is an undeniable fact.

Your task might become a search for proof and evidence that supports the
writer's assertion.

Inference is the writer's assumption or interpretation of the evidence.

We may infer that today's students are smarter, more motivated,
receive a better education, or—on the other side—infer that the
students now benefit from grade inflation.

Drawing inferences and making assumptions are acts of reasoning from factual knowledge, and they enable the writer to draw implications.

Implication is an insinuation, proposition, proposal, or suggestion. It usually occurs after the inference has been drawn from the evidence (e.g., the
implication of these findings . . . or the evidence suggests . . .).

The evidence implies that high school teachers have succumbed
to demands imposed by college scholarship programs.

7d Evaluating a Writer's Theory and/or Hypothesis

A theory establishes a position that is subject to research for its verifica-
tion. The hypothesis provides the search for proof. Thus, your critical reading must discover a writer's basic theory. You can employ three processes to
pinpoint the writer's scientific approach to the topic.

- Locate the writer's hypothesis.
- Identify the supporting evidence.
- Judge the implications suggested in the conclusion.

These techniques will help you in summarizing the article and in select-
ing portions you wish to quote or paraphrase in your own paper. Keep in mind
that every hypothesis has a special form to test the theory, as displayed below.

Theory: Call to Action

Hypothesis: The younger beneficiaries of the civil rights movement should use the pro bono policies of their law firms or businesses to take leaves of absence to work a year or two for civil or human rights groups.

This hypothesis asks readers to confront a problem, face up to a decision, cast their lot, and take action. This writer will examine the implications for young African-Americans who might become fully engaged in a cause or movement. You will find this type of assertion in articles on social, political, and religious issues.

Theory: Assertion of a Cause

Hypothesis: The federal program entitled No Child Left Behind has imposed an unnecessary burden on teachers, school systems, and the traditional goals of learning.

You will find this type of hypothesis in papers advocating a cause, asking for a reasonable response, pleading for proper behavior, or defending a social cause. In this instance, the writer will discuss implications for ending a federally mandated program.

Theory: Interpretation

Hypothesis: Nonsense sounds, such as *uh* or *um*, improved the clarity of speech, according to a recent study (Wilson, 2004).

This type of hypothesis appears in papers that explain and clarify human behavior. This writer in the field of education will offer implications on human speech patterns and effective pauses and breaks in the flow of words.

Theory: Evaluation

Hypothesis: Online college courses have served the special needs of homebound students.

Writers evaluate products, social policies, government regulations, airline travel, nursing homes—you name it. The writer will offer implications for distance learners, such as mothers, persons with disabilities, and even people in prison.

Theory: Search for Truth

Hypothesis: In truth, online students demonstrated a lack of motivation, for only one-half of the students who enrolled in online classes completed their assignments.

Revealing truth is the standard for writers who present this type of paper. This writer will cite the factual evidence and offer implications, such as "Students enrolling in online classes need an introductory session on self-motivation as well as instructions on using the system."

Finally, keep in mind that factual articles have no argument, as with reports on SAT scores, directions for logging onto the library's computer system, or a description of a test cage for rats in an experimental mode. A writer cannot argue against basic facts. In like manner, personal feelings have no argument. They are subjective and beyond reasonable measurement—"I don't like online classes." To become an argument, the writer's focus must be altered—for example, "An effective college class has a professor present, and online classes fail this requirement."

Finding a Writer's Support

For support, writers most often use a combination of statistics, examples, textual evidence, results, anecdotes, and comparison.

Statistics

If the article is about social, educational, or political issues, statistics are used to support the hypothesis. Papers on education, for example, cite empirical data drawn from written tests and classroom observation. A social science paper on the move of textile manufacturing to foreign countries would benefit from statistical data on the number of closed plants, lost jobs, shifts in the labor force, and the dollars lost in county and state taxes. In a report on head injuries, Lindsey Tanner employs statistics by citing scientific studies and providing a chart from the *Archives of General Psychiatry*. Here's a sample of her statistics:

The study involved 1,718 veterans hospitalized for various ailments during the war and questioned 50 years later. About 11% who had experienced head injuries said they currently had major depression, compared with 8.5% of those hospitalized during the war for other reasons.

Examples

The use of examples is popular in all types of writing, but your critical reading should ascertain that the examples are representative, relevant, and truly supportive of the writer's hypothesis. In a paper about the social consequences of the demise of the textile industry, an example of one town's experiences with lost jobs and lost taxes might serve the writer's argument, but substantial data on many afflicted towns would improve the paper.

Textual evidence

Look for evidence from writers interpreting a passage or speech. Quotations, summaries, and paraphrases of a text can provide the primary support and background for a study. The review of the literature is mandatory for a scientific study. It establishes the basis on which the new study will emerge and develop. Thus, the literature on the textile industry is vital to a study on lost jobs and the depression that afflicts small towns. The selections drawn from the literature should be highly selective and bear precisely on the issue under discussion. The citation of experts gives credibility both to the article and to the writer who has done his or her research.

> Along with their colleagues, Holsinger and Plassman (2002) reported in *Archives of General Psychiatry* on major depression. Overall, the lifetime prevalence of major depression was reported to be 18.5% for the head injury group, and 13.4% among the other veterans.

Anecdotes

A brief story about an experience or event can enliven and illustrate one aspect of the argument. Of course, the brief story must be true to life, believable, and a dramatic illustration in support of the writer's hypothesis. An anecdote often initiates an article to make an issue realistic and vital to a social condition. For example, a writer might interview one family directly affected by the closing of a textile mill. The case study would serve as primary evidence for the paper's argument.

Comparison

Writers often lay out two ideas, activities, or positions for comparison and contrast. By showing two comparable items, the writer supports and clarifies the thesis of an article or essay. For example, Caleb Carr, in *The Lessons of Terror* (page 96), compares modern terrorism that targets civilians to the Roman terms *destructive war* and *punitive war*. He makes the comparison to clarify the Roman position for punitive war.

7e   Considering the Writer's Logic

This text cannot dwell in depth on the formal aspects of logic, but as a critical reader you should understand the ebb and flow of inductive and deductive reasoning. Most assertions you will encounter are based on **inductive reasoning,** which reaches a theory but not a final conclusion. The evidence is often inconclusive:

Identifying Inductive and Deductive Reasoning

- Does the writer base the conclusion on premises, declarations, or propositions that have been confirmed by study and research? It is deductive.
- Does the writer base the conclusion on observation and gathered evidence? It is inductive.
- Does the writer use such words as *all, every, certainly, without fail, always*? It is deductive.
- Does the writer use such words as *some, most, almost, probably, very likely*? It is inductive.

Electronic classrooms via the Internet will continue to grow each year. The demand is greater than current offerings because students are enrolling in E-courses for a number of reasons: employment conflicts, children at home, distance from campus, and the convenience of working at home.

The writer uses the word *likely* in the first sentence because the theory— growth in electronic classrooms—might slow at a semester's notice. Thus, if an article is inconclusive based on the limited inductive evidence, the writer must set a limit on the claim by inserting *some, most, almost, probably, very likely,* or *almost certainly,* as in "Electronic classrooms via the Internet will likely grow each year."

Deductive thinking moves in the opposite direction, using a hypothesis (see pages 17–19):

Dyslexia is caused by a failure of communication between the hemispheres of the brain.

Observation and testing will provide support for or against the likelihood of the hypothesis. When the deductive reasoning and testing reaches a firm conclusion, the writer uses indicator words such as *all, every, certainly, without fail, is, was,* and *always.* An illustration illuminates the difference in the thinking process.

A child had a toy glider that she threw into the sky, and she watched it glide to earth. She tried again with the same result. She said to her father, "I guess I can't make it fly. Every time it always comes back down. Here, Daddy, you throw it, and I bet it comes back down for you too!"

The father replied, "Yes, it will certainly come back down. That's Newton's law of gravity, Susie. Everything that goes up will be pulled back down by the force of earth's gravity."

The child was thinking inductively: She observed the plane's pattern and arrived at a theory. The father was thinking deductively because, for him, Newton already had confirmed the hypothesis.

Identifying Fallacies That Damage a Conclusion

The word *fallacy* names a defective argument, one that is either reasoned incorrectly or based on invalid premises. When you find an article with specific passages you wish to use in your own writing, pause for a moment to judge the overall stance of the writer. Look for bias and unsound arguments. The writer may not maintain a clear line of reasoning from one argument to another. The writer may even misrepresent the evidence or take quotations out of context. Every writer who launches an essay has an agenda that he or she wants to defend. Before you cite a source, judge the essay for fairness to the issues and the validity of the evidence. Fallacies slip into a piece of writing with or without the writer's realization, and they affect readers who readily accept the printed word.

Here are a few of the most common errors:

1. *Argument directly against the person* attempts to discredit a person holding the opposing viewpoint rather than confront the opposing argument.
2. *Appeal to authority* is valid if the person is truly an expert, but writers sometimes promote a person as an expert who is not reputable, up-to-date, objective, or truly the final authority in the area of discussion. Is an athlete really qualified to judge the best deodorant or shave cream? Is the

---

CHECKLIST

Finding Fallacies in Logic

The conclusion of an essay is suspect if:

- An assertion grows from a premise or inference that is not convincing.
- The chain of reasoning breaks down, with the result that the assertion does not follow logically from the evidence offered.
- The evidence is manipulated or distorted with some type of fallacy.
- The writer misdirects the argument, appeals to a false authority, misinterprets the cause and effect, or jumps to hasty conclusions.

National Enquirer a good source of information about the future of oil prices? Good sources are vital.

3. *Arguing that a first event caused the second event* often makes a false assumption because there is no evidence in support.

4. *Circular reasoning* simply restates the conclusion as a premise. It begs the question and offers no proof.

5. *Hasty generalization* draws a conclusion quickly from inadequate evidence.

6. *False analogy* makes an illogical comparison of two items that do not belong together.

7. *Using the either/or fallacy* creates a false dilemma by arguing that a complicated issue has only two answers when, in truth, a multitude of options may be available. It reflects oversimplification by the writer.

8. *False emotional appeal* is a fallacy that comes in several well-disguised packages. For example, *flattery* uses insincere and excessive praise of the audience to disguise shallow reasoning. *Snob appeal* and the *bandwagon* encourage readers to join a cause or buy a product because the "best" people do it and because it will raise their self-esteem. *Racial and sexist slurs* demean one class in a perverse appeal from one bigot to another.

9. A conclusion may not follow from the premises. Called a *non sequitur,* this fallacy arrives at an assertion without valid evidence.

10. *Dodging the real issue* shifts the reader's attention to an unrelated issue. Sometimes called a *straw man* or a *red herring,* the fallacy diverts attention from the real target.

YOUR RESEARCH PROJECT

1. Create an outline of one of your sources and submit it to your instructor. This assignment requires you to make a commitment to critical reading of your sources. Evaluate each major idea before placing it in your outline.

2. Submit to your instructor a short passage (one or two paragraphs) from a source, together with your own passage containing your inferences on the topic and the source writer's approach to it. Is the writer reliable? Look again at the guidelines for judging the assertions of others on pages 97–98.

3. Learn to search out a writer's hypothesis or claim, which is the basis for the essay. See pages 98–101 for ways that a writer can make assertions. Submit an opening to an article with the hypothesis highlighted.

4. Always examine the writer's support for an argument. Look for statistics, examples, textual evidence, use of authorities, and effective comparisons, yet be on guard against misleading reasoning. Submit an article to your instructor that has your marginal notations about the content and any bias you might find in the writer's assertions.

8 Organizing Ideas and Setting Goals

Initially, research is haphazard, and your desk may be cluttered with bits of information scattered in your research journal and on photocopies or print-outs from electronic sources. Careful organization for a paper in APA style requires the presentation of evidence to augment your report and give it a touch of authority. In truth, researching and organizing occur simultaneously, so use this chapter in harmony with the next chapter on notetaking.

Your needs become clear when you draw plans, such as a research pro-posal, a list of ideas, a set of questions, or a rough outline. In addition, the design of your study should match an appropriate organizational model, often called a paradigm or pattern.

8a Charting a Direction and Setting Goals

Instead of plunging too quickly into research, first decide *what* to look for and *why* you need it. One or more of these exercises will help your organization:

- Chart the course of your work with a basic order.
- Revisit your research proposal, if you developed one, for essential issues.
- List key words, ideas, and issues you must explore in the paper.
- Rough out an initial outline.
- Ask a thorough set of questions.

A hypothesis on organ donation can point toward various issues and concerns.

Hypothesis: Misunderstandings about organ donation distort reality and set serious limits on the availability of those persons who need an eye, a liver, or a healthy heart.

ISSUE 1   Many myths mislead people into believing that organ donation is unethical.

ISSUE 2   Some fear that as patients they might be put down early.

ISSUE 3   Religious views sometimes get in the way of donation.

The plan above, although brief, will give the writer three categories that require detailed research in literature.

Arrangement by Cause/Effect

In other cases, a theory may suggest development by cause/effect issues. Notice that the next writer's concept on television's educational values points the way to four very different areas that are worthy of investigation.

Hypothesis: Television provides positive influences on a child's language development.

CONSEQUENCE 1   Television introduces new words.

CONSEQUENCE 2   Television reinforces word usage and proper syntax.

CONSEQUENCE 3   Literary classics come alive visually and verbally on television.

CONSEQUENCE 4   Television provides the subtle rhythms and musical effects of accomplished speakers.

Arrangement by Correlation

A correlation shows the relationship of two factors. In a positive correlation, the behavior of the subjects in one area directly affects their performance in another. Thus, the theory points toward analysis of student behavior:

Hypothesis: The less students study, the worse their grades will be.

1. Analysis of study time of students in the experimental group in contrast with the students in the control group.

2. Analysis of the change in performance by a study of the grades.

3. Discussion of the correlations and the implications of the study.

Arrangement by Interpretation

Interpretation evolves from a theory that requires classification of the issues and a corresponding analysis. Notice how this next theory requires interpretation and will eventually lead to testing.

Theory: The id, ego, and superego interact to shape our actions.

1. Define *id*.

2. Define *ego*.

3. Define *superego*.

4. Show the correlation of the three.

Evaluating Your Overall Plan

- What is the theory I want to evaluate? Will my notes and records defend and illustrate my proposition? Is the evidence convincing?
- What is the hypothesis I want to investigate and subject to testing in the lab or field?
- Have I found the best plan for developing the report with focus on the issue, cause/effect, correlations, interpretation, or comparison?
- Should I use a combination of elements—that is, do I need to evaluate the subject, examine the causes and consequences, and then set out the issues?

Arrangement by Comparison

Sometimes a comparison evaluates two sides of an issue, as shown in one student's preliminary outline:

Theory: Discipline often involves punishment, but child abuse adds another element: the gratification of the adult.

COMPARISON 1: Spanking versus a beating. A spanking has the interest of the child at heart, but a beating or a caning has no redeeming value.

COMPARISON 2: Timeouts versus lockouts. Timeouts remind the child that relationships are important and to be cherished, but lockouts in a closet only promote hysteria and fear.

COMPARISON 3: Parent's ego versus welfare of the child. The parent's ego and selfish interests often take precedence over the welfare of the child or children.

Many other methods of research require careful outlining of the issues, such as the case study, observational study, statistical correlations, longitudinal research, and empirical research. Consult with your instructor for advice.

8b Drafting a Research Proposal

Your research proposal, if you develop one, will introduce issues worthy of research. For example, the following proposal names specific topics:

> This paper is designed to address the reader who has concerns about child abuse. In particular, the research will examine the distinctions between discipline and abuse. Discipline may involve punishment, but it has the best interests of the child in mind. Abuse only gives gratification to the adult. Thus, research will clarify spanking and a beating, a timeout and a lockout, and, ultimately, the welfare of the child played against the selfish interests of the caregiver.

This writer will search the social work literature and write notes to build an examination of child abuse in comparison with reasonable discipline.

Another writer sketched the following research proposal, which lists the types of evidence necessary to accomplish the project:

> This paper will study the social issues affecting donation programs for human organs and tissue. It will expose the myths that prevail in the public's imagination and, hopefully, dispel them. The project will also explore the serious need as well as the benefits derived from donated organs and tissue. Finally, it will itemize the organs and their use to rehabilitate the diseased and wounded. It will evaluate the social issues, but it will also be a proposal—sign the donor card!

You should also consult Chapter 2, pages 20–24, for a detailed discussion of the research proposal and for various ways to focus the topic and its issues by listing key words, asking questions, or building notes *with definition, analysis,* or other modes of development. For example, one student recorded this note, which describes and defines the subject:

> Organ and tissue donation is the gift of life. Each year, many people confront health problems due to diseases or congenital birth defects. Organ transplants give these people the chance to live a somewhat normal life. Organs that can be successfully transplanted include the heart, lungs, liver, kidneys, and pancreas (Barnill, 2001). Tissues that can be transplanted successfully include bone, corneas, skin, heart valves, veins, cartilage, and other connective tissues (Taddonio, 2003).

A proposal can also produce valuable notes as the student searches for answers in the literature, as shown in this note:

Wolcott (2001) conducted a study on the interactions of juveniles and the police in Chicago, Detroit, and Los Angeles. Wolcott gathered data for 1890–1940, a period that determined the nature of the nation's juvenile courts. The abstract to his article stated that Wolcott found "the exercise of discretionary authority by the police shaped juvenile justice." The police made decisions on which children to handle on their own and which should be referred to juvenile court. As a result, the police "could discipline young offenders in their own fashion" to filter who was referred to the juvenile courts.

From Walcott, D. (2001). "The cop will get you": The police and discretionary juvenile justice, 1890–1940. *Journal of Social History, 35,* 349–371.

8c Drafting an Academic Pattern

A traditional outline is content-specific for only one paper, while an academic pattern governs all papers within a certain design. For example, a general, all-purpose model gives a plan for almost any research topic. Others are more specific, as explained in several examples shown below.

A General, All-Purpose Pattern

If you are uncertain about the design of your paper, start with this basic model and expand it with your material. Readers, including your instructor, are accustomed to this sequence for research papers. It offers plenty of leeway.

- Identify the subject in the *introduction.* Explain the problem, provide background information, mention some of the literature on the subject, and discuss briefly the theory you will examine.
- Analyze the subject in the *body* of the paper. You can compare, analyze, correlate, trace patterns, and give details of a case study, and—in general—present the results of your work.
- Discuss your findings in the *conclusion.* You can challenge an assumption, interpret the findings, discuss implications, provide solutions, or reaffirm the validity of a theory.

Academic Pattern for Advancing Your Ideas and Theories

If you want to advance a theory in your paper, use the following design, but adjust it to eliminate some items and add new elements as necessary.

Introduction:

    Establish the problem, question, or theory.

    Discuss its significance.

    Provide the necessary background information.

    Introduce experts who have addressed the problem.

    Provide a literature review (see pages 191–200) if yours is a long paper (8+ pages).

Body:

    Evaluate the issues involved in the problem.

    Develop a past-to-present examination.

    Compare and analyze the details and minor issues.

    Interpret results and discuss correlations.

    Continue to cite experts who have addressed the same problem.

Conclusion:

    Advance and defend the theory, or show its negative values.

    Offer directives or a plan of action.

    Suggest additional work and research that is needed.

See Chapter 12, pages 163–174, for a complete discussion of writing the theoretical paper.

Academic Pattern for Argument and Persuasion Papers

If you write persuasively or argue from a set position, your paper should conform, in general, to this next paradigm. Select the elements that fit your design.

Introduction:

    In one statement, establish the problem or controversial issue your paper examines.

    Summarize the issues.

    Define key terminology.

    Make concessions on some points of the argument.

    Use quotations and paraphrases to clarify the controversial nature of the subject.

    Provide background information to relate the past to the present.

    Establish the position you wish to defend.

Body:

    Develop arguments to defend one side of the subject.

    Analyze the issues, both pro and con.

    Give evidence from the sources, including quotations as appropriate.

Conclusion:

    Expand your conclusion to make clear your position, which should be one that grows logically from your analysis and discussion of the issues.

Academic Pattern for Analysis of Political Activities and Events

If you are writing a political science paper that analyzes events and their causes and consequences, your paper should conform, in general, to the following plan.

Introduction:
> Identify the event.
> Provide the background leading up to the event.
> Offer quotations and paraphrases from experts.
> Give the theory and the hypothesis being tested.

Body:
> Analyze the background leading up to the event.
> Trace events from one historic episode to another.
> Offer a chronological sequence that explains how one event relates directly to the next.
> Cite authorities who have also investigated this event in history.

Conclusion:
> Reaffirm your theory and your methods for testing it.
> Discuss the consequences of this event, explaining how it altered the course of history.

Academic Pattern for a Comparative Study

A comparative study requires that you examine two schools of thought, two issues, two works, or the positions taken by two persons. The paper examines the similarities and differences of the two subjects, generally using one of three arrangements for the body of the paper.

Introduction:
> Establish A.
> Establish B.
> Briefly compare the two.
> Introduce the central issues.
> Cite source materials on the subjects.
> Present your thesis.

Body (choose one of these three possible arrangements):

Examine A	Compare A & B	Issue 1
		Discuss A & B
Examine B	Contrast A & B	Issue 2
Compare and	Discuss the central	Discuss A & B
Contrast A & B	issues	Issue 3
		Discuss A & B

Conclusion:
>   Discuss the significant issues.
>   Write a conclusion that ranks one over the other.
>   or
>   Write a conclusion that rates the respective genius of each side.

Academic Pattern for a Laboratory Investigation or Field Report

This model is rigid, with little flexibility. Instructors will expect your report to remain tightly focused on each of these items.

Introduction:
>   Provide the title, the experiment number, and the date.
>   Describe the experiment.
>   List the literature consulted.
>   Objectively describe what you hope to accomplish.

Method:
>   Explain the procedures used to reproduce an experiment.
>   Explain the design of the test.
>   Identify the tools or apparatus used.
>   Identify the variables that affected your research (weather conditions, temperatures, and so on).

Results:
>   Give your findings, including statistical data.

Discussion:
>   Provide your interpretation of the data.
>   Discuss the implications of your research.
>   Comment on what you learned from the experiment (optional).

Academic Pattern for a Review of Scientific Literature

In this situation, you are working with the literature on a scientific issue, so you have more flexibility than with a report on a lab experiment.

Introduction:
>   Identify the issue and its relevance.
>   Cite the literature.
>   State the problem.
>   State the objectives of the study, with a hypothesis at the end.

Body:
>   Classify the issues.
>   Analyze, define, and compare each aspect of the topic.
>   Suggest a testable hypothesis.
>   Make a detailed inquiry into all relevant issues.

Conclusion:

> Explain the current findings of scientific studies related to your topic.
> Advance your reasons for continued research.
> Suggest possible findings.
> Discuss the implications of your analysis.

Academic Pattern for a Report of Empirical Research

This pattern is similar to the one for a laboratory investigation, so follow it closely to fill all the required items.

Introduction:

> Present the point of your study.
> Provide the theoretical implications.
> Explain the manner in which your study relates to previously published work.
> State the hypothesis and how it tests the problem.

Method:

> Describe the subject (what was tested, who participated, whether human or animal, and where the fieldwork was accomplished).
> Describe your equipment and explain how you used it.
> Summarize the procedure and the execution of each stage of your work.

Results:

> Summarize the data you collected.
> Provide statistical treatment of your findings with tables, graphs, and charts.
> Include findings that conflict with your hypothesis.
> Discuss the implications of your work.
> Evaluate the data and its relevance to the hypothesis.
> Interpret the findings as necessary.
> Discuss the implications of the findings.
> Qualify the results, limiting them to your specific study.
> Make inferences from the results.
> Suggest areas worthy of additional research.

Remember that the models provided above are guidelines, not ironclad rules. Adjust each as necessary to meet your special needs.

8d Writing a Formal Outline

Not all papers require a formal outline, nor do all researchers need one. You might build a short research paper from one of the patterns shown earlier in section 8c, or by expanding a well-designed proposal. However, a formal outline is sometimes important because it classifies the issues of your study into clear, logical categories with main headings and one or more levels of subheadings. An outline can change miscellaneous notes, computer drafts, and photocopied materials into an ordered progression of ideas. You may wish to experiment with the outline feature of your software, which will allow you to view the paper at various levels of detail and to highlight and drop the essay into a different organization.

> **HINT:** A formal outline is not rigid and inflexible; you may, and should, modify it while writing and revising. In every case, treat an outline or organizational pattern as a tool. Like an architect's blueprint, it should contribute to, not inhibit, the construction of a finished product.

Using Standard Outline Symbols

List your major categories and subheadings in this form:

I _____	First major heading
A. _____	Subheadings of first degree
1. _____	Subheadings of second degree
2. _____	
a. _____	Subheadings of third degree
b. _____	
(1) _____	Subheadings of fourth degree
(2) _____	
(a) _____	Subheadings of fifth degree
(b) _____	
B. _____	Subheading of first degree

The degree to which you continue the subheads will depend, in part, on the complexity of the subject. Subheads in a research paper seldom carry beyond subheadings of the third degree, the first series of lowercase letters.

Writing a Formal Topic Outline

If your purpose is to arrange quickly the topics of your paper, the outline may use noun phrases. The following roman numeral list begins with III.

III. The senses

  A. Receptors to detect light

    1. Rods of the retina

    2. Cones of the retina

It may also use gerund phrases:

III. Sensing the environment

  A. Detecting light

    1. Sensing dim light with retina rods

    2. Sensing bright light with retina cones

It may also use infinitive phrases:

III. To use the senses

    A. To detect light

        1. To sense dim light

        2. To sense bright light

No matter which grammatical format you choose, you should follow it consistently throughout the outline.

Writing a Formal Sentence Outline

The sentence outline requires full sentences for each heading and subheading. It has two advantages over the topic outline:

1. Many entries in a sentence outline can serve as topic sentences for paragraphs.
2. The subject/verb pattern establishes the logical direction of your thinking—for example, the phrase "Vocabulary development" becomes "Television viewing can improve a child's vocabulary."

Consequently, the sentence outline brings into the open possible organizational problems rather than hiding them as a topic outline might do. The time devoted to writing a complete sentence outline, like writing complete, polished notes (see pages 120-127), will serve you well when you write the rough draft and revise it.

One student's sentence outline is shown below.

Outline

Theory: Computer matchmaking has social and psychological

implications that affect behavior in multiple ways.

    I. Introduction

        A. Human behavior is being modified by online dating services.

        B. The literature discusses the magnitude of the issue.

        C. Online dating reverts to the prearranged meetings of two
           young people by their elders.

    II. Method

        A. Procedures for accessing an Internet date vary.

           1. Internet dating services have made romance a commodity.

           2. Meeting on the Internet is now like a phone call.

           3. Courtship is conducted across keyboards.

      4. The system allows the modest person a chance to explore the personality of another person before making any commitments.

  B. A case study uncovers the results of one Internet match.

      1. Two subjects met in an Internet chat room.

      2. They chatted anonymously for nine months.

      3. Online romance gave them protection of their privacy and time to prearrange a positive meeting.

III. Results

  A. Online romance can have negative consequences.

      1. It entices people into adultery.

      2. It affects the workplace in negative ways.

      3. It produces online infidelity and addiction.

      4. It invites escape from reality.

      5. It can damage self-esteem.

  B. Online romance can have positive consequences.

      1. It offers a type of prearranged courtship.

      2. It protects the privacy of the individuals until they make a commitment.

      4. It forces participants to talk, which is something most women want prior to any intimacy.

      5. Online romance has produced healthy relationships and successful marriages.

IV. Discussion

  A. Online romance has several social implications.

      1. It affects the workplace and damages professional reputations.

      2. It affects marriages because of online infidelity and adultery.

      3 It replaces the church, workplace, bars, and so forth as the place for meeting a partner.

      4. It offers a new form of prearranged dating and prearranged marriage.

B. Online romance has several psychological implications.

  1. It offers men an opportunity to explore their motives and psychological balance before plunging into an affair.

  2. It offers women especially an opportunity to explore the relationship before ever meeting somebody in person.

  3. It has developed a new role for psychotherapy.

  4. The phenomenon requires further study by experts in the field.

YOUR RESEARCH PROJECT

1. Scratch out a preliminary plan for your project. List a theory or hypothesis and, below it, establish several divisions that will require careful and full development. Test more than one plan. Do you need several criteria of judgment? causal issues? arguments? evidence from field research? Which seems to work best for you? Consult with your instructor, if possible, before going to assignment 2.

2. Select one of the academic patterns, as found on pages 109–113, and develop it with the information from your preliminary notes. Submit this pattern to your instructor for his or her approval.

3. If you are familiar with the design of Web pages, you probably realize that the hierarchical ideas have value because readers can click hot keys that will carry them deeper into the files. Test your final outline by constructing a plan like the one below, filling the blanks downward from the large block (hypothesis), to major issues (medium blocks), to evidence (small blocks). The chart, which you can redraw roughly on a sheet of paper, looks like this:

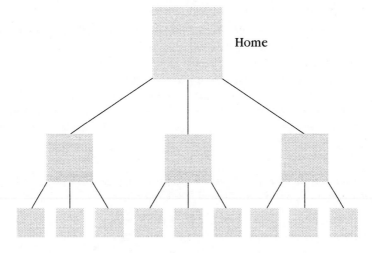

Home

9 Writing Notes

The primary reason for any scholarly research is to announce and publicize new findings. A psychologist investigates the reluctance of a homeless person to accept any sort of organized, unified sanctuary. A sociologist announces the results of a two-year pilot study of Native Americans in the Appalachian region. A political scientist explains his discoveries on the effects of absentee ballots in a presidential race. Another researcher examines the effects of women in combat. For each topic, APA style is employed in research to reach the desired result.

Similarly, students may be asked to conduct research—perhaps an investigation of student behavior in campus parking lots. One student might interview 20 others on campus parking issues, a second might develop a questionnaire and submit it to a fairly large sample of students, and a third might observe behavior by watching students come and go from campus parking lots. Accurate notes from the personal research will join with carefully paraphrased notes from experts on the topic to form the support of a hypothesis. The researcher's goal is to share verifiable information so that others can learn from it and extend it to new dimensions. Excellent notes in a variety of forms are vital to that process.

9a Developing a Research Journal

A research journal collects your data for use in developing a research report. The journal can take many forms, so you must choose wisely. You can start with a paper file; however, today's technology makes it easy to print Internet articles, scan graphic images, and photocopy articles and pages of books. Yet this convenience comes at a price: *You must somehow make sense of it all!* Therefore, keep everything. You must cite each source in the text and in a bibliography entry, so do not write a note and throw away the printout or photocopy.

Literature Journal

Build a folder in which you place photocopies, printouts, and scanned articles about your subject. It serves several purposes:

- Shows the history of research on the topic.
- Focuses the issues.

- Offers models of the report you will need to write.
- Reviews the literature that might be a part of your introduction.
- Quotes or paraphrases the words of authorities on the topic.

Response Journal

The response journal is a set of personally written pages in which you reflect on aspects of your research. It too serves several purposes:

- Records your comments on the literature as you gather pertinent articles.
- Provides a set of summary notes valuable to your work (see pages 125–127).
- Contributes to the Observation Log or the Laboratory Journal to demonstrate your responses to the results of your work.

Laboratory Journal

The laboratory journal records all your research data, accompanied by your commentary on the implications of your experiment—for example, "Were there variables at play?" and "Did the findings correspond with the norm?" The lab journal serves several purposes:

- Serves as a powerful catalyst for thinking through the various ingredients, procedures, and experiments.
- Focuses on the concepts of scientific inquiry.
- Teaches you the terminology to use in your paper.
- Records successes and failures in conducting the lab work.
- Stores the data you will need for writing the lab reports.
- Represents, usually, a portion of your grade.
- Builds your confidence in written, drawn, photographic, and electronic communication.

Note: When computers are a component of your laboratory study, you may need to learn new methods for electronic manipulation of the data. In most cases, you are allowed to print out results and tape them into your journal.

Field Research Journal

A research journal records your findings for special projects. It lists your observations and active involvement with subjects of the study and includes your responses to and discussion of the findings, their implications, and further work that might be done. It too serves several purposes:

- Gives evidence supporting your hypothesis.
- Maintains a commentary that might form the basis of your report.
- Records behavior of the subjects as you watch from a distance and records words and sounds if you move closer to the subjects.
- Establishes the distinctions in behavior of control and experimental groups, but only if they serve in your research.

CHECKLIST

Writing Effective Journal Notations

- Write one notation with commentary for each aspect of your work.
- List the source with name, year, and page to be ready for in-text citations.
- Label each notation—for example, "Saturday, observation at Student Center."
- Write important notations in well-developed sentences to speed the writing of your first draft.
- Keep everything, including photocopies and scribbled notes, in order to authenticate dates, page numbers, or full names.

Note: If your journal is maintained on a computer, keep material well labeled in distinct files and folders.

- Label your personal notes with "my idea" or "personal note" to distinguish them from the sources.

- Collects drawings, maps, designs, tables, and figures that are central to your work.
- Records the conversation of an interview with the subject and serves as a backup to audiotapes and videotapes.

Writing Notes of High Quality

Journal writing is the heart of research. If you write notes of high quality, the notes may need only minor editing to fill the appropriate places in your first draft. Prepare yourself to write different types of notations in the journal—quotations of well-phrased passages by authorities but also paraphrased or summarized notes to maintain your voice. This chapter explains the following types of notes:

Personal notes (9b) express your ideas or record your personal responses to laboratory and field research.

Quotation notes (9c) preserve the wisdom and distinguished syntax of an authority.

Paraphrase notes (9d) interpret the wisdom of an authority in your words.

Summary notes (9e) distill factual data in a condensed form; several options exist.

9b   Writing Personal Notes

Instructors and readers are primarily interested in *your* methods and *your* response to the test, experiment, or observation. Therefore, during your research, record your thoughts on the issues by writing plenty of personal notes in your research journal, or in your computer files. Personal notes:

- Record your discoveries.
- Reflect on your findings.
- Make connections with various points of view.
- Question prevailing views and patterns of thought.

Personal journal notes should conform to these three standards:

1. The idea in the notation is yours as you respond during the investigation.
2. The note is labeled with "my idea," "mine," or "personal thought," to distinguish it from borrowed ideas.
3. The notation is a rough summary, a sketch of ideas, or, preferably, a complete sentence or two.

A sample follows:

Personal thought

     I'm beginning to notice patterns in the behavior of students searching for a parking space. Some just drive around frantically searching here and there for an empty space. Others sit at the end of a row and wait patiently for somebody to leave. A third set has a designed plan in which student A leaves class and arrives at her parking place, just as her friend arrives to fill the slot. I see their cell phones at work. A fourth group looks through the lot first, finds nothing, and parks in a restricted spot or a faculty space, gambling that they can attend one class without getting a ticket.

9c   Writing Direct Quotation Notes

Citing the words of another person is the easiest type of note to write. These notes allow you to:

- Capture the authoritative voices of the experts on the topic.
- Feature essential statements.
- Provide proof that you have researched the subject carefully.
- Offer conflicting points of view.
- Show the dialog that exists about the topic.

In the process, you must follow these basic conventions:

1. Select quoted material that is important and well phrased, not trivial or a matter of common knowledge.

   TRIVIAL: "The brain is a complex network of nerve cells" (Rupert, 2004, p. 16).

   PERTINENT: Rupert (2004) commented, "Chemicals in the brain, called neurotransmitters, help you receive accurate information, process the information (make sense of it), and make decisions based on the information you receive and process" (p. 16).

2. Use quotation marks. Do not copy the words of a source into your paper in such a way that readers will think *you* wrote the material.
3. Use the exact words of the source.
4. Provide an in-text citation to author, year, and page number, such as (Henson, 2004, pp. 34–35), or give the author's name at the beginning of the quotation and put the page number after the quotation, like the Rupert citation above.
5. The in-text citation goes *outside* the final quotation mark but *inside* the period.
6. Try to quote key sentences and short passages, not entire paragraphs. Find the essential statement and feature it; do not force your reader to fumble through a long quoted passage in search of the relevant statement. Make the brief quotation a part of your sentence in this manner:

   Many Americans get caught in a psychological trap with the so-called yo-yo dieting pattern, in which they try a diet for a few weeks only to abandon it. Later, they try another, so the failed diets, said Nelson (2003), "cost citizens billions of dollars every year without any positive benefit" (p. 755).

7. Quote from both primary sources and secondary sources.

Quoting Primary Sources

Primary sources are pilot studies, tests, experiments, surveys, interviews, case studies, and the statistics and discussions that flow from them. Quote from primary sources for these seven specific reasons:

1. To draw on the wisdom of a researcher's findings, surveys, charts, and discussion.
2. To let readers hear the precise words of the author.

3. To reproduce graphs, charts, and statistical data.
4. To share the voices of others as drawn from interviews and case studies.
5. To cite the president and other government officials.
6. To share and compare tests and experiments.
7. To cite from pilot studies, test data, observations, statistics, and computer data.

Quoting from Secondary Sources

Secondary sources are journal and magazine articles and textbooks that comment on discoveries and findings. Often they appear as reviews or explain complex research findings for laymen in scientific magazines like *Discovery* and *Psychology Today.* Quote from secondary sources for these five specific reasons:

1. To explain complex issues through the secondhand commentary of experts on the topic.
2. To make clear the purpose and extent of a research project.
3. To review the research work of another person.
4. To group into one review several research reports that touch on a common topic.
5. To provide a review of the literature in your introduction.

However, the overuse of direct quotations from secondary sources indicates either (1) that you neglected primary sources (see above), or (2) you did not have a clear focus and copied verbatim just about everything related to the subject. Limit quotations from secondary sources by using only a phrase or a sentence, as shown here:

> The ethnic conflicts on the Mexican border continue to require "intensive political analysis" (Herman, 2004, p. 611).

If you quote an entire sentence, make the quotation a direct object. It tells *what* the authority says.

> In response to the ethnic conflicts on the Mexican border, one scholar noted, "The American government must exercise caution and conduct intensive political analysis of the various clans and subcultures" (Herman, 2004, p. 611).

Blend material from several sources to build strong paragraphs, as shown here:

> A search of the literature produced by a limited number of journals. Maheu (2004) discussed methods of helping clients, "even to

the point of counseling in cyberspace itself," which would establish professional relationships online (p. 82). Schneider and Weiss (2003) described this new trend but offered little insight. Cooper (2003) provided an excellent collection of articles in his guidebook for clinicians. All agreed that counseling can help persons who "substitute fantasy sex online for a true relationship" (Cooper, 2003, p. iv).

> Note: For additional examples of handling quoted materials, see Chapter 10, pages 131–148.

9d Writing Paraphrased Notes

A paraphrase requires you to restate in your own words the thought, meaning, and attitude of someone else. With *interpretation,* you act as a bridge between the source and the reader as you capture the wisdom of the source in approximately the same number of words. A paraphrase serves these purposes:

- Maintains your voice in the paper.
- Sustains your style.
- Avoids an endless string of direct quotations.
- Interprets the source as you rewrite it.

Keep in mind five rules for paraphrasing a source:

1. Rewrite the original in about the same number of words.
2. Provide an in-text citation to the source (the author, year, and page number only if the location is buried in a long work).
3. Retain exceptional words and phrases from the original by enclosing them in quotation marks.
4. Preserve the tone of the original by suggesting moods of satire, anger, humor, doubt, and so on. Show the author's attitude with appropriate verbs: "Edward Zigler condemned . . . defended . . . argued . . . explained . . . observed . . . defined . . . ."
5. Put the original aside while paraphrasing to avoid copying word for word. Compare the finished paraphrase with the original source to be certain that (1) the paraphrase truly rewrites the original, and (2) encloses within quotation marks key words retained from the original.

HINT: When your instructors see an in-text citation but no quotations marks, they will assume you are paraphrasing, not quoting. Be sure that their assumption is true.

The following examples show the differences between a quoted passage and a paraphrased idea.

Quotation:

> Hein (2004) explained, "Except for identical twins, each person's heredity is unique" (p. 294).

Paraphrase:

> Hein (2004) explained that heredity is special and distinct for each of us, unless a person is one of identical twins.

Quotation (more than 40 words must be indented as a block):

> Hein (2004) has clarified the phenomenon:
>
> > Since only half of each parent's chromosomes are transmitted to a child and since this half represents a chance selection of those the child could inherit, only twins that develop from a single fertilized egg that splits in two have identical chromosomes. (p. 294)

Paraphrase:

> Hein (2004) has specified that twins have identical chromosomes because they grow from one egg that divides after it has been fertilized. He affirmed that most brothers and sisters differ because of the "chance selection" of chromosomes transmitted by each parent (p. 294).

Note: As shown above in the paraphrase, enclose exact wording within quotation marks and provide a page number; otherwise a page number is not required.

9e   Writing Summary Notations

You should learn to write several types of summaries. All provide a quick sketch of the data or material, but they differ in form and purpose.

The basic summary describes and paraphrases source material to preserve ideas quickly without quotation or paraphrase. For example, you might reference several works that address the same issue, as shown in this example:

> The logistics and cost of implementing a reading program for pre-kindergarten children has been examined in books by West (2003) and Loveless (2004) and in articles by Jones et al. (2002), Coffee and Street (2004), and Abernathy (2004).

Success with the basic summary requires the following:

1. Keep it short.
2. Avoid quotations and paraphrases by jotting down rough ideas.
3. Provide author documentation.

In addition to the basic summary, you may also create five additional summaries:

- Summary of a book or an article.
- Review of an article or book.
- Abstract to introduce your report.
- Annotation for a bibliography entry.
- Field and laboratory notes.

Each one differs significantly from the other three.

Summary of a Single Book or Article

Use the summary to describe an entire work. In just a few sentences, a writer can summarize a scholarly essay or book, a textbook, a novel, or literary work. This is an objective description, not an evaluation, as with a review.

Weir and Faulkner (2004) have published a new anthology on feminism entitled *Voices of a New Generation*. The book of essays has three headings. The first, "Uses and Limitations of Feminism and Feminist Theory," provides a diverse set of essays on economics, race, and abortion, with titles like "Seeing in Color" and "Laundry: Writing on Feminism." The second, "Defining Ourselves; Others Defining Us," focuses issues of identity with such titles as "The Curse," "Criminalizing Black Women," and "Imagining Cinematic Lesbian Identity." The third section, "Contradictions: Theory and Activism," focuses on the women's movement with essays on women's studies, social justice, men within the movement, Native Americans, and activists in the streets. The anthology could serve nicely for courses in women's studies, gender, and the sociology of women.

Furnish a summary of this nature as a courtesy to your readers to cue them about the contents of a work. The summary helps you avoid a full-blown retelling of the whole work.

Review

The review is an evaluation of the work as well as a summary. Note this example of the short review by one student:

Tannen (1990) considered gender-based differences that distinguished male and female communication in her book *You Just Don't Understand: Women and Men in Conversation*. She argued that ignoring differences can be hazardous. She explained that for the majority of women a conversation helps to connect and negotiate. Thus, their chats over coffee focus on private conversation. In contrast, she said men use conversation to attain status in social and business environments. Men, less personal, speak out on issues of the day, which Tannen considered report tones. Her research examined the dialog differences of men and women. She remained firm in presenting differences in gender for men and women attempting to bridge communication failures of the sexes. She would like to change the spots on the leopard, a daunting task.

For more instructions on preparing a review, see pages 191–200.

Abstract

An abstract is a brief summary that appears as a separate paragraph at the beginning of an essay or report to summarize the contents. Usually, the author writes it to help readers decide whether to read or skip the article. You can find entire volumes devoted to abstracts, such as *Psychological Abstracts* and *Social Work Abstracts*. Most database search engines at your library, such as SilverPlatter and PsycINFO, display an abstract for each essay. You will discover that most of your instructors in all fields of the social sciences demand abstracts as the opening element of your reports.

When filed electronically, the key words of an abstract go into electronic storage for recovery by other researchers. Thus, an abstract should include the following:

- One fully developed summary of about 100 key, essential words.
- An organization that features the report's purpose, design, results, and implications as expressed in the conclusion.
- An objective tone that makes complex issues understandable to the average reader.

Here is a sample abstract by one student; another example is found on pages 178 and 179.

Abstract

Computer matchmaking was investigated to examine the theoretical implications of marriages arranged in part by online dating. The goal was to determine the effect of Internet activity on the private lives of participants. The social and psychological implications were determined by an examination of the literature, a profile of the participants, and a case study that interviewed an affected couple. Results were mixed, with failures balanced against successful matches. The social implications affect the workplace as well as the private lives of the men and women who are active in chat rooms and dating services. The psychological and behavioral implications include infidelity, damage to self-esteem, addiction, and motivation based on the chance for true and lasting love.

Annotated Bibliography

An *annotation* is a summary of the contents of a book or article. A *bibliography* is a list of sources on a selected topic. Thus, an annotated bibliography does two important things: (1) it gives a bibliographic list to a selection of sources, and (2) it summarizes the contents of each book or article. Writing an annotated bibliography may at first appear to be busywork, but the exercise will help you evaluate the strength of your sources.

The annotated bibliography that follows provides a summary to a few sources on the social pressure placed on young people to get and maintain a tan. It includes a discussion of key issues, especially the manner in which young people ignore the dangers of skin cancer.

Norman Levenson

Professor Davidson

24 July 2003

Annotated Bibliography

Brown, E. W. (1998). Tanning beds and the 'Safe Tan' myth. *Medical Update 21*, 6.

> Like others, Brown is mystified by the desire of young persons to burn their skin. Social pressure or not, Brown declared that there is "no such thing as a 'safe' or 'healthy' tan. He explained that tanning is the skin's reaction to radiation damage, and "tanned skin is damaged skin" (p. 6). He cautioned that tans from tanning beds are no different than those produced by the sun. Like others, he encouraged the use of SPF 15 or higher.

Cohen, R. (2003). Tanning trouble: Teens are using tanning beds in record numbers. *Scholastic Choices 18*, 23–28.

> Cohen warned that tanning beds "can be just as dangerous as the sun's rays" (p. 23). Tanning salons have become a social

gathering place, yet the writer explained that tanning salons are not well regulated and can be really dangerous. The writer also explained how skin type affects tanning and the dangers of cancer.

Geller, A. C., et al. (2002). Use of sunscreen, sunburning rates, and tanning bed use among more than 10,000 U. S. children and adolescents. *Pediatrics 109,* 1009–1015.

> The objective of this study was to examine the psychosocial variables associated with teens seeking suntans. It collected data from questionnaires submitted by 10,079 boys and girls, ages 12 to 18. It concluded that many children are at risk for skin cancer because of failure to use sunscreen.

Segilia, A. (2000, June 13). Sunscreens, suntans, and sun health. American Cancer Society. Interview. Retrieved June 4, 2003, from http://www.intelihealth.com/search

> In this article, Segilia, a coordinator of Cancer Control Programs for the American Cancer Society, answered questions about tanning, including the use of sunscreen of SPF 15 or higher, use of suntan lotions, the effects of the sun, and the dangers of skin cancer.

Zazinski, J. (2003, August 11). A Legion of Ladies' Lesions. *Research Briefs.* Boston U. Retrieved June 4, 2003, from http://www.bu.edu/news/research/2000/8-11-suntans-chf.htm

> This article cited M. Demierre, a professor of dermatology, who sees the desire for a good tan as just another addiction. In truth, women have joined men in contracting and dying of melanoma, in great part because of tanning beds. Zazinski cautioned youngsters against becoming addicted to sun worship.

Field and Laboratory Notes

You will be expected to conduct field research in many social and physical science courses. This work requires different kinds of notes kept on charts, cards, notepads, laboratory notebooks, a research journal, or the computer.

If you interview knowledgeable people, make careful notes during the interview and transcribe those notes to your draft in a polished form. A tape recorder can serve as a backup to your notetaking.

If you conduct a questionnaire, the tabulated results of the survey become valuable data for developing information on the findings along with graphs and charts for the Results section of your report.

If you perform an observation, you will need carefully drawn descriptions of what you observed—behavior, speech, gestures, interaction of subjects with one another, facial expressions, and similar details. These notations become the fulfillment of your methodology and serve to build your Results section.

Note: See pages 27–28 for one student's notations on an interview and pages 179–185 for a research project that incorporates a student's questionnaire survey.

If you conduct experiments, tests, and measurements, the findings serve as your tabulated notations for the Results section of the report and as the basis for the Discussion section.

YOUR RESEARCH PROJECT

1. Look carefully at each of the sources you have collected so far—sections of books, journal articles, Internet printouts. Try writing a summary of each one. At the same time, make decisions about material worthy of direct quotation and material that you wish to paraphrase or summarize. Submit one of your summaries to your instructor.

2. Decide how you will keep your notes—in a research journal, on handwritten notecards, or in computer files. Note: The computer files will serve you well because you can transfer them into your text and save typing time.

3. Write various types of notations—that is, write a few that use direct quotations, some that paraphrase, some that summarize, and some that show tabulated data. Submit to your instructor three notes: one that uses a direct quotation, one that paraphrases the source in about the same number of words, and one that summarizes the source.

4. Dedicate yourself to writing as many personal notes as possible. These ideas will establish your voice and position. In other words, do not let the sources speak for you; let them support your position.

5. If you have access to *Take Note!* or some other notetaking program, take the time to consider its special features. You can create notes, store them in folders, and even search your own files by keyword, category, and reference.

10 Blending Reference Material into Your Report

As you might expect, writing a research report carries with it certain obligations. You should read the literature on your subject, gather citations from the articles and books, and display the words of authorities prominently in your writing, especially in the introduction, where you must provide a brief history of the work that has been done in your area of study. APA style requires you to identify each source mentioned using the authority's last name, the year of publication, and page numbers to quotations. Of course, page numbers are not expected for lectures, news broadcasts, and most Internet sources. As a general policy, keep citations brief:

> Munon (2004) found that exposure duration affected eyewitness accuracy and confidence.

Remember, your readers will have full documentation to each source on the References page (see Chapter 11). However, make no entry on the References page for letters, e-mail, and informal interviews that cannot be recovered by other researchers. In those cases, give a more complete description of the source in your text with initials, surname, year, and the type of source:

> The chief investigator for the police department, W. M. Warren (2004), reported during a recent interview that his personnel had great difficulty in gathering effective witnesses for most trials.

10a Writing in the Proper Tense for Papers in the Social Sciences

Verb tense is an indicator that distinguishes papers written in APA style for the social sciences. Citations that refer to reports and articles by your sources require either the past tense or present perfect tense ("Jeffries *stipulated*" or "the work of Mills and Maguire *has demonstrated*"). However, this style does require present tense in two instances: (1) when you discuss the results (e.g., "the results confirm" or "the study indicates"), and (2) when you mention established knowledge (e.g., "the therapy offers some hope" or "salt contributes to hypertension"). Here's an example to show the differences in verb tense for a passage written in the humanities and one written in the social sciences.

Humanities style:

The scholarly issue at work here is the construction of reality. Cohen, Adoni, and Bantz label the construction a social process "in which human beings acts both as the creators and products of the social world" (34). These writers identify three categories (34–35).

Social sciences style:

The scholarly issue at work here is the construction of reality. Cohen, Adoni, and Bantz (2004) labeled the construction a social process "in which human beings act both as the creators and products of the social world" (p. 34). These writers have identified three categories.

The social science passage on the right shows the present tense used for generalizations and references to stable conditions, but it displays the present perfect tense or the past tense for sources cited (e.g., the sources *have tested* a hypothesis or the sources *reported* the results of a test). This next sentence uses tense correctly:

> The dangers of steroid use exists for every age group, even youngsters. Lloyd and Mercer (2003) reported on six incidents of liver damage to 14-year-old swimmers who used steroids. Since that time, several scientists have examined the connection between steroid use and liver damage (Boston, 2003; Randolph, 2002; Watson, 2003).

As shown in the example, use the present tense *(exists)* for established knowledge, the past tense *(reported)* for an action that has occurred, or the present perfect *(have examined)* for an action that began in the past and continues to the present. For example, "Grunfeld reported" (past tense) but "Responses of participants in the past six months have varied" (present perfect).

10b Using In-Text Citations in Your Reports

Use the following conventions for in-text citations:

- Cite last names only for sources listed on the References page.
- List author names in alphabetical order in the citation.
- Cite the year, within parentheses, immediately after the name of the author.
- Cite page numbers with a direct quotation but not with a paraphrase.
- Use *p.* or *pp.* before page numbers.

Citing Last Name Only and the Year of Publication

An in-text citation in social sciences style requires the last name of the author and the year of publication.

Devlin (2003) and Watson (2004) have advanced the idea of combining the social sciences and mathematics to chart human behavior.

If you do not use the author's name in your text, place the name(s) within the parenthetical citation.

Two studies have advanced the idea of combining the social sciences and mathematics to chart human behavior (Devlin, 2003; Watson, 2004).

If necessary, add initials to distinguish the person, especially if two people with the same last name are listed on the References page (e.g., G. W. Bush and G. H. Bush or E. Roosevelt and F. D. Roosevelt).

Providing a Page Number

If you quote the exact words of a source, provide a page number and use *p.* or *pp.* Place the page number in one of two places: after the year (2003, p. B4) or at the end of the quotation.

George (2004) advanced the idea of "soft mathematics," which is the practice of "applying mathematics to study people's behavior" (p. B4).

Citing a Block of Material

Present a quotation of 40 words or more as a separate block, indented five spaces or 1/2 inch from the left margin. Because it is set off from the text in a distinctive block, do not enclose it with quotation marks. Do not indent the first line an extra five spaces; however, do indent the first line of any additional paragraphs that appear in the block an extra five spaces, that is, ten spaces from the left margin. Set parenthetical citations outside the last period.

Albert (2003) reported the following:

> Whenever these pathogenic organisms attack the human body and begin to multiply, the infection is set in motion. The host responds to this parasitic invasion with efforts to cleanse itself of the invading agents. When rejection efforts of the host become visible (fever, sneezing, congestion), the disease status exists. (pp. 314–315)

Citing a Work with More Than One Author

When one work has two or more authors, use *and* in the text but use *&* in the citation.

> Werner and Throckmorton (2003) offered statistics on the toxic
> levels of water samples from six rivers.

but

> It has been reported (Werner & Throckmorton, 2003) that toxic
> levels exceeded the maximum allowed each year since 1983.

For three to five authors, name them all in the first entry (e.g., Torgerson, Andrews, Smith, Lawrence, & Dunlap, 2003), but thereafter use *et al.* (e.g., Torgerson et al., 2003). For six or more authors, employ *et al.* in the first and in all subsequent instances (e.g., Fredericks et al., 2004).

Citing More Than One Work by an Author

Use small letters *(a, b, c)* to identify two or more works published in the same year by the same author—for example, (Thompson, 2004a) and (Thompson, 2004b). Then use 2004a and 2004b on your References page (see page 161 for an example). If additional items will clarify the citation for the reader, add them as necessary:

> Horton (2003; cf. Thomas, 2002a, p. 89, and 2002b, p. 426)
> suggested an intercorrelation of these testing devices. But after
> multiple-group analysis, Welston (2004, esp. p. 211) reached an
> opposite conclusion.

Citing Indirect Sources

Although it is desirable to use information from the original source, you may use a double reference to cite somebody quoted in a book or article—that is, you may use the original author(s) in the text and cite your source for the information in the parenthetical citation.

> In other research, Massie and Rosenthal (2002) studied home
> movies of children diagnosed with autism, but determining criteria
> proved difficult because of the differences in quality and dating of the
> available videotapes (cited in Osterling & Dawson, 2003, p. 248).

See also "Textbook, casebook, anthology" (page 151), for additional details about citing this type of source on the References page.

Citing from a Textbook or Anthology

If you make an in-text citation to an article or chapter of a textbook, casebook, or anthology for which many authors are listed, you should use the in-text citation to refer only to the person(s) you cite:

> One writer stressed that two out of every three new jobs in this decade will go to women (Rogers 2003).

The list of references will clarify the nature of this reference to Rogers (see "Textbook, casebook, anthology," page 151).

Citing Classical Works

If an ancient work has no date of publication, cite the author's name in the text followed by *n.d.* within parentheses.

> Sophocles (n.d.) saw psychic emotions as. . . .

Cite the year of any translation you have used, preceded by *trans.*, and give the date of the version used, followed by *version*.

> Plato (trans. 1963) offered a morality that. . . .
>
> Plato's *Phaedrus* (1982 version) explored. . . .

If you know the original date of publication, include it before the date of the translation or version you used.

> In his "The Poetic Principle," Poe (1850/1967) announced the doctrines upon which he built his poetry and fiction.

> Note: Entries on your References page need not cite major classical works and the Bible. Therefore, identify in your text the version used and the book, chapter, line, verse, or canto.

> In Exodus 24:3–4 Moses erected an altar and "twelve pillars according to the twelve tribes of Israel" (King James Version).
>
> The Epic of Gilgamesh demonstrated, in part, the search for everlasting life (Part 4).
>
> Homer (n.d.) took great efforts in describing the shield of Achilles (18:558–709).

Abbreviating Corporate Authors in the Text

Corporate authors may be abbreviated after a first, full reference:

> One source questioned the results of the use of aspirin for arthritis
> treatment in children (American Medical Association [AMA], 2003).

Thereafter, refer to the corporate author by initials: (AMA, 2003).

Citing an Anonymous Work

When no author is listed for a work, cite the title as part of the in-text citation (or use the first few words of the material).

> The cost per individual student has continued to rise rapidly as
> states cut funding and shift the expense to students and their parents
> (Money concerns, 2003, p. 2).

Citing Personal Communications

E-mail, telephone conversations, memos, and conversations do not provide recoverable data, so exclude them from your list of references. Thus, you should cite personal communications in the text only. In so doing, give the initials as well as the last name of the source, provide the date, and briefly describe the nature of the communication.

> M. C. Gaither (personal communication, August 24, 2003)
> described the symptoms of Wilson's disease.

Citing Internet Sources in Your Text

Material from electronic sources presents special problems. Currently, most Internet sources have no prescribed page numbers or numbered paragraphs. You cannot list a screen number because monitors differ. You cannot list the page numbers of a downloaded document because computer printers differ. Therefore, in most cases, do not list a page number or a paragraph number. Here are basic guidelines.

Omit a page or paragraph number. The marvelous feature of electronic text is that it is searchable, so your readers can find your quotation quickly with the Find feature. Suppose you have written the following:

> The UCLA Internet Report (2003) advised policy makers that "a
> better understanding of the impact of the Internet requires rigorous
> study."

A reader who wants to investigate further will find your complete citation in your References list. With the Internet address for the article and the Edit and Find features, the passage can be found quickly within the essay. That is much easier than counting through 46 paragraphs.

Provide a paragraph number. Some scholars who write on the Internet number their paragraphs. Therefore, if you find an article on the Internet that has numbered paragraphs, by all means supply that information in your citation.

> The Insurance Institute for Highway Safety (2003) has
>
> emphasized restraint first, saying, "A federal rule requiring special
>
> attachments to anchor infant and child restraints in vehicles is making
>
> installation easier, but not all child restraints fit easily in all
>
> vehicles" (par. 1).
>
> Recommendations for treating non-insulin-dependent diabetes
>
> mellitus (NIDDM), the most common type of diabetes, include a diet
>
> that is rich in carbohydrates, "predominantly from whole grains, fruit,
>
> vegetables, and low-fat milk" (Yang, 2003, par. 3).

Provide a page number. In a few instances, you will find page numbers buried within brackets here and there throughout an article. These refer to the page numbers of the printed version of the document. In these cases, you should cite the page just as you would a printed source. Here is the Internet source with the page numbers buried within the text to signal the break between page 17 and page 18:

> What is required is a careful reading of Chekhov's subtext, that elusive [pp17–18] literature that lingers in psychological nuances of the words, not the exact words themselves.—Ward, *Drama and Psychology*, 2001.

The page number may be included in the citation:

> One source has argued the merits of Chekhov's subtext and its
>
> "psychological nuances of the words" (Ward, 2001, p. 18).

In some instances, the Web site reproduces the original pagination, as in the case of JSTOR, which photocopies the original pages and makes them available electronically:

The figure shows a reproduction of a JSTOR database page with the following text:

XL
SHAKESPEARE'S CONCEPTION OF *HAMLET*

What was Shakespeare's conception of *Hamlet?* That is the question. It is one which inevitably resolves itself into a reconstruction of the materials at his disposal, the dramatic problems with which he had to deal, and the means whereby he sought to satisfy contemporary dramatic taste. For such a reconstruction modern scholarship provides abundant information about both the theatrical practices and intellectual interests of the time and Shakespeare's habits as a craftsman. In particular should be noted his exceptional preoccupation with character portrayal and the scrupulous motivation of action; his conformity with changing theatrical fashion, yet at the same time his reluctance to pioneer in experiment; his sensitive, if sketchy, acquaintance with matters of contemporary interest; and his success as a skilled and inspired adapter rather than as an innovator. In the application of this knowledge two principles are fundamental. First, *Hamlet* must not be viewed as isolation, but in close conjunction with the theatrical environment which produced it. Second, Shakespeare must be recognized as primarily a practical playwright, a business man of the theater with obligations to fulfill, specific theatrical conditions to meet, and an audience to divert. For the rest, it is a pleasant exercise for the recreative imagination to try to think oneself into Shakespeare's mind, to face the problem of *Hamlet* as he faced it, and to trace the solution as he must have found it.

I

Shakespeare's *Hamlet* is a philosophical melodrama. Theatrically it is one of his most spectacular plays. For all its discursiveness it is crammed with action of the most sensational sort. Ghosts walk and cry "Revenge!" Murder is fully done. Conspirators plot and counterplot. Two characters go mad. A queen is terrified nearly to death. A play breaks up in a near-riot. An insurrection batters the palace gates. A brawl desecrates a suicide's grave. A duel explodes into murder and general butchery. There are poison, incest, war, and debauchery. This is not closet drama for the philosopher's study; it is blood and thunder for the popular stage.

Nevertheless, *Hamlet* is also one of Shakespeare's most thoughtful plays. Permeated with moralizing and philosophical speculation, it presents in its center character a most elaborate psychological study. As for the reader these are unquestionably the most enduring elements, so to the elucidation of these criticism has devoted most of its attention.

777

778   *Shakespeare's Conception of "Hamlet"*

Indeed, not infrequently is it implied that the play exists for the express purpose of expounding Shakespeare's views on life and death, or that the play is primarily a peg upon which to hang the character of Hamlet. Such a view, however, scarcely squares with the known practice of Shakespeare, or, for that matter, of any successful playwright. The one play of the period which openly advertised itself as a philosophical character study–Chapman's *Revenge of Bussy D'Ambois*–was an inglorious failure. Contrast with this the extraordinary popularity of *Hamlet*, and one may see how much of it depends upon the scrupulous subordination of those very philosophical elements which make Chapman's play so insufferably dull to the modern reader. To Shakespeare, doubtless, both character study and philosophical speculation were distinctly subsidiary to plot and stage business; and in the excised version, which must have been necessary for stage presentation, they probably interfered little with the more congenial business of swift melodrama.[1]

You may cite these page numbers because JSTOR photocopies the original publication

Harold R. Walley   779

session with a few restricted preoccupations. The peculiarity of Hamlet's madness is that, no matter how insane his ravings may seem to his hearers, without exception they contain *double entendre* and make perfect sense from Hamlet's point of view. The method is substantially that which underlies the contemporaneous intellectual interest; namely, the surprise association of apparently incongruous elements linked by a submerged chain of thought. Thus whatever madness Hamlet exhibits is an integral part of his own mental attitude.

This mental obsession, which issues in the evidences of Hamlet's supposed madness, is intimately connected with two other important features of the play. Hamlet is much concerned with his inability to carry forward his revenge. This delay is essential to the plot; that it is a delay for which Hamlet is himself responsible Shakespeare makes clear throughout.[2] Much, however, as Hamlet endeavors to understand the reason, he is incapable of explaining it to himself; it is an ingrained part

FIGURE 10.1 Sample page from JSTOR database

A citation to an article from the JSTOR database would include the page number:

> Kandiyoti (1998) argued that "women strategize within a set of concrete constraints that reveal and define the blueprint of what I will term the *patriarchal bargain* of any given society . . . " (p. 275).

The citation on the References page would also include the pages:

> Kandiyoti, D. (1998). Bargaining with patriarchy. *Gender and Society, 2*(3), 274–290.

Internet article

> Commenting on the distinction between a Congressional calendar day and a legislative day, Dove (2003) stated that "a legislative day is

the period of time following an adjournment of the Senate until
another adjournment."

One source gave this cautionary notice: "Reports of abuses in the
interrogation of suspected terrorists raise the question of how—or
whether—we should limit the interrogation of a suspected terrorist
when our national security may be at stake" (Parry & White, 2003,
abstract).

HyperNews posting

Ochberg (2003) examined the use of algae in paper that "initially
has a green tint to it, but unlike bleached paper which turns yellow
with age, this algae paper becomes whiter with age."

Online magazine

BusinessWeek Online (2002) reported that the idea of peer-to-peer
computing is a precursor to new Web applications.

Government document

The Web site *Thomas* (2003) outlined the amendments to the
Homeland Security Act of 2002, which will implement the READICall
emergency alert system.

Other Electronic Sources

E-mail

Personal communications such as e-mail, which others cannot retrieve,
should be cited in the text only and not mentioned at all in the bibliography.

One technical writing instructor (March 8, 2003) has bemoaned
the inability of hardware developers to maintain pace with the
ingenuity of software developers. In his e-mail message, he indicated
that educational institutions cannot keep pace with the hardware
developers. Thus, "students nationwide suffer with antiquated
equipment, even though it's only a few years old" (clemmerj@APSU.edu).

However, electronic discussion groups have gained legitimacy in recent
years, so in your text you might wish to give an exact date and provide the
e-mail address *only* if the citation has scholarly relevance and *only* if the
group has made public the e-mail address with the expressed wish for correspondence.

Discussion group (listserv)

Postings available to others should be cited in the text and in the References page.

> Blackmore (May 7, 2005) has identified the book *Echoes of Glory* for those interested in detailed battlefield maps of the American Civil War.

> Funder (April 5, 2004) argued against the "judgmental process."

Posting to a newsgroup site

> In an essay in *Electronic Antiquity,* Whitehead (2003) explored the issue of ancient Athenian oratory from the 420s to the 320s, including the opening or introduction of the speech:

Note: Maintain any special spelling in the original, as shown above. Signal to the reader that the spelling is original by following the word with *sic* (see page 145).

> Proem [sic] is the condition which a speaker needed to create at the beginning of his speech that would have been universally understood. He had to win his audience's goodwill.

FTP sites

> Del Reyes (2003) demonstrated in the following graph that "enrollment in radiology programs of study has increased by 67% in the past ten years" (p. 54).

CD-ROM

> *Grolier's Multimedia Encyclopedia* (2003) explained that in recent decades huge swaths of the rain forest have been toppled; as the trees disappeared, so, too, did the flora and fauna that thrived under their canopy.

10c Punctuating Citations Properly and Consistently

Keep page citations outside quotation marks but inside the final period, as shown here:

Smith (2004) argued, "The benefits of cloning far exceed any harm that might occur" (p. 34).

If there is a page citation to a paraphrase, which is not required, the period follows the page citation.

Smith (2004) argued that cloning will bring benefits to medical science that will outweigh any disadvantages within the field (p. 34).

See page 133 on placing the page citation with a block quotation.

Commas and Periods

Place commas and periods inside quotation marks unless the page citation intervenes. The example below shows (1) how to put the mark inside the quotation marks, (2) how to interrupt a quotation to insert the speaker, (3) how to use single quotation marks within the regular quotation marks, and (4) how to place the period after a page citation.

"Modern advertising," said Rachel Murphy (2004), "not only creates a marketplace, it determines values." She added, "I resist the advertiser's argument that they 'awaken, not create desires'" (p. 192).

Sometimes you may need to change the closing period to a comma. Suppose you decide to quote this sentence: "Scientific cloning poses no threat to the human species." If you start your sentence with the quotation, you must change the period to a comma, as shown:

"Scientific cloning poses no threat to the human species," declared Wineberg (2004) in a recent article (p. 357).

However, retain question marks or exclamation marks, and no comma is required:

"Does scientific cloning really pose a threat to the human species?" wondered one scientist (Durham, 2004, p. 546).

Let's look at other examples. Consider this original material:

The Russians had obviously anticipated neither the quick discovery of the bases nor the quick imposition of the quarantine. Their diplomats across the world were displaying all the symptoms of improvisation, as if they had been told nothing of the placement of the missiles and had received no instructions what to say about them.

—Arthur M. Schlesinger, Jr., *A Thousand Days,* (New York: Houghton, 1965), 820.

Punctuate citations from this source in one of the following methods.

"The Russians," wrote Schlesinger (1965), "had obviously anticipated neither the quick discovery of the [missile] bases nor the quick imposition of the quarantine" (p. 820).

Schlesinger (1965) noted, "Their diplomats across the world were displaying all the symptoms of improvisation . . . " (p. 820).

Schlesinger (1965) observed that the Russian failure to anticipate an American discovery of Cuban missiles caused "their diplomats across the world" to improvise answers as "if they had been told nothing of the placement of the missiles . . . " (p. 820).

Note that the last example correctly changes the capital *T* of *their* to lower-case to match the grammar of the restructured sentence, and it does not use ellipsis points before *if* because the phrase flows smoothly into the text.

Semicolons and Colons

Both semicolons and colons go outside the quotation marks, as illustrated in the following examples:

Zigler (2004) admitted that "the extended family is now rare in contemporary society"; however, he stressed the greatest loss as the "wisdom and daily support of older, more experienced family members" (p. 42).

Sutton-Smith (2004) said, "Adults don't worry whether their toys are educational" (p. 64); nevertheless, parents want to keep their children in a learning mode.

The example immediately above shows how to place the page citation after a quotation and before a semicolon. The next example shows a clause following the colon that could stand alone as a complete sentence, so it begins with a capital letter.

Zigler (2004) lamented the demise of the "extended family": The family suffers by loss of the "wisdom and daily support of older, more experienced family members" (p. 42).

If the word group following the colon cannot stand alone as a sentence, do not capitalize the first word after the colon.

> Zigler (2004) lamented the demise of the "extended family" for this primary reason: the loss of the "wisdom and support of older, more experienced family members" (p. 42).

Question Marks and Exclamation Marks

When a question mark or an exclamation mark serves as part of the quotation, keep it inside the quotation mark. Put the page citation with the year to avoid a conflict with the punctuation mark.

> Thompson (2004, p. 16) passionately shouted to union members, "We can bring order into our lives even though we face hostility from every quarter!"
>
> "We face hostility from every quarter!" declared the union leader.

Question marks may appear inside the closing quotation mark when they are part of the original quotation; otherwise, they go outside.

> The philosopher Bremmer (2004, p. 16) asks, "How should we order our lives?"

but

> Did Brackenridge (2004) say that we might encounter "hostility from every quarter" (p. 16)?

Single Quotation Marks

When a quotation appears within another quotation, use single quotation marks with the shorter one.

> George Loffler (2004, p. 32) confirmed that "the unconscious carries the best of human thought and gives man great dignity, but it also has the dark side so that we cry, in the words of Shakespeare's Macbeth, 'Hence, horrible shadow! Unreal mockery, hence.'"

Remember that the period always goes inside the quotation marks unless the page citation intervenes, as shown below:

> George Loffler (2004) confirmed that "the unconscious carries the best of human thought and gives man great dignity, but it also has the dark side so that we cry, in the words of Shakespeare's Macbeth, 'Hence, horrible shadow! Unreal mockery, hence'" (p. 32).

10d Altering Some Capital Letters and Lowercase Letters

Social sciences style permits you to change some initial capital letters to lowercase letters when you incorporate them into your text, and on occasion to change lowercase letters to capital letters.

Change Some Initial Capital Letters to Small Letters

If you change a sentence to quote only a subordinate clause or a phrase, you integrate the words into your sentence; thus, the first letter of the quotation should be small *even though it was a capital letter in the original:*

> E. Roosevelt (1937) warned her audience that "you will have to rise above considerations which are narrow and partisan" (p. 45).

Compare to "E. Roosevelt warned, "You will. . . .""

> Plath (1945) surprised her readers with unusual similes, as in "love set you going like a fat gold watch" (p. 432).

The original line reads: "Love set you going like a fat gold watch."

Change Some Small Letters to Capitals

Change a small letter to a capital letter within a separated citation—that is, if a quotation that is only part of a sentence in the original forms a complete sentence as quoted, the initial lowercase letter may be changed to a capital where your introductory structure permits it. For example, in the next quotation note that the word *the* is in lower case.

> "Men can never lead if they are afraid, for the leader who is afraid will never be followed" (Roosevelt, 1937, p. 43).

Notice next how the word *the* may be changed to a capital letter:

Eleanor Roosevelt (1937) wisely observed, "The leader who is afraid will never be followed" (p. 43).

10e Editing a Quotation with [*sic*], Ellipsis Points, and Brackets

You are permitted to include additional information in a quotation under certain circumstances. You must use brackets around material you insert, and you must use ellipsis if you delete any part of an entire sentence.

Use [*sic*] to Signal a Mistake in a Quotation

When a quotation has a questionable spelling or word usage, let your reader know that you are quoting exactly and that the structure is not your error. The word *sic* ("thus," "so," "in this manner") is placed in brackets immediately after the word in question. In the next example, the student writer makes clear that the year *1964* was the error of Lovell. The assassination occurred in 1963.

Lovell (2004) said, "John F. Kennedy, assassinated in November of 1964 [*sic*], became overnight an immortal figure of courage and dignity in the hearts of most Americans" (p. 92).

The word *sic* is not an abbreviation and therefore takes no period. Because of its Latin roots, it is usually set in italics. Do not overuse the device. In a linguistics study, for example, it is unnecessary to call attention to every variant:

Whan that Aprille with his shoures sote
The droghte of Marche hath perced to the rote.

Chaucer

Use Brackets to Enclose Interpolation, Corrections, Explanations, Translations, or Comments within Quoted Matter

Use square brackets, not parentheses, to clarify a statement:

E. Roosevelt (1936) warned, "You [the Democratic delegates] will have to rise above considerations which are narrow and partisan" (p. 367).

Use the brackets, without ellipsis, to correct the grammar within an abridged quotation:

ORIGINAL:	"Eleanor Roosevelt, who served in the United Nations after FDR's death, gained international attention, especially as a champion of the impoverished people around the globe."—Orin Roberts, 2003, p. 15
ABRIDGED:	"Eleanor Roosevelt [became] a champion of the impoverished people around the globe," reported Orin Roberts (2003, p. 15).

Use brackets to note any addition or change you make in the quotation:

E. Roosevelt (1943) observed, "You gain *strength, courage, and confidence* [my emphasis] by every experience in which you really look fear in the face"; then she added, "You must do the thing you think you cannot" (p. 342).

Lovell (2004) said, "John F. Kennedy, assassinated in November of [1963], became overnight an immortal figure of courage and dignity in the hearts of most Americans" (p. 92).

Compare the citation of Lovell, above, with the one on page 145 that retains the wrong date and marks it with *sic.*

Use brackets to substitute a proper name for a pronoun, such as *she*:

Roberts (2003, p. 7) added, "We all know [Roosevelt] implored us into action by saying 'look fear in the face.'"

> Note: Use parentheses to enclose the comments or explanations that fall outside the quotation, as shown in this example:
> Boughman (46) and other experts have child care providers to "instruct their employees on responding *wisely* to medical emergencies with CPR and other life-saving techniques" (emphasis added).

Use Ellipsis Points to Omit Portions of a Quotation

An ellipsis shows an omission of a word, phrase, line, paragraph, or more from a quoted passage. The ellipsis is marked with points, not asterisks, printed on the line like periods, separated from each other by a space and from the text by a space. Three points indicate an omission within a quoted sentence.

ORIGINAL:	"Success in marriage depends on being able, when you get over being in love, to really love," advised Eleanor Roosevelt, who added, "You never know anyone until you marry them."
ELLIPSIS:	"Success in marriage depends on being able . . . to really love," advised Eleanor Roosevelt (1937), who added, "You never know anyone until you marry them" (p. 45).

When the ellipsis occurs at the end of a sentence and what remains is still grammatically complete, use a period followed by three spaced points.

ORIGINAL:	Osburn observed, "The final years of Eleanor Roosevelt's life were filled with public service to the needy and the private love of her family in travels around the world that always brought her back to the New York mansion" (p. 23).
ELLIPSIS:	Osburn (2000, p. 23) observed, "The final years of Eleanor Roosevelt's life were filled with public service to the needy and the private love of her family. . . ."

Three spaced dots without the period show the omission of a quoted sentence that is purposely and grammatically incomplete:

Everybody knows that the "Gettysburg Address" begins with the line, "Four score and seven years ago . . . " But who can recite the entire speech?

Note: Consult a grammar handbook for issues beyond what is discussed here.

YOUR RESEARCH PROJECT

1. Make a critical journey through your draft with one purpose: to examine your handling of the sources. Have you introduced them clearly so the reader will know when the borrowing began? Have you provided last name

and year for each citation? Have you placed quotation marks at the beginning and the end of borrowed phrases as well as borrowed sentences? Have you provided a page number for quoted matter as appropriate?

2. If you have used any Internet sources, look at them again to see if the paragraphs on the Internet site are numbered. If so, use the paragraph numbers at the end of your citation(s); if not, use no numbers—not the page numbers on a computer printout and not paragraph numbers if you must count them.

3. If you have used a table, graph, figure, or photograph, be sure you have labeled it correctly (see pages A-9–A-10 for examples).

4. Did you keep verb tenses in the correct form—past tense or present perfect tense for citations and present tense for discussing results and making a conclusion? Compare your work with the instructions in section 10a.

11 Preparing the References List

When you write a final document for your instructor in APA style, place an entry for each of your sources in an alphabetical list using the hanging indention form shown below.

> Kharif, O. (2003, June 11). The net: Now, folks can't live without it.
>
> *BusinessWeek Online.* Retrieved June 18, 2003, from
>
> http://www.businessweek.com/technology/content/jun2003/
>
> tc20030610_1865_tc104.htm

Note: Do not use a period at the end of the URL.

The default style as explained in Section 11a applies to research reports written in APA style for the social sciences:

Education	Home Economics	Physical Education	Political Science
Psychology	Social Work	Sociology	Women's Studies

11a Preparing the List of References

At the end of your paper, create a References page to list the sources you cite in the paper, in footnotes, in figures and illustrations, and in an appendix. Alphabetize the entries and double-space throughout.

Note: Do not list an e-mail or other personal correspondence that is not retrievable by others (see page 27).

Type the first line of each entry flush left, and indent succeeding lines five spaces. You may italicize or underscore the names of books, periodicals, and volume numbers. List the author with surname first and initials only for given names. Include the year of publication within parentheses, followed by the title of a book or journal, italicized or underscored. Capitalize only the first word of the title and the first word of any subtitle; do capitalize proper nouns. Finish with the publication data, as demonstrated in the following examples.

Books

Turlington, C. (2003). <u>Living yoga: Creating a life practice.</u> New York: Hyperion.

For books, close the citation with the place of publication and the name of the publisher. In the publisher's name you may omit the words *Publishing,* *Company,* and *Inc.,* but otherwise give the full name: Florida State University Press; Pearson Longman; HarperCollins.

> Note: If you underline the titles, be sure to underline any punctuation marks at the end of titles and volume numbers.

Two authors

List chronologically, not alphabetically, two or more works by the same author—for example, Fitzgerald's 2003 publication would precede a 2004 publication.

Fitzgerald, R. A. (2003). *Psychological persuasion in marriage.*

Fitzgerald, R. A. (2004). *Marriage, emotions, and surrender.*

References with the same author in the same year are alphabetized and marked with lowercase letters *(a, b, c)* immediately after the date:

Murphy, T. B. (2004a). *Addressing preschool childcare needs.*

Murphy, T. B. (2004b). *Marketing a revolutionary reading program.*

Entries of a single author precede multiple-author entries beginning with the same surname without regard for the dates:

Martin, D. C. (2003). *Principles of sociology.*

Martin, D. C., & Smith, A. F. (2001). *Handbook to sociology.*

References with the same first author and different second or third authors should be alphabetized by the surname of the second author:

Bacon, D. E., & Smithson, C. A. (2004). <u>A primer in political science.</u>

Bacon, D. E., & Williamson, T. (2003). <u>The nuances of political power.</u>

Part of a book

List author(s), date, chapter or section title, editor (with name in normal order) preceded by *In* and followed by *(Ed.)* or *(Eds.),* the name of the book (underscored or italicized), page numbers to the specific section of the book cited (placed in parentheses), place of publication, and publisher.

Graham, K. (2003). The male bashing stereotype. In P. Elbow & P. Belanoff (Eds.), *Being a writer* (pp. 249–254). New York: McGraw Hill.

If no author is listed, begin with the title of the article.

Obadiah. (1999). In C. Wellington (Ed.), *Who was who in the Bible* (p. 245). Nashville: Nelson.

Textbook, casebook, anthology

Make a primary reference to the anthology:

VanderMey, R., Meyer, V., Van Rys, J., Kemper, D., & Sebranek, P. (Eds.) (2004). *The college writer*. Boston: Houghton Mifflin.

You have several options for identifying individual sources drawn from the anthology. First, you can cite each author with a cross-reference to the VanderMey book.

Bulthuis, J. (2002). Education through application. In VanderMey et al., p. 271.

Loeb, P. R. (1999). Soul of a citizen: Living with conviction in a cynical time. In VanderMey et al., pp. 287-289.

Turner, L. (2002). The media and the ethics of cloning. In VanderMey et al., pp. 323–327.

> Note: These entries should be placed in alphabetical order with all others on the reference page so that cross-references may appear before or after the primary source. The year cited should be that in which the cited work was published, not the anthology itself; such information is usually found in a headnote, footnote, or list of credits at the front or back of the anthology.

An alternative to the style shown above is to provide a double reference in your text by naming the authority cited and, within parentheses, the source, as shown below. Only Vander-Mey et al. would be listed on the References page.

Turner (2002) examined the media's rather dubious role in examining the ethics of cloning (as cited in VanderMey et al., 2004).

> Note: Full information on Turner is *not* provided with this method.

Finally, you may prefer to provide a complete entry for each of the authors cited from the casebook, in which case you do not need a separate entry to VanderMey:

Bulthuis, J. (2002). Education through application. In R. VanderMey, V. Meyer, J. Van Rys, D. Kemper, & P. Sebranek (Eds.), (2004), *The college writer* (p. 271). Boston: Houghton Mifflin.

Loeb, P. R. (1999). Soul of a citizen: Living with conviction in a cynical time. In R. VanderMey, V. Meyer, J. Van Rys, D. Kemper, & P. Sebranek (Eds.), (2004), *The college writer* (pp. 287–289). Boston: Houghton Mifflin.

Turner, L. (2002). The media and the ethics of cloning. In R.
VanderMey, V. Meyer, J. Van Rys, D. Kemper, & P. Sebranek (Eds.),
(2004), *The college writer* (pp. 323–327). Boston: Houghton
Mifflin.

Encyclopedia or dictionary

To cite an entry:

Foley, A. F. (2004). Cognitive psychology. In *Encarta 2004 encyclopedia
standard* [CD]. Redmond, WA: Microsoft.

To cite the entire work:

Vogt, P. (1999). *Dictionary of statistics & methodology: A nontechnical
guide for the social sciences.* Thousand Oaks, CA: Sage.

Book with corporate author

American Medical Association. (2003). *American medical association
complete medical encyclopedia.* New York: Random House.

Brochure or booklet

Mathis, R. (2002). *Human resource management: Student resource guide*
(10th ed.) [Brochure]. Washington, DC: Thompson.

Edition

Acredolo, P., Goodwyn, S., & Abrams, D. (2002). *Baby signs* (Rev. ed.).
Boston: McGraw.

Chapter in one volume of a series

Fuchs, A., & Milar, K. S. (2000). Psychology as a science. In I. B.
Weiner (Series Ed.) & D. K. Freidman (Vol. Ed.). (2003). *Handbook
of psychology: Vol. 1. History of psychology* (2nd ed, pp. 1–20).
New York: Wiley.

Numbered report

Raveis, V. H. (2003). *Aging families and breast cancer:
Multigenerational issues* (NTIS Rep. No. ADA418090). New York:
Columbia University.

Proceedings

Kvale, S. (2000). *The church, the factory, and the market: Scenarios for psychology in a postmodern age.* Paper presented at the proceedings of the International Congress of Psychology. Stockholm, Sweden.

If the presentation is published as an article in a journal or a chapter in a book, provide publication data:

Kvale, S. (2003). *The church, the factory, and the market: Scenarios for psychology in a postmodern age.* Paper presented at the International Congress of Psychology, Stockholm, Sweden. In *Theory and Psychology, 13,* 579–603.

Periodicals

Journal

List author(s), year, title of the article without quotation marks and with only the first word (and any proper nouns) capitalized, name of the journal underscored or italicized and with all major words capitalized, volume number underscored or italicized, and inclusive page numbers *not* preceded by *p.* or *pp.*

Smiler, A. P., Gagne, D. D., & Stine-Morrow, E. A. L. (2003). Aging, memory load, and resource allocation during reading. *Psychology and Aging, 18,* 203–209.

Article retrieved from ERIC, InfoTrac, Silverplatter, Proquest, or other library servers

Wakschlag, L. S., & Leventhal, B. L. (1996). Consultation with young autistic children and their families. *Journal of the American Academy of Child and Adolescent Psychiatry, 35,* 963–965. Retrieved August 8, 2003, from *Expanded Academic Index* database.

Magazine

List author, the date of publication (year, month without abbreviation, and the specific day for magazines published weekly and fortnightly [every two weeks]), title of the article without quotation marks and with only the first word capitalized, name of the magazine underlined with all major words capitalized, the volume number if it is readily available, and inclusive page numbers preceded by *p.* or *pp.* if you do not provide the volume number. If a magazine prints the article on discontinuous pages, include all page numbers.

> Creedon, Jeremiah. (2003, May/June). The greening of Tony Soprano. *Utne, 14*, 73-77.
>
> Harman, T. D. (2003, August). The unchanging plan. *Civil War Times*, 43-47, 52.

Newspaper

List author, date (year, month, and day), and title of the article with only first word and proper nouns capitalized, the complete name of newspaper in capitals and underlined or italicized, and the section number of letter with all inclusive and discontinuous page numbers.

> Haynes, T. (2003, June 10). Saving the Columbia. *Boston Globe*, pp. C12-13, C24.

Abstract of a published article

> Tasker, F. L. (1992). Anti-marriage attitudes and motivations to marry amongst adolescents with divorced parents. [Abstract]. *Journal of Divorce & Remarriage, 18*, 105-120.

Abstract of an unpublished work

> Gandhi, J. (2003). Political institutions under dictatorship [Abstract]. New York: New York University.

Abstract retrieved from Infotrac, Silverplatter, Proquest, or other servers

> Gryeh, J. H., et al. (2000). Patterns of adjustment among children of battered women. *Journal of Consulting and Clinical Psychology, 68*, 84-94. Abstract retrieved August 15, 2004 from *PsycINFO* database.

Review of a book

> Sharpe, K. (2003, Summer). The whole world in your hands [Review of the book *World Atlas of Biodiversity*]. *Nature Conservancy*, 86.

Review article

Review articles are devoted to an examination of the literature on a subject, not just a review of one book.

Tindale, R. (2003). Self-harm and domestic violence. *Emergency Nurse,*

11, 7.

Report

Gorman, L.(2003). Why pay more? Simple insurance reform would save

Coloradoans millions (No. 2003-2). Golden, CO: Independence

Institute.

Nonprint material

If the source is not printed, insert a description of the product within
brackets.

Ford, B., & Ford, S. (Producers). (2003). *Child Care Reading Programs.*

[Videotape]. Brentwood, CA: Images in Motion.

Howe, C. (Speaker). (2004, March 25). *Relationships: The Path to self-*

discovery [Cassette Recording]. Orlando: Howe Press.

Excel 2003 [Computer software]. (2003). Redmond, WA: Microsoft.

Remember that sources that cannot be recovered by others (e.g., some
e-mail messages, personal interviews, unpublished letters, and private papers)
should be described in your text but not included as an entry in the References list. For example, write into your text this type of description:

I. Barstow (2003, May 22) submitted to an interview with the

author in Chattanooga, Tennessee, on the role of palm reading in

predicting a person's future.

To maintain the anonymity of the source, write this in-text citation:

In an anonymous interview (2003, April 6) in Chattanooga,

Tennessee, an alleged medium revealed several interesting aspects of

palm reading as a predictor of a subject's future behavior.

Electronic Sources

When citing electronic sources in the References section of your paper,
provide the following information if it is available:

1. Author/editor last name, followed by a comma, given-name initials, and
   a period.
2. Year of publication, followed by a comma, then month and day for magazines and newspapers, within parentheses, followed by a period.
3. Title of the article, not within quotations and not underscored, with the
   first word and proper nouns capitalized, followed by the total number of

paragraphs within brackets only if that information is provided. You do not need to count the paragraphs yourself; in fact, it is better that you do not. This is also the place to describe the work within brackets, as with [Abstract] or [Letter to the editor].

4. Name of the book, journal, or complete work, underscored or italicized, if one is listed.
5. Volume number, if listed, underscored or italicized.
6. Page numbers only if you have that data from a printed version of the journal or magazine. If the periodical has no volume number, use *p.* or *pp.* before the numbers; if the journal has a volume number, omit *p.* or *pp.*
7. The word *Retrieved,* followed by the date of access, followed by the URL. URLs can be quite long, but you must provide the full data so other researchers can find the source.

Abstract of an online article

Townsend, J. W. (2003). Reproductive behavior in the context of global

population. *American Psychologist, 58.* Abstract retrieved October

13, 2003, from http://www.apa.org/journals/amp/303ab.html#2

Article from an online journal

Clune, A. C. (2002). Mental disorder and its cause. *Psycoloquy, 13*(18).

Retrieved September 23, 2003, from

http://psycprints.ecs.soton.ac.uk/archive/00000210/

Article from a printed journal reproduced online

Many articles online are reproduced in the Portable Document Format (PDF files) by Adobe Reader. These electronic pages are the exact duplicates of their print versions, so if you view an article in its electronic form and are confident that the electronic form is identical to the printed version, add within brackets *Electronic version.* This notation allows you to omit the URL. Your clue is the appearance of the original pages with the original page numbers.

White, A. M., Jamieson-Drake, D. W., & Swartzwelder, H. S. (2002).

Prevalence and correlates of alcohol-induced blackouts among

college students: Results of an e-mail survey [Electronic version].

Journal of American College Health, 51, 117–131.

However, give the URL and date of access of any article that is not an exact reproduction with original page numbers. Most electronic articles do not have page numbers and do not look like a reproduction. Be aware that in many instances with InfoTrac and other servers, you may choose a PDF version or a text version. The next example shows how to cite the text version:

White, A. M., Jamieson-Drake, D. W., & Swartzwelder, H. S. (2002). Prevalence and correlates of alcohol-induced blackouts among college students: Results of an e-mail survey. *Journal of American College Health, 51.* Retrieved July 2, 2004, from http://morris.lib.apsu.edu:2062/itw/infomark/177/153/52565w2.htm

Article from a library database

University libraries, as well as public libraries, feature servers that supply articles in large databases, such as PsycInfo, ERIC, and netLibrary. Use the examples below as models that give the date of your retrieval, the name of the database, and—only if readily available—the item number within parentheses. You need not cite the URL. If you cite only from an abstract, mention that fact in your reference entry (see the Kang entry below).

Coleman, L., & Coleman, J. (2002). The measurement of puberty: A review. *Journal of Adolescence, 25.* Retrieved April 2, 2004, from ERIC database (EJ65060).

Firestone, D. (2000, August 10). The south comes of age on religion and politics. *New York Times.* Retrieved November 24, 2004, from UMI-ProQuest database.

Kang, H. S. (2002). What is missing in interlanguage: Acquisition of determiners by Korean learners of English. *Working Papers in Educational Linguistics, 18.* Abstract retrieved April 2, 2004, from ERIC database.

Article from a printed magazine reproduced online

If original pagination is listed with a PDF reproduction, use this form:

Creedon, Jeremiah. (2003, May/June). The greening of Tony Soprano [Electronic version]. *Utne, 4,* 15–19.

If original pagination is not listed, use this form:

Hanner, N. (2003, February 10). Demystifying the adoption option: Was taking in my brother-in-law's kids a noble act? I quickly realized the answer is beside the point. *Newsweek.* Retrieved July 2, 2004, from http://web7.infotrac.galegroup.com

Article from an online magazine, no author listed

Children make every day special. (2004, February 3). *Capper's.* Retrieved July 2, 2004, from http://web7.infotrac.galegroup.com

Article from an online newspaper

Because online newspapers have their own archival files with a search engine, a reference to the Web site is often sufficient:

Zaino, J. S. Learning a little discipline. (2003, June 12). *Chronicle of*

Higher Education. Retrieved June 12, 2003, from

http://chronicle.com

Otherwise, provide the URL:

Ippolito, M. (2003, June 12). Delta Moon rising locally. *Atlanta*

Journal-Constitution Online. Retrieved June 12, 2003, from

http://www.accessatlanta.com/hp/content/entertainment/features/

0603/12delta.html

Article from an Internet-only newsletter

Tau, M. (2000, August 16). Data-jacking prevention for the

psychologist. *Telehealth News.* Retrieved July 18, 2003, from

http://telehealth.net/articles/datajacking.html

Compact disc

Encyclopedias, music, movies, and instructional matter are often stored on compact diskettes; use this form:

African American history: Abolitionist movement. (2003). In *Encarta*

2004 encyclopedia standard [CD]. Redmond, WA: Microsoft.

Miller, A. (2003). What is the Power of Attorney? In *Family Lawyer*

[CD]. Novato, CA: Broderbund.

Bulletins and government documents

Murphy, F. L. (2003). *What you don't know can hurt you.* Preventive

Health Center. Retrieved October 19, 2003, from

http://www.mdphc.com/education/fiber.html

U.S. Cong. House. (2003, January 7). *Unlawful Internet gambling*

funding prohibition act. House Resolution 21. Retrieved

September 18, 2003, from http://thomas.loc.gov/cgibin/query/

D?c108:2:./temp/~c108k7golG::

Document, no date

National Broadband Task Force. (n.d.). *An action plan for achieving*

basic broadband access by 2004. Retrieved October 17, 2003, from

http://broadband.gc.ca/Broadband-document/english/
recommendation.htm

Document, section, or chapter

Benton Foundation. (2003). *What is the initiative's purpose in 21st
century skills initiative?* (sec. 1). Retrieved June 25, 2004, from
http://www.benton.org/initiatives/skillsinitiative.html#Q1

Document, no author identified, no date

Begin the reference with the title of the document if the author of the
document is not identified.

GVU's 10th WWW user survey. (n.d.). Retrieved September 11, 2003,
from http://www.gvu.gatech.edu/user_surveys/survey-1998-10/

Document from a university, available on a private organization's Web site

University of Illinois at Chicago, Health Research and Policy Centers.
(2000). *Partners with tobacco use research centers: Advancing
transdisciplinary science and policy studies.* Retrieved September
9, 2003, from the Robert Wood Johnson Foundation Web site at
http://www.rwjf.org/programs/npoDetail.jsp?id=TRC

Message posted to an online discussion group or forum

Lettevall, E. (2003, January 7). Analysis of small population size.
Retrieved July 18, 2003, from Population Discussion Group at
http://canuck.dnr.cornell.edu/HyperNews/get/marked/marked/289/
1.html

Message posted to an electronic mailing list

Cheramy, R. (2004, April 18). Inexpensive and easy site hosting.
Message posted to Fogo mailing list, archived at http://
impressive.net/archives/fogo/20030418170059.GA23011@bougan.org

Newsgroup message

Burke, G. V. (2003, November 5). Narrative bibliography [Msg. 33].
Message posted to jvmacmillan@mail.csu.edu

Symposium report, abstract

Eisenfeld, B. 2003, October 19). *Tutorial: CRM 101: The basics.* Paper

presented at the Gartner Symposium ITxpo, Orlando, Florida.

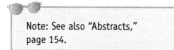

Abstract retrieved October 22, 2004, from

Note: See also "Abstracts,"   http://www.gartner.com/2_events/

page 154.   symposium/2003/asset_46841.jsp

Usenet, Telnet, FTP message

Haas, H. (2004, August 5). Link checker that works with cold fusion

[Msg. 34]. Message posted to impressive.net/archives/fogo/

200000805113615.AI4381

Virtual conference, Report

A virtual conference occurs entirely online, so there is no geographic location. Treat a conference report as a book.

Verhey, S. D., Stefanides, S., & Pinkart, H. C. *Geonomics and education:*

An undergraduate genome project. Paper presented at the Second

Virtual Conference on Genomics and Bioinformatics. Retrieved

October 1, 2004, from http//www.ndsu.nodak.edu/

virtual-genomics/Proc_VCGB2002.pdf

11b Presenting the References Page

Every scientific report requires a References page that alphabetically
lists each source cited in the paper. The next example shows the references for a student paper on the social and political implications of
ancient warfare. Additional examples of the References page are shown
on pages 173, 183, and 199.

References

Adams, M. (1998). The 'Good War' myth and the cult of nostalgia. *The*

Midwest Quarterly, 40. Retrieved May 23, 2004, from InfoTrac

database.

Cooper, L. D. (1999). *Rousseau, nature, and the problem of the good*

life. University Park: Pennsylvania State University Press.

Ferrill, A. (n.d.) Neolithic warfare. Frontline Educational Foundation. Retrieved May 22, 2004, from http://eserver.org/history/neolithic-war.txt

Hanson, V. D. (2002). War will be war: No matter the era, no matter the weapons, and the same old hell. *National Review, 54.* Retrieved May 22, 2004, from *InfoTrac* database.

Harder, B. (2002, April 29). Ancient Peru torture deaths: Sacrifices or war crimes? *National Geographic News.* Retrieved May 20, 2004, from http://news.nationalgeographic.com/ news/2002/ 04/0425_020426_mochekillings.html

Jones, P. (2003). Ancient and modern. *Spectator, 291.* Retrieved May 23, 2004, from *InfoTrac* database.

Kagan, D. (1997). History's largest lessons. Interview by Fredric Smoler. *American Heritage, 48.* Retrieved May 20, 2004, from *InfoTrac* database.

LeBlanc, S. A. (2003a). *Constant battles: The myth of the peaceful, noble savage.* New York: St. Martin's Press.

LeBlanc, S. A. (2003b, May/June). Prehistory of warfare. *Archaeology, 17,* 34–42.

Parsell, D. L. (2002, March 21). City occupied by Inca discovered on Andean peak in Peru. *National Geographic News.* Retrieved May 19, 2004, from http:// news.nationalgeographic.com/news/2002/03/ 0314_0318_vilcabamba.html

Shy, J. (1993). The cultural approach to the history of war. *The Journal of Military History, 57.* Retrieved May 20, 2004, from *InfoTrac* database.

Thorpe, N. (2000). Origins of war: Mesolithic conflict in Europe. *British Archaeology, 52.* Retrieved May 28, 2004, from http://www.birtarch.ac.uk/ba/ba52/ba52feat.html.

Webster, D. (1999). Ancient Maya warfare. In K. Raaflaub & N. Rosenstein (Eds.), *War and society in the ancient and medieval worlds* (pp. 246–340). Cambridge, MA: Center for Hellenic Studies.

Yates, R. (1999). Early China. In K. Raaflaub & N. Rosenstein (Eds.), *War and society in the ancient and medieval worlds* (pp. 216–246). Cambridge, MA: Center for Hellenic Studies.

YOUR RESEARCH PROJECT

Submit to your instructor the initial draft of your References list. The instructor's response will indicate the quality of your work and its precision. You may have time to revise it carefully before final submission of your report.

12 Writing the Theoretical Essay

As an undergraduate student, you will be asked by some instructors to write a theory paper, which is an essay that draws on existing research to trace the development of a theory or to make a comparison of two or more theories. Written in APA style, a theoretical analysis examines the current thinking about a social topic, such as criminal behavior, the human tendency to fight and go to war, dysfunctional families, class size for effective learning, or learning disorders. The theoretical paper, in most instances, has four major components:

1. The theoretical paper identifies a problem or hypothesis that has current as well as historical implications in the social science community. For example, it might examine this theory: "Cutters, usually young women, slice their arms, legs, and torsos to match their damaged physiques with their wounded psyches." Or this one: "Humans have always upset social stability by waging war on each other and against other tribes or nations."

2. The theoretical paper traces the development and history of the evolution of the theory. It calls for a review of the relevant literature, so your task includes the gathering of all available literature on the subject, such as articles on the phenomenon of cutters or on the prehistoric wars by Bronze Age tribes. While you might draw some information from magazine and newspaper articles, most of your information should come from technical and scholarly journals and from the statistical data of empirical studies.

3. The theoretical research project provides a systematic analysis of the articles that have explored the problem to trace the various issues, not so much in chronological order but in relation to issues you identify in your introduction. Hence, your goal is analysis and exploration of the problem, not a literature review or a mere history of research, although those are part of your introductory work.

4. The theory paper arrives at a judgment and discussion of the prevailing theory. Usually, the writer advances one theory as more valid than another. In the case of the theory about humans and their penchant for war, the study either supports or contradicts the theory. The paper by Jamie Johnston, shown later in this chapter, arrives at this conclusion, among others:

Yet in a final analysis, people want power over others—men beat their wives, mothers overly spank their children, the better team overpowers an opponent, and, yes, a larger, stronger nation will demolish another if self-interest prevails.

Finally, the theoretical paper is arranged much like a typical research paper, with three basic sections: introduction, body, and conclusion.

12a Writing the Introduction to a Theoretical Paper

The theoretical paper should include a clear and concise introduction that advances the research topic. For example, if your topic focuses on cutters, or teenagers who abuse their bodies by cutting themselves with razors and knives, you should introduce the subject, indicate that it merits examination, and show (1) how prevalent the practice of cutting has become, and (2) how it is affecting the lives of more and more young women. You may want to discuss background information to relate this practice, if appropriate, to other practices, such as tattooing, branding, and piercing. In another example, Jamie Johnston (pages 166–174), gives evidence to demonstrate that people have always fought to seek revenge, protect trade routes, honor their gods, and defend their honor. Yet the social and political motivation for war derives from both culture and biology. Johnston's paper balances the society that fights to preserve its civilization against the human love for aggressive behavior and power over others.

The introduction should provide a brief review of the key literature; keep in mind that the body of your paper will provide in-depth analysis of the findings. In this early review you should quote from a few of the sources, for scholarly quotations can set the academic tone of your project.

Your introduction should establish the problem under examination by stating the hypothesis or theory to be examined. You must discuss its significance to the scientific community to provide a rationale for your study. You may give your initial perspective on the issue, and, in an undergraduate paper but not a graduate paper, you might explain your personal interest in the subject—a roommate or a good friend who is a cutter or a good friend who has gone to war and lost a leg or an arm.

Thus, the introduction should:

- Establish the problem under examination.
- Discuss its significance to the scientific community.
- Provide a review of the literature (see pages 191–200 for more information).
- Quote experts who have commented on the issue.
- Provide a thesis sentence to identify an initial perspective on the issue.

12b Writing the Body of the Theoretical Paper

The body of your paper traces the various issues; each may be listed with its own side head. Under each issue you should establish a prevailing theory and examine the literature. You might establish a historical perspective—a past-to-present narrative timeline that establishes contemporary perspectives in light of their history. In the body, you can also compare and analyze the various aspects of the theories.

Throughout, you should cite extensively from the literature on the subject. Let the experts, and sometimes the subjects, speak for themselves. You are not pretending to be an expert, just the messenger. Your task is analysis rather than detailed explanation, reporting rather than investigative research, classification of the issues rather than providing a solution. Do not take on a task greater than you can handle without the tools and skills of empirical research.

Thus, the body of the theoretical paper must:

- Trace the various issues.
- Establish a past-to-present perspective.
- Compare and analyze the various aspects of the theories.
- Cite extensively from the literature on the subject.

12c Writing the Conclusion of the Theoretical Paper

The conclusion of the theoretical paper must offer several ingredients. You might again explain the significance of the issue and give a general overview of the prevailing theories. Your discussion of the implications is vital. In many cases, you will defend one theory as it grows from the evidence in the body. In some instances, if appropriate, you might suggest additional research work to be done in pursuit of more answers to the problem or issue.

Thus, the conclusion of the theoretical paper must:

- Defend one theory as it grows from the evidence in the body.
- Discuss the implications of the theory.
- Suggest additional work that might be launched in this area.

12d Sample Theoretical Essay

In the research paper that follows, Jamie Johnston researches the social and political forces of war, but not just recent wars. Rather, he looks closely at wars of prehistoric times. The writer offers substantial evidence to prove that early tribes had a social history of warfare and even brutality toward captives. The tools of war are reviewed, and then Johnston poses the crucial question: Why did early civilizations fight? He lists many reasons, such as fights for resources, slaves, precious metals, revenge, and honor. Ultimately, he poses the key issue: Was human behavior motivated by biology or culture? Johnston reaches an interesting conclusion, so read on.

Prehistoric Wars 1   *Page header*

PREHISTORIC WARS: A STUDY IN SOCIAL HATRED AND CRUELTY   *Running head*

Prehistoric Wars: A Study in Social Hatred and Cruelty   *Title*

Jamie Johnston

Austin Peay State University

5 May 2004

Prehistoric Wars 2

Abstract

The existence and nature of prehistoric wars were investigated. The evidence determined that prehistoric wars did exist with evidence attested by archaeology in fortification, weapons, cave paintings, and skeletal remains. Reasons for early wars have been advanced for armies that went in search of resources, women, slaves, sacrificial victims, and precious metals. Evidence has demonstrated that early people fought to seek revenge, protect trade routes, honor their gods, and defend their honor. The cause for fighting has centered on two issues—biology and culture. Some experts have argued that a society fought to preserve its civilization, but others have argued, more persistently, that humans possess an aggressive behavior and want power over others. Further research might reveal whether one government should use its power to impose its sense of order on other countries in the international community.

Prehistoric Wars: A Study in Social Hatred and Cruelty

Here we are, a civilized world with reasonably educated people, yet we constantly fight with one another. These are not sibling squabbles either; people die in terrible ways. We wonder, then, if there was ever a time when men and women lived in harmony with one another and with the natural environment. The Bible described the Garden of Eden, and the French philosopher Jean-Jacques Rousseau advanced the idea in the 1700s of the "noble savage"; as he stated, "nothing could be more gentle" than an ancient colony of people. Wrong!

LeBlanc (1999), an archaeologist at Harvard University, along with several other scholars, has argued instead that "humans have been at each others' throats since the dawn of the species" (p. 15). For example, Yates (1999) said the ancient ancestors of the Chinese used "long-range projectile weapons" as long ago as 28,000 BC for both hunting and "intrahuman conflict" (p. 9). Ferrill (2003) observed, "When man first learned how to write, he already had war to write about." Ferrill added, "In prehistoric times man was a hunter and a killer of other men. The killer instinct in the prehistoric male is clearly attested by archaeology in fortifications, weapons, cave paintings, and skeletal remains."

Evidence proves that savage fighting occurred in the ancient history of human beings. We have evidence of the types of weapons employed. We can also list reasons for the prehistoric fighting. The crux of the debate in the literature centers on two theories: inducement or instinct. Were early humans motivated by biological instincts or by cultural demands for a share of limited resources? That is the issue this paper will address.

First, we need to look briefly at the evidence. Harder (2003) has reported on the work of one forensic anthropologist,

Establish the topic along with social and/or psychological issues that will be examined

A theoretical study depends heavily upon the literature, which must be cited in correct APA form.

John Verano, who investigated a series of "grisly executions" in the valleys of Peru during the Moche civilization. Victims "were apparently skinned alive. Others were drained of blood, decapitated, or bound tightly and left to be eaten by vultures" (cited in Harder). Verano has the proof of the executions, but not the reason, although speculations center on religious ceremonies. UCLA anthropologist C. B. Donnan has studied Moche art and suggests "the suffering of the losers may have had a ritualistic meaning in Moche society much as the pain of Christ does in Christianity" (cited in Harder). At the same time, Verano thinks the victims were prisoners of war and not the losers of ritual combat. In either case, the ancients were less than noble savages.

LeBlanc's book *Constant Battles* (2003) provided a catalog of prehistoric fighting. Webster (1999) described the savage fighting of the ancient Mayans. Thorpe (2003) described massacres that occurred in Europe over 8,500 years ago— decapitation, scalping, axe blows, and other nasty methods. Indeed, articles are now available on wars in ancient Japan, Egypt, Greece, and the Southwestern areas of the United States.

The weapons, too, have been uncovered: clubs, arrowheads, bows, slings, daggers, maces, and spears. Each weapon graduated from the previous ones and served new purposes as armies gathered for combat. One Internet source pointed out that "the bow and the sling were important for hunting, but the dagger and mace were most useful for fighting other humans" (Prehistoric warfare, n.d.). The spear required close combat. The bow and arrow had a range of about 100 yards. The sling was a significant weapon because in the right hands it was accurate from long distances and very powerful, launching stones that could crush skulls. The mace gave way to the battleaxe to cut through armor. Then with copper, bronze, and finally iron, the sword gained great popularity and remains a weapon of choice even today (Prehistoric warfare, n.d.).

Prehistoric Wars 5

Horses, mules, and even elephants gave primitive armies mobility. Ultimately, however, the primary weapon was the soldier, and over time the ragged fighting groups were organized into armies that could march in columns and lay siege to other villages and cities. Accordingly, archaeologists have examined walls, pits, ditches, moats, and barriers of all sorts, even villages with all the rooms built against each other with access only from the roof (LeBlanc, 1999, p. 20). Fortress cities were built on mountaintops, as with the Acropolis at Athens. And researchers have found an ancient Peruvian city high atop a mountain peak in the Andes (Parsell, 2002). Thus, archaeologists have uncovered many offensive weapons but also gigantic earthen defenses, and the Great Wall of China springs forward as one great example.

Why fight? Many reasons have been advanced by different researchers, and we can take our pick from quite a list, as armies went out in search of:

- Food, resources, water, and cattle.
- Women for concubines and wives.
- Slaves.
- Sacrificial victims.
- Gold, bronze, copper, and other valuable metals.

And they fought to:

- Seek revenge.
- Protect and secure the best trade routes.
- Honor their God and their religion.
- Defend their honor.

Shy (2003) argued that early people, like today, fought to protect their culture and way of life. Adams (1998) said the four principles used by the Allies in World War II would serve all armies of all times—"freedom from want, freedom from fear, freedom of speech, freedom of religion." Thorpe (2002) offered this theory:

Prehistoric Wars 6

My own belief is that warfare, in earliest prehistory, arose over matters of personal honor—such as slights, insults, marriages going wrong, or theft. In a small hunter-gatherer community, everyone is related. An attack on one group member is an attack on the whole family. A personal feud may quickly involve the whole community. From there it is a small step to war.

Kagan (1997) echoed that concept with his focus on the word *honor:*

If a state finds that its honor is at risk, that it is treated with contempt, the other two elements of the triad immediately become part of the story. Men get fearful that in light of this contempt others will take advantage and damage their real interests.

Yet I recall reading *Beowulf* for one of my literature classes, and Beowulf fought for *wergild* (money and riches), and he made no bones about it. Victory brings economic bonanzas. LeBlanc (*Constant Battles*, 2003, p. 194) showed that ancient battles shifted from total annihilation of the enemy to economic control of villages, cities, and even large states:

Conflict waged by complex societies results in a new twist. Warfare was controlled by the elite, and wealth and prestige began to play a role. The commoners became valuable as a means to supply wealth to the elite, so warfare began to include conquest instead of annihilation as a goal (p. 194).

Thus, we must add "the search for wealth" as a prime reason for war in primitive times and also in contemporary times because it was whispered about George W. Bush's conquest of Iraq—he did it for the oil.

Ultimately, the key question about the cause of war, whether ancient or current, centers on one's choice between biology and culture. On the one side we have the historian, like Hanson (2002), who argued, "Culture largely determines how people fight. The degree to which a society embraces freedom, secular rationalism, consensual government, and capitalism often determines—far more than its geography, climate, or population—whether its armies will be successful over the long term." Hanson added, "No nation has ever survived once its citizenry ceased to believe that its culture was worth saving."

The society as a whole wants to preserve its culture, in peace if possible. In 500 BC Herodotus said, "No one is so foolish that he prefers war to peace. In peace sons bury their fathers, in war fathers their sons" (cited in Jones, 2003).

Yet, in conclusion, the biological history of men and women suggests that we love a good fight. I recall reading an article that said twins inside the womb actually fight, and one fetus might actually devour or absorb the other one. Siblings just naturally fight, as I did with my older sister and younger brother. His anger exploded one time, and he broke my arm by hitting me with a shovel. We all have witnessed the terrible fights at sporting events, and a few years ago at Glenbrook North High School in Northbrook, Illinois, hazing turned into a terrible beating for some girls. Oh sure, we can give reasons for our eagerness to fight—to preserve our honor ("Don't diss me!), to preserve our freedom ("Don't encroach!"), or because of fear ("Don't hit me 'cause I'll be hitting back even harder!"). Yet in a final analysis, people want power over others—men beat their wives, mothers overly spank their children, the better team overpowers an opponent, and, yes, a larger, stronger nation will demolish another if self-interest prevails.

This is human nature. The men of Al Qaeda who flew their suicide missions into the World Trade Center and the Pentagon knew exactly what they were doing—exercising their power. In effect, they said, "We'll show the United States that we can inflict great damage." Kagan (1997) observed:

> In the end what people really go to war about is power, by which I simply mean the ability to have their will prevail. . . . Every being and every nation requires power for two purposes. The first is to be able to do what it wishes to and must do, some of which will be good and perfectly natural things. Second, one needs power to keep others from imposing their will, to prevent evil things from being done.

The sport of boxing continues to thrive, despite attempts to end it because of its brutality. The fans have a vicarious thrill as one boxer gets pounded to the canvas. At NASCAR races the greatest shouts occur as the fenders crash and cars go tumbling topsy-turvy down the asphalt. The aggressive behavior of humans is not always a pretty sight, such as the eager willingness of some to loot and pilfer a neighborhood that has been hit by a tornado or another natural disaster.

At the same time, a country like the United States governs itself, imposing order by law and moral behavior by religion. When chaos develops, as in Baghdad during the 2003 war, lawless looting and violence emerged because neither the religious leaders nor an absent police force could maintain order. The breakdown of the culture opened a vacuum filled quickly by primitive behavior. Our government, our culture, and our sense of honor have prevailed in a world of nations gone berserk and lawless. Whether we should use our power to impose our sense of democracy on other countries is an international question without a clear answer. My brother, with the shovel in his hand, would say "yes."

Prehistoric Wars 9

References

Adams, M. (1998). The 'Good War' myth and the cult of nostalgia. *The Midwest Quarterly, 40.* Retrieved May 4, 2004, from *InfoTrac* database.

Cooper, L. D. (1999). *Rousseau, nature, and the problem of the good life.* University Park: Pennsylvania State Univ. Press.

Ferrill, A. (n.d.). Neolithic warfare. Frontline Educational Foundation. Retrieved May 5, 2004, from http://eserver.org/history/neolithic-war.txt

Hanson, V. D. (2002). War will be war: No matter the era, no matter the weapons, and the same old hell. *National Review, 54.* Retrieved April 30, 2004, from the *InfoTrac* database.

Harder, B. (2002, April 29). Ancient Peru torture deaths: Sacrifices or war crimes? *National Geographic News.* Retrieved May 3, 2004, from http://news.nationalgeographic.com/news/2002/04/0425_020426_mochekillings.html

Jones, P. (2003). Ancient and modern. *Spectator, 291.* Retrieved May 6, 2004, from *InfoTrac* database.

Kagan, D. (1997). History's largest lessons. Interview by Fredric Smoler. *American Heritage, 48.* Retrieved May 3, 2004, from *IntroTrac* database.

LeBlanc, S. A. (2003). *Constant battles: The myth of the peaceful, noble savage.* New York: St. Martin's Press.

LeBlanc, S. A. (2003, May/June). Prehistory of warfare. *Archaeology, 56*(3). Abstract retrieved May 3, 2004, from http://www.archaeology.org/ found.php.page=10305/ abstracts/warfare.html

References begin on a new page.

References are listed in alphabetical order.

Prehistoric Wars 10

Parsell, D. L. (2002, March 21). City occupied by Inca discovered on Andean peak in Peru. *National Geographic News.* Retrieved May 3, 2004, from http://news.nationalgeographic.com/ news/2002/03/0314_0318_vilcabamba.html

Prehistoric warfare. (n.d.). Retrieved May 1, 2004, from *InfoTrac* database.

Shy, J. (1993). The cultural approach to the history of war. *The Journal of Military History, 57.* Retrieved May 9, 2004, from *InfoTrac* database.

Thorpe, N. (2000). Origins of war: Mesolithic conflict in Europe. *British Archaeology 52.* Retrieved May 3, 2004, from http://www.britarch.ac.uk/ba/ba52/ba52feat.htm

Webster, D. (1999). Ancient Maya warfare. In K. Raaflaub & N. Rosenstein (Eds.), *War and society in the ancient and medieval worlds* (chap. 13). Cambridge, MA: Center for Hellenic Studies.

Yates, R. (1999). Early China. In K. Raaflaub & N. Rosenstein (Eds.), *War and society in the ancient and medieval worlds* (chap. 2). Cambridge, MA: Center for Hellenic Studies.

YOUR RESEARCH PROJECT

Submit to your instructor your theoretical essay. Check to be sure it conforms to the standards and design advocated in this chapter.

13 Report of an Empirical Study

Empirical research requires you to conduct original research in the field or lab. It means designing a questionnaire for conducting a survey or interviewing subjects in person or by e-mail. It can also mean manipulating or stimulating a nest of laboratory rats, testing the manner in which elementary teachers administer examinations, or observing the behavior of automobile drivers at a busy intersection. Thus, empirical research is hands-on field or lab investigation, and you should understand its implications for work in the social sciences. As a student, you must work closely with your instructor to (1) plan a proposal, (2) conduct the research, and (3) write the report.

Note: Your instructor may request only the proposal, in which you explain a hypothesis and the manner in which a study might be conducted, even though you will not actually conduct the research (see pages 19–24 and 186–190 for an example of such a proposal).

Typically, the report of an empirical study in APA style has four major elements:

1. The report identifies a problem or issue and expresses a hypothesis that requires investigation and testing.
2. The report describes the design and methodology of the research, explaining the subjects, procedures, and tools employed.
3. The report describes in detail the results of the investigation or test. Here you display the data you collected and the findings you discovered, even if the results contradict your hypothesis or presuppositions. These findings are displayed in this section without editorial comment, which is reserved for the Discussion section.
4. The report comments on the findings and examines their implications in light of the hypothesis that launched the study. Thus, a Discussion section explains, interprets, and analyzes the work reported in the results section.

Each of these four parts is a vital element of your research and the polished report, as explained below.

13a Writing the Introduction to a Report on Empirical Research

The Introduction names your theory to explain the general nature of your project, the rationale for conducting the investigation, and suggestions about what might be found or what results are expected. For example, you might wish to study the peer responses to self-cutting by secondary school adolescents—that is, how do friends respond when a fellow student appears with unexplained cuts on an arm or leg? The interviews and written survey become the primary vehicles for conducting the research. In another example, a student might investigate the implications of marriages arranged, in part, by online dating. The research might determine the effect of Internet activity on the private lives of participants. You can read this type of introduction on pages 179–180.

An effective introduction also provides a review of the literature on the topic in order to establish the study's veracity as scholarly research.

Thus, the Introduction should:

- Introduce a theory addressing a problem that can be examined by testing in the field or the laboratory.
- Explain how you addressed the problem by a hypothesis to be proved or disproved as your research explores it.
- Relate your work to other research in this area with a review of the literature.
- Suggest briefly the possible implications, keeping in mind that the Discussion section will explore these findings fully.

13b Writing the Method Section of the Report on Empirical Research

The Method section describes the investigation to answer several questions:

What was tested?
Who participated, human or animal?
Where was the field work accomplished?
What was the apparatus (or equipment) and how did you use it?

In other cases, the Method section explores your use of a control group and an experimental group along with your methods for stimulating the experimental group. It can also explain your methods for conducting a survey with a questionnaire or for gathering information by e-mail responses. The Method section summarizes the procedure and execution of each stage of your investigation. An appendix is the appropriate place to display a copy of a questionnaire, test questions, and similar forms used to collect data.

Thus, the Method section should:

- Explain the design of the study so others can see clearly how you conducted the work.
- Give sufficient information so that other researchers in the lab or field can duplicate your work.
- Identify the subjects, show how they are representative of the population under study, and explain how they were selected and assigned to a group.
- Describe your apparatus for conducting the study—laboratory equipment, questionnaire, a classroom with a viewing window, and so forth.
- Explain the procedure by giving a step-by-step description of the process, from initial instructions to the participants to details on how an experimental group was manipulated or a test was performed.

13c   Writing the Results Section of the Report on Empirical Research

This section provides the data discovered by your investigation—charts, graphs, statistics, tables, and general data to substantiate your work. It reports in detail but without editorial comment because your interpretation is reserved for the Discussion section. You should display your findings in detail even if the results contradict your hypothesis or presuppositions. Individual scores should not be included but placed in an appendix where interested readers can examine the statistics and tabulations. Consult with the instructor for accuracy in the statistical analysis.

Thus, the Results section should:

- Provide a summary of the data collected.
- Supply graphs, charts, and figures to illustrate the findings.
- Present statistical tables that tabulate the results in meaningful patterns.
- Keep the Results presentation objective without discussion of the study's implications.

13d   Writing the Discussion Section of the Report on Empirical Research

In this section, you must discuss the implications of the study and its findings. Here you interpret and evaluate the results with commentary. Explain how the test supported or failed to support the hypothesis. You can verify the validity of the results yet acknowledge any failures or variations you encountered.

The discussion can, and often does, explain applications to be pursued and areas demanding further research and analysis. This section is the place to comment on the importance of your research, delineating how it extends the current work in the field by adding another data set to illuminate the problem or issue.

Thus, the Discussion section should:

- Explain how the results of the study yield implications with regard to your original hypothesis.
- Discuss how the findings support or fail to support the hypothesis.
- Comment on the discoveries and explain how the findings might be applied in addressing the theory underlying the work.
- Identify implications for future research in this area.

13e Writing the Title Page, Abstract, References, and Appendix

Each of your papers opens with a title page followed on the next page by an abstract. The title page gives essential information, and the abstract overviews the study. These two pages may be the only ones read by readers who examine an abstract to decide on reading or skipping the complete report. Therefore,

- The *title page* gives the official title of the paper, the byline of the writer, his or her academic affiliation, and a running head that appears on every page with a page number.
- The *abstract* establishes clearly the theory on which the whole work is based, the hypothesis under experimentation, the methods used, the findings, and the implications drawn from the testing. In just a few words, from 50 to 200, it provides an accurate and self-contained description of the problem. It explains the topic and problem, the purpose of the study, the kind of evidence gathered, the experimental method, the findings, the implications, and issues for additional research or theoretical study.
- The *References* page(s) provides the bibliography of sources cited in the paper, in tables and graphs, and in content notes. Pages 173, 183, and 199 provide detailed examples of Reference pages, and pages 149-162 provide an explanation of these forms.
- An *appendix* furnishes research material that contributed to the study but was not essential to the content of the paper itself. This information— tests, experiments, interviews, surveys, questionnaires, and so forth— may or may not serve the reader. See pages 184-185 for an example.

13f Sample Report of Empirical Research

The student paper that follows, written in APA style, provides an example of one student's investigation into Internet romance—that is, the effect of online matchmaking services such as Match.com. She examines this hypothesis: Online dating services provide, among other things, an opportunity for people to meet, chat, and reveal things about themselves yet, like ancient matriarchs, set the criteria for determining a good match.

Arranged Marriages 1   Page header

ARRANGED MARRIAGES: THE REVIVAL IS ONLINE   Running head

Arranged Marriages: The Revival Is Online   Title
Valerie Nesbitt-Hall   Byline
Sociology 2020, Austin Peay State University   Affiliation

Arranged Marriages 2

Abstract

Computer matchmaking was investigated to examine the
theoretical implications of marriages arranged in part by online
dating. The goal was to determine the effect of Internet activity on
the private lives of the participants. One researcher started with a
theory that arranged marriages exist from a variety of procedures,
but the researcher can use a hypothesis to support or refute by
experimentation and observation of one issue. Thus, a case study
that interviewed an affected coupled determined social and
psychological implications. The social implications might affect the
workplace as well as the private lives of the men and women who
are active in chat rooms and dating services. The psychological
implications involve hesitation in romance procedures, but they
suggest the possibility for discovering a true and lasting love.

Arranged Marriages 3
Arranged Marriages: The Revival Is Online
Arranged marriages display a theory, but with a twist.
Online dating services provide today, among other things, an
opportunity for people to meet, chat, reveal things about
themselves, and—as one source has expressed it—"play the role
of patriarchal grandfathers, searching for good matches based

Establish the topic along with social and/or psychological issues that will be examined

on any number of criteria that you select" (Razdan, 2003, p. 71). In addition, hundreds of Internet groups draw people together by the millions, so computer matchmaking has social implications that psychologists examine carefully. This study examined the implications of marriages arranged by online dating to test this hypothesis: Online dating revised ancient matchmaking by the patriarchs and matriarchs of the family.

Statistics vary greatly on the amount of activity. Sources show the figure is in the millions, and that is substantial. *People Weekly* (2004) reported that 50 million Americans were registered online, and that figure climbs considerably each year. People have visited, many have found a mate, and some have even married. Match.com and America Online's dating areas credit themselves for hundreds of marriages that began as personal online messages. Can it be called a social revolution? Some have said "yes" to that question because about one-fifth of all singles in the country are online, prearranging their meetings and their lives, assuring themselves a better match than an evening's trip to a local nightclub. For example, Cooper (2002) argued that online dating has the potential to lower the nation's divorce rate. Kass (2003) identified the "distanced nearness" of a chat room that "encourages self-revelation while maintaining personal boundaries" (cited in Razdan, 2003, p. 71). Fein and Schneider (2002) insisted that many arranged marriages, by parents or by cyberspace, have produced enduring love because of a deliberation performed in rational moments before moments of passionate impulse.

With the divorce rate at 50 percent, marriage has become a roll of the dice, so some experts agreed that online dating reverts to the prearranged meetings of two young people identified as compatible by economic, political, religious, and social reasons.

Meanwhile, persons online can enjoy a distance, even hiding their real names to enjoy "an intimate but protected (cyber)space" (Kass, 2003, cited in Razdan, p. 71). Participants

A theoretical study depends heavily upon the literature, which must be cited in correct APA form.

Arranged Marriages 5

online have erected and maintained personal fences of privacy but at the same time revealed private feelings that they might never express in face-to-face meetings.

Method

An e-mail technique for collecting evidence was used. It featured a case study in which the subjects were interviewed with regard to their online romance.

Subjects

The subjects of the interview preferred to remain anonymous; they were Stephen of Scotland and Jennifer of the United States. This research uncovered a match that resulted in marriage.

Procedure

The subjects were interviewed on cyber romance by e-mail correspondence. The interview as recorded appears in the Appendix, pp. 10–11, and is described next as a case study.

Case Study

Research uncovered a match that resulted in marriage. The two subjects, Jennifer and Stephen, were interviewed on the matter of cyber romance. What follows is a brief summary of the interview, which is on file. The couple met online in September of 1996 in a chat room, not on a matching service. Stephen initiated the first contact, and they chatted anonymously for nine months before Jennifer initiated an exchange of phone numbers, addresses, and photographs. Stephen initiated the first meeting in person after 11 months, inviting Jennifer to travel from the United States to Glasgow, Scotland. Seven months later they married; it was 1.5 years from the time they met at the Internet newsgroup.

When asked if online romance protected her privacy and gave her time to prearrange things, Jennifer answered in the affirmative with emphasis. When asked who was more aggressive

Arranged Marriages 6

in pushing forward the romance, Stephen said it was a mutual thing. Both agreed that when they finally met in person, they really knew the other person—spiritually, emotionally, and intellectually. The matter of different nationalities also played a role on two fronts—immigration matters and the concern of Jennifer's parents that she would fly to Scotland to see someone she had never met.

When asked if the relationship had been excellent to this point, both replied with affirmative answers. When asked if they would recommend online dating to others who are seeking mates, Stephen and Jennifer said, yes, under the right circumstances—"be cautious and take your time." Thus, online dating in this instance was successful.

It should be noted that the people who participate in online romance run the whole range of human subjects. Millions now consider meeting someone over the Internet is like phoning them or sending a fax. It has become an everyday thing to send dozens of e-mails, so the next logical step would be finding romance on the Internet.

Procedure

Stephen and Jennifer received a set of questions as an e-mail attachment. They answered each question, as shown in the Appendix, pages 10–11. Procedures to access a matching partner are varied, yet each has one thing in common—to bring two compatible people together on the Web, where they can e-mail each other, participate in IM chats, send attachments of favorite songs or personal photographs, and eventually exchange real names, phone numbers, and addresses. Newsgroups work in a similar fashion with back-and-forth discussion, even argument, about a variety of topics.

Discussion

In conclusion, the world of online romance is growing at a staggering rate with millions signing on each year, with thousands finding happiness, and with thousands more finding sexual chaos and dangerous liaisons. Yet little research is being done in this area. My search of the literature produced a surprisingly limited number of journal articles. Various sources have discussed methods of helping clients, even to the point of counseling in cyberspace itself, which would establish professional relationships online. Schneider and Weiss (2001) describe it but offer little psychoanalysis. Cooper (2002) has an excellent collection of articles in his guidebook for clinicians. Counseling needs to be in place for persons who substitute fantasy sex online for a true relationship. However, numerous case studies also show that online romance can produce healthy relationships and successful marriages (Brooks, 2003; Cha, 2003; Fein, 2002; Nussbaum, 2002; and Young, et al., 2002).

Arranged Marriages 8

References

Brooks, L. (2003, February 13). The love business. *The Guardian* (London), p. 6. Retrieved April 8, 2003, from InfoTrac database.

Cha, A. E. (2003, May 4). ISO Romance? Online matchmakers put love to the test. *Washington Post,* p. A01. Retrieved April 9, 2003, from Lexis-Nexis database.

Cooper, A. (Ed.). (2002). *Sex and the Internet: A guide book for clinicians.* New York: Brunner-Routledge.

Fein, E., & Schneider, S. (2002). The rules for online dating. New York: Pocket Books.

Nussbaum, E. (2002, December 15). The year in ideas: Online personals are cool. *New York Times,* Sec. 6, p. 106. Retrieved April 8, 2003, from http://www.nytimes.com

Razdan, A. (2003, May-June). What's love got to do with it? *Utne,* pp.69-71.

Arranged Marriages 9

Schneider, J., & Weiss, R. (2001). *Cybersex exposed: Simple fantasy or obsession?* Center City, MN: Hazelden.

Young, K., Griffin, S., Shelley, E., Cooper, A., O'Mara, J., & Buchanan, J. (2002). Online infidelity: A new dimension in couple relationships with implications for evaluation and treatment. *Sexual Addiction and Compulsivity, 7,* 59–74. Abstract retrieved April 4, 2003, from InfoTrac database.

Arranged Marriages 10

Appendix

Following is the set of 12 questions and the answers by Stephen and Jennifer:

1. When did you first meet online?

   Answer: September of 1996

2. What prompted you to try an online matching service?

   Answer: We didn't really try online matching services. We chatted in a chat room, became friends there, and met in person later.

3. Who initiated the first contact?

   Answer: Stephen initiated the first online chat.

4. How long into the relationship did you correspond by e-mail before one of you gave an address and/or phone number? Who did it first, Steve or Jennifer?

   Answer: We chatted and corresponded by e-mail for nine months before Jennifer shared her phone number.

5. How long into the relationship did you go before sharing photographs?

   Answer: At nine months we began to share written correspondence and photographs.

6. Who initiated the first meeting in person? Where did you meet? How long were you into the relationship before you met in person?

Arranged Marriages 11

Answer: Stephen first requested the meeting, and Jennifer
flew from the States to Glasgow, Scotland. This was
about a year into the relationship.

7. How much time elapsed between your first online discovery
of each other and your marriage?

Answer: One and a half years after our first chat we were
married.

8. Did you feel that online romance enabled you to prearrange
things and protect your privacy before meeting in person?

Answer: Yes, we were cautious and at times reluctant to
continue, but we kept coming back to each other online
until we knew the other well enough to trust in the
relationship. Once we got offline into what we might call
real-time dating, the love blossomed quickly.

9. Did you feel, when you finally met in person, that you really
knew the other person spiritually? emotionally?
intellectually?

Answer: Yes.

10. Not to put you on the spot, but do you feel as a couple that
the relationship has been excellent to this point?

Answer: Yes, super.

11. Has the difference in nationalities been a problem?

Answer: Yes, but only in relation to sorting out immigration
matters. Also, Jennifer's parents were concerned that she was
going to another country to see someone she had never met.

12. Finally, would you recommend online matching services or
chat rooms to others who are seeking mates?

Answer: Yes, in the right circumstances. We were lucky; others
might not be.

13g Writing the Proposal for Conducting Empirical Research

In some instances, instructors might require a proposal for empirical research but not the actual research. In other words, your grade will be based only on the proposal—its presentation of the problem, its review of the literature on the topic, and its design of a method for conducting the research. The general design of a proposal, like the finished report, should conform to the following guidelines. The *introduction* should:

- Establish a problem or topic worthy of examination.
- Provide background information, including a review of literature on the subject.
- Give the purpose and rationale for the study, including the hypothesis that serves as the motivation for the experiment.

The *body* of the proposal for empirical research should:

- Provide a Methods section for explaining how you will design the study with regard to subject, apparatus, and procedure.
- Offer a Results section for listing any potential findings of the study.

The *conclusion* of a proposal for empirical research should:

- Suggest implications to be drawn from the possible findings in relation to the hypothesis.
- Offer suggestions for additional research by others.

Effects of Communication Skills 1

Proposal: The Effects of Communication

Skills on Development of Interpersonal Relationships

Julie A. Strasshofer

Department of Psychology

Austin Peay State University

May 4, 2004

Effects of Communication Skills 2

Abstract

Marital and premarital counselors have used communication skills training on a regular basis to enhance a couple's relationship. This study explores the theory that communication training can affect an adolescent's ability to develop constructive relationships with friends and family members. Hypothesis: In-class instruction to students to express themselves and listen to others will improve their relationships as measured by a revised version of the Interpersonal Relations Questionnaire (IRQ). The discussion explores the expected results of this study.

Effects of Communication Skills 3

The Effects of Communication Skills

on the Development of Interpersonal Relationships

The ability of a student to relate with others in personal relationships, as opposed to public, has been an important aspect of classroom training. The breakdown of the American family has led society into crime, violence, and a decay in moral values. Feindler and Starr (2003) stated: "Teaching children and adolescents to recognize how they feel when they are angry and what pushes their buttons enables them to make better choices about how they express their anger" (p. 158).

Mongrain and Vettese (2003) argued that young women are often ambivalent in their emotional expression, which "entails less congruent communication" and "less positivity in close relationships" (abstract). Black (2002) showed that young women rated lower than young men in withdrawal and higher than the men in communication skills during a test of their conflict resolution in conversations with their best friends. Since the family structure depends highly upon the relationship of husband and wife, a breach in that relationship can destroy the family unit. Thus, teaching communication skills to married couples before problems arise can reduce marital distress.

This concept has carried over into the realm of premarital counseling. Numerous churches extending across the denominations have come to require premarital counseling weighed heavily with communication skills in order to prevent distressed marriages and to decrease divorce rates.

Effects of Communication Skills 4

Other types of close relationships include those of parent-child, sibling-sibling, and same-sex friendships. The ability of a person to relate with others in social and intimate settings begins when children interact with others by observation and instruction. Even though this acquisition of knowledge steadily increases in childhood, many young adults are not sufficiently prepared to deal with the types of social interaction they face as they proceed through adolescence and young adulthood. Since communication has an important role in relationships and since relationships have such an impact on society, then the effects of training adolescents in communication skills should be further examined.

This study will test the hypothesis that training high school students in the applied use of communication skills will enable these students to develop healthy and constructive interpersonal relationships as measured by a revised version of the Interpersonal Relations Questionnaire (IRQ). They will have a definition of their opinions, develop accurate expression of these options, and build a courteous reception to the opinions and emotions of others.

Method

Subjects

The subjects will consist of high school students in grades 10, 11, and 12. They will be selected from a local high school through contact with the principal by letter. Only a school that has a mandatory Health and Wellness class will be accepted because interpersonal relationship is a relevant issue to the mental and emotional well-being of students. Two classes from the school will be allowed for a control group and a treatment group.

Instrumentation

Characteristics of the students' interpersonal relationship will be measured by using a test based on the standard IRQ. This test measures personal adjustment in adolescents aged 12 to 15 and will be adjusted for 16- to 18-year-olds.

Effects of Communication Skills 5

An open-ended questionnaire will also be developed to inquire about the perceived quality of past and present relationships by the students. It will question these items:

- Average length of past and present relationships.
- Satisfaction of communication in family and friendly relationships.
- The ability to solve conflicts verbally.
- The awareness in his or her ability to communicate since taking the course.

Procedure

Communication skills will be taught to one class for six weeks, preferably when the students return from Christmas break. This will allow the students time to develop relationships during the school year prior to skill training and also allow time after the training, but before the school year ends, so that students might notice tendency changes in their relationships.

The skills taught will stress the definition and expression of feelings and opinions, along with listening techniques. These skills will be focused toward those strategies used in a variety of interpersonal relationships as administered by an instructor. The students will once again take the IRQ, and the open-end questionnaire will be administered to all students at the completion of the school year.

Results

The IRQ pretest and posttest scores will be compared, and open-ended questionnaires will be examined for pattern changes and perceived changes in relationship quality. The results between the treatment and non-treatment group will be compared in order to examine whether any changes or trends could be related to normal growth. The results might also be compared to the IRQ results in the attempt to expose any sensitivity created by pretesting.

Effects of Communication Skills 6

Discussion

If the results of this study actually do show a positive correlation between communication skills and interpersonal relationships in the students tested, then consideration should be given to refining this technique and using it in Wellness classes in an attempt to prepare adolescents for their growth into young adults.

Effects of Communication Skills 7

References

Black, K. A. (2002). Gender differences in adolescents' behavior during conflict resolution tasks with best friends. *Women and Language, 25*. Abstract retrieved March 7, 2004, from InfoTrac database.

Feindler, E. L., & Starr, K. E. (2003). From steaming mad to staying cool: A constructive approach to anger control. [Electronic version]. *Reclaiming Children and Youth, 12*, 158–161.

Mongrain, M., & Vettese, L. C. (2003). Conflict over emotional expression: Implications for interpersonal communication. *Personality & Social Psychology Bulletin, 29*. Abstract retrieved March 7, 2004, from the InfoTrac database.

YOUR RESEARCH PROJECT

1. Write a report on your empirical research. Conform to the standards established in this chapter and the preceding sections of the text. Submit your report to your instructor.

2. As an alternative, write a proposal for empirical research, as demonstrated in this chapter on pages 186–190. Submit the proposal to your instructor.

14 Writing the Review of Literature on a Topic

The review of literature is an educational activity that trains you in the investigation of sources. It does not require empirical research, but it does involve theory—that is, you examine the theoretical basis for each article in order to describe the work and compare it with others. Accordingly, the literature review written in APA style has several goals:

1. The review discovers conflicts, contradictions, and variables, for you show how several scholars, under differing circumstances, examined the issues. It compares the key theories in one small area of research.
2. It shows gaps in the research to pinpoint areas worthy of additional study. Along the way, it explains the ramifications of the problem to show how each article contributes another aspect of the problem and solution.
3. The literature review classifies current research to show relationships. Thus, it should not be a chronological listing of the sources, nor should each paragraph be devoted to a single source. The articles that address the same issue should be grouped to show the various positions. Some will agree on an answer while others disagree, and immediately you have two classifications.
4. The review of literature, as shown on pages 194–200, can be a short paper of its own or part of the introduction to your theoretical study or your report of empirical research.
5. Your review serves other researchers who might be interested in the topic and who want to know how other scholars have addressed the problem.

14a Choosing a Topic

Three factors affect the selection of an effective topic for review purposes: relevance, currency, and a narrow focus.

First, choose a topic of interest to you, if you have that option. For example, you may know a person with an addiction to drugs or another who suffers with depression. Examining such topics has relevance to your life and will keep you interested.

Second, select a subject of current interest so you can find articles published in recent years. Glance at a few magazines and journals to see what the experts are writing about, and use an electronic search engine to find articles.

For example, entering the topic "cutters" in the PsycINFO search engine will produce 30 to 40 current articles on this subject of adolescents who are purposely cutting themselves.

Third, you can begin with a broad subject, such as hypnosis, abortion, same-sex marriage, and so forth, but you will soon need to narrow the topic to a specific issue. The topic "hypnosis," for example, will show over 12,000 articles in the PsycINFO database. Try narrowing it to "hypnosis and addictions" or, even tighter, "hypnosis and smoking." The search engine also allows you to narrow the search to recent articles of the last five or ten years. See pages 58–61 for more information on conducting searches.

14b Reading the Articles

Give each article a careful, critical reading. In particular, look for differences and similarities in the theoretical outlook of the writers, which will enable you to classify the articles, such as those that examine peer response, those that advocate pharmacological remedies, and those that promote parental intervention. The classifications should become evident as you move from one article to the next. Make notes

> Note: See Chapter 7, "Responding to the Evidence," pages 94–104, for complete details on the techniques for examining the literature.

that summarize, paraphrase, or quote the authors, for these materials will form the basis of your review. You must be able to explain what the various writers are saying in defense of their theoretical positions.

14c Writing the Literature Review

The length of your review depends primarily on the number of articles you have included, which may number from six to seven or as many as 25, depending on the assignment, the subject, and available articles.

Introduction

The introduction establishes the theme, theory, or research question you review. All articles should then, of course, address the central issue, which you have narrowed as much as possible. Not *abortion* but *grief responses in women following abortion* and not *gender bias* but *gender bias toward African-American women*.

If you wish, the introduction is a good place to trace the history of research in the subject because the body of your review will comment on *recent* works.

The introduction describes the organization of the paper. In the case of a controversy, show how you describe research that supports one side and then the other. If you have three classifications of critical approaches, explain them briefly, as with *bias in the workplace, bias in the schools,* and *bias in the courts.* Thus, the introduction of the review should:

- Identify the problem or subject to be reviewed.
- Explain its currency and its significance.
- Briefly describe the organization of the essay.

Body

The body of the review traces the various issues, and explains for each the articles that pertain to it. Under your classifications, you compare and evaluate the studies to address each article's contribution to research on the subject. You should identify and describe each article in detail, especially to explain how the work contributes to the overall design of research on the subject.

Depend heavily on paraphrase to describe what each author or set of authors has advanced. Reserve direct quotations for statements that are truly germane to the issues.

In each major section of your review, you should compare the research projects of various scientists and discuss the implications of each. Your comparisons of the sources will advance your reader's understanding of the central issues. For example, you might compare:

- Hypotheses advanced by various writers.
- Assumptions drawn from the research by the writers.
- Theories that have been tested.
- The designs or methods used for the research.
- The results of the research.
- The writers' interpretations of their findings.

Every literature review must find its own way, and yours will fall into place as you read, analyze, and compare the various approaches to the problem or question at hand. Be courageous enough to evaluate the research, not just describe it. In that way, your paper becomes a critical review, not merely an objective description of articles. Only by evaluation can you make the essay your own.

Thus, the body of the review should:

- Provide a systematic analysis of each article.
- Compare the articles that fall within a specific classification.
- Discuss the relevance of the findings by each piece of research.
- Comment on the apparent significance of the results.

Conclusion

The conclusion of the review should explain again the significance of the subject under review. It can also give a general overview of the prevailing theories you examined in the body. Of vital importance is your discussion of the implications drawn from your examination of several research reports. You might wish to defend one theory, and you might also suggest additional research work to launch in pursuit of more answers to the problem or question.

Thus, the conclusion of the literature review should:

- Discuss the implications of the findings.
- Make judgments as appropriate.
- Evaluate the relative merits of the various works of research.
- Defend one theory.
- Suggest additional research.

14d   Sample Literature Review

The paper that follows classifies several articles on gender communication under a progression of headings: the issues, the causes (both environmental and biological), the consequences for both men and women, and possible solutions. You also should arrange the sources to fit your selected categories or to fit your preliminary outline, and, like Kaci Holz in the paper below, use centered heads and side heads to identify the sections of your APA-style paper.

Gender Communication 1

GENDER COMMUNICATION: A REVIEW OF THE LITERATURE

Kaci Holz

Women's Studies 2040

April 23, 2004

Gender Communication 2

Gender Communication: A Review of the Literature

Several theories have existed about different male and female communication styles. These ideas have been categorized below to establish the issues, to show causes for communication failures, to describe the consequences for both men and women, and to discuss the implications.

The Issues

Tannen (1990) identified basic gender patterns or stereotypes. She said men participate in conversations to establish "a hierarchical social order" (*You Just Don't Understand*, p. 24), while women most often participate in conversations to establish "a network of connections" (p. 25).

Gender Communication 3

She distinguished between the way women use "rapport-talk" and the way men use "report-talk" (p. 74).

In similar fashion, Basow and Rubenfeld (2003) explored in detail the sex roles and how they determine and often control the speech of each gender. They noticed that "women may engage in 'troubles talk' to enhance communication; men may avoid such talk to enhance autonomy and dominance" (p. 186).

In addition, Yancey (1993) has asserted that men and women "use conversation for quite different purposes" (p. 71). He provided a 'no' answer to the question in his title, "Do Men and Women Speak the Same Language?" He claimed that women converse to develop and maintain connections, while men converse to claim their position in the hierarchy they see around them. Yancey asserted that women are less likely to speak publicly than are men because women often perceive such speaking as putting oneself on display. A man, on the other hand, is usually comfortable with speaking publicly because that is how he establishes his status among others. Similarly, masculine people are "less likely than androgynous individuals to feel grateful for advice" (Basow & Rubenfeld, p. 186). In similar fashion, Woods (2002) claimed that "male communication is characterized by assertion, independence, competitiveness, and confidence [while] female communication is characterized by deference, inclusivity, collaboration, and cooperation" (p. 440). This list of differences described why men and women have such opposing communication styles.

In another book, Tannen (1998) addressed the issue that boys, or men, "are more likely to take an oppositional stance toward other people and the world" and "are more likely to find opposition entertaining—to enjoy watching a good fight, or having one" (*The Argument Culture*, p. 166). Girls try to avoid fights.

Causes

Two different theories suggest causes for gender differences.

Environmental Causes. James and Cinelli (2003) made this observation: "The way men and women are raised contributes to differences in conversation and communication . . . " (p. 41). Another author, Witt (1997), in "Parental Influence on Children's Socialization to Gender Roles," discussed the various findings that support the idea that parents have a great influence on their children during the development of their self-concept. Witt stated, "Children learn at a very early age what it means to be a boy or a girl in our society" (p. 253) and added that parents "[dress] infants in gender-specific colors, [give] gender-differentiated toys, and [expect] different behavior from boys and girls" (p. 254).

Yancey (1993) noticed a cultural gap, defining culture as "shared meaning" (p. 68). He said, "Some problems come about because one spouse enters marriage with a different set of 'shared meanings' than the other" (p. 69). The cultural gap affects the children. Yancey also talked about the "Battle of the Sexes" as seen in conflict between men and women. Reverting back to his 'childhood gender pattern' theory, Yancey claimed, "Men, who grew up in a hierarchical environment, are accustomed to conflict. Women, concerned more with relationship and connection, prefer the role of peacemaker" (p. 71).

Like Yancey, Tannen (1990) also addressed the fact that men and women often come from different worlds and different influences. She argued, "Even if they grow up in the same neighborhood, on the same block, or in the same house, girls and boys grow up in different worlds of words" (*You Just Don't Understand*, p. 43).

Gender Communication 5

<u>Biological Causes</u>. Though Tannen (1990) addressed the environmental issue in her early research, she has also considered the biological issue in her book *The Argument Culture* (1998). Tannen observed, "Surely a biological component plays a part in the greater use of antagonism among men, but cultural influence can override biological inheritance" (*Argument*, p. 205). She summed up the nature versus nurture issue by saying, "the patterns that typify women's and men's styles of opposition and conflict are the result of both biology and culture" (p. 207).

Glass (1992) addressed the issue that different hormones found in men and women's bodies make them act differently and therefore communicate differently. She also discussed how brain development has been found to relate to sex differences.

Mann (1997) said, "Most experts now believe that what happens to boys and girls is a complex interaction between slight biological differences and tremendously powerful social forces that begin to manifest themselves the minute the parents find out whether they are going to have a boy or a girl" (cited in McCluskey, p. 6).

Consequences of Gender Differences

Now that we have looked at different styles of gender communication and possible causes of gender differences, let us look at the possible results. M. Weiner-Davis (1996), author of *Divorce Busting,* said to this point, "Ignorance about the differences in gender communication has been a major contributor to divorce" (cited in Warren, p. 106).

Through various studies, Tannen has concluded that men and women have different purposes for engaging in communication. In the open forum that Tannen and Bly (1993) gave in New York, Tannen (on videotape) explained the different ways men and women handle communication throughout the day. She explained that a man constantly talks during his workday in order to impress those around him and to establish his status in the office. At home, he wants peace and quiet. On the other hand, a woman is constantly cautious and guarded about what she says during her workday. Women try hard to avoid confrontation and avoid offending anyone with their language. So when a woman comes home from work, she expects to be able to talk freely without having to guard her words. The consequence? The woman expects conversation, but the man is tired of talking.

Implications

Answers for better gender communication seem elusive. What can be done about this apparent gap in communication between genders? In an article published in *Leadership,* Arthurs (2002) suggested that women should make an attempt to understand the male model of communication and that men should make an attempt to understand the female model of communication.

However, in an article entitled "Speaking Across the Gender Gap," Cohen (2003) mentioned that experts didn't think it would be helpful to teach men to communicate more like women or for women to communicate more like men. This attempt would prove unproductive because it would go against what men and women have been taught since birth. Rather than change the genders to be more like one another, we could simply try to "understand" each other better.

In addition, Weaver (1995) made this observation: "The idea that women should translate their experiences into the male code in order to express themselves effectively . . . is an outmoded, inconsistent, subservient notion that should no longer be given credibility in modern society" (p. 439). Weaver suggested three behavioral patterns we can change:

1. Change the norm by which leadership success is judged.
2. Redefine what we mean by power.

Gender Communication 7

3. Become more sensitive to the places and times when inequity and inequality occur (p. 439).

Similarly, Yancey offered advice to help combat "cross-cultural" fights. He suggested:

1. Identify your fighting style.

2. Agree on rules of engagement.

3. Identify the real issue behind the conflict (p. 71).

McCluskey (1997) argued that men and women need honest communication that shows respect, and they must "manage conflict in a way that maintains the relationship and gets the job done" (p. 5). McCluskey said, "To improve relationships and interactions between men and women, we must acknowledge the differences that do exist, understand how they develop, and discard dogma about what are the 'right' roles of women and men" (p. 5).

The most obvious implication is that differences exist in the way men and women communicate, whether they are caused by biological and/or environmental factors. We can consider the possible causes, the consequences, and possible solutions. Using this knowledge, further research should more accurately interpret communication between the genders.

Gender Communication 8

References

Arthurs, J. (2002, Winter). He said, she heard: Any time you speak to both men and women, you're facing cross-cultural communication. *Leadership, 23.1*, 49.

Basow, S. A., & Rubenfeld, K. (2003). Troubles talk: Effects of gender and gender typing. *Sex Roles: A Journal of Research*. Retrieved April 24, 2003, from http://web5.infotrac.galegroup.com/search

Cohen, D. (1991). Speaking across the gender gap. *New Scientist 131*, 36. Retrieved September 28, 2003, from *InfoTrac* database.

Gender Communication 9

Deborah Tannen and Robert Bly: Men and women talking together. (1993). [Videocassette]. New York: Mystic Fire Video.

Glass, L. (1992). *He says, she says: Closing the communication gap between the sexes.* New York: G.P. Putnam's Sons.

James, T., & Cinelli, B. (2003). Exploring gender-based communication styles. *Journal of School Health, 73,* 41–61.

McCluskey, K. C. (1997). Gender at work. *Public Management, 79(5),* 5–10.

Tannen, D. (1990). *You just don't understand: Women and men in conversation.* New York: Ballantine.

Tannen, D. (1998). *The argument culture: Moving from debate to dialogue.* New York: Random House.

Warren, A. (1996, March). How to get him to listen. *Ladies' Home Journal, 113,* 106.

Weaver, R. L. (1995). Leadership for the future: A new set of priorities. *Vital Speeches of the Day, 61,* 438–441.

Witt, S. D. (1997). Parental influence on children's socialization to gender roles. *Adolescence. 32,* 253–264.

Woods, J. T. (2002). *Gendered lives.* San Francisco: Wadsworth.

Yancey, P. (1993). Do men and women speak the same language? *Marriage Partnership, 10,* 68–73.

YOUR RESEARCH PROJECT

1. Write a review article that evaluates at least four sources on a topic of your choice. Conform to the standards established in this chapter. Submit the review article to your instructor.

2. As an alternative, write a review of one article and submit it to your instructor.

15 Preparing Electronic Research Projects

Creating your research paper electronically has a number of advantages:

- *It's easy.* Creating electronic research papers can be as simple as saving a file, and your school probably has resources for publishing your paper electronically.
- *It offers multimedia potential.* Unlike paper documents, electronic documents enable you to include anything available in digital form—including text, illustrations, sound, and video.
- *It can link your reader to more information.* Your readers can click a hyperlink to access additional sources of information. A hyperlink or link is a highlighted word or image that, when clicked, lets readers jump from one place to another—for example, from your research paper to a Web site on your subject.

15a Getting Started

Before you decide to create your research paper electronically, consider three questions:

1. What support does your school provide? Most institutions have the technology and the personnel to support electronic publication. Investigate how your college will help you publish in an electronic medium.
2. Is electronic publishing suitable for your research paper? Ask yourself what your readers will gain from reading an electronic text rather than the traditional paper version. Will an electronic format really help you send ideas to your audience?
3. What form will the paper take? Electronic research papers appear generally in one of the following forms:
   - A word-processed document (see section 15b).
   - An electronic presentation or slide show (see section 15c).
   - A Web site (see section 15d).

15b Using Word Processing to Create Electronic Documents

The easiest way to create an electronic document is by using word processing programs such as Microsoft Word® or Corel WordPerfect® and then distributing your report in its electronic form rather than printing it out. (See the following for an example of how such a research paper might look.)

Gender Communication: A Review of the Literature

Several theories have existed about different male and female communication styles. These ideas have been categorized below to establish the issues, show causes for communication failure, examine the consequences for both men and women, and discuss the implications.

The Issues

Tannen (1990) has identified basic gender patterns or stereotypes. She said men participate in conversations to establish "a hierarchical social order" (*You Just Don't Understand,* p. 24), while women most often participate in conversations to establish "a network of connections" (p. 25). She distinguished between the way women use "rapport-talk" and the way men use "report-talk" (p. 74).

In similar fashion, Basow and Rubenfeld (2003) explored in detail the sex roles and how they determine and often control the speech of each gender. They noticed that "women may engage in 'troubles talk' to enhance communication; men may avoid such talk to enhance autonomy and dominance" (p. 186). See also http://www.eff.org/Net_culture/Gender_issues/cross_gender_communciation.paper.

Most popular word processing programs include tools for handling features like these:

- *Graphics.* Word processors can accommodate graphics in a variety of formats, including .gif and .jpg (see the graphics above for an example; see section 15e on page 206 for more information on .gif and jpg formats).
- *Sound and video.* Word processors can include several common audio and video clip formats. Usually, the reader has to click on an icon to activate the clip (see the sound link in Figure 15.1).
- *Hyperlinks.* Readers can click to go to a Web site on the Internet for further reading (see the underlined hyperlink in the text of the research paper in Figure 15.2).

15c Building a Slide Show

If you plan an oral presentation, an electronic slide show can help illustrate your ideas. Electronic presentations differ from word-processed documents in that each page, or slide, comprises one computer screen. By clicking, you (or another reader) can move to the next slide (see Figure 15.1).

Because slides can hold only limited information, condense the content of each.

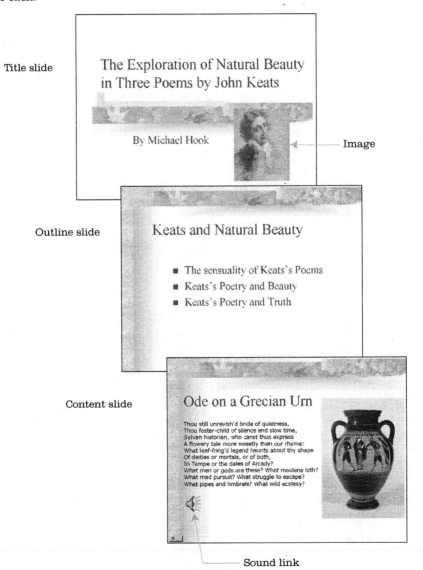

FIGURE 15.1 Opening image of a researched slide presentation

15d Creating Pages with Hypertext Markup Language

Creating a Web page or a Web site involves collecting or making a series of computer files—some of them as HTML files that contain the basic text and layout for your pages and others that contain graphics, sounds, or video.

Using a Web Page Editor to Create Web Pages

The easiest way to create your pages is with a Web page editor such as Microsoft FrontPage®, Adobe Page Mill®, or Netscape Composer®. These programs work differently, but they each create Web pages. Using them is like using a word processor; you enter or paste in text, insert graphics or other multimedia objects, and save the file to your computer or a CD-ROM disk. You can also specify fonts, font sizes, font styles (like bold), alignment, bulleted lists, and numbered lists. Here are a few tips for entering text into a Web page:

- Use bold rather than underlining for emphasis and titles. On a Web site, links are underlined, so any other underlining causes confusion.
- Do not use tabs. HTML does not support tabs for indenting the first line of a paragraph. You also won't be able to use hanging indents for your bibliography.
- Do not double-space. The Web page editor automatically single-spaces lines of text and double-spaces between paragraphs.
- Make all lines flush left on the References page; HTML does not support hanging indentions.

HINT: For more information on building Web pages and Web sites, go to NCSA Beginner's Guide to HTML at http://archive.ncsa.uiuc.edu/General/Internet/www/HtmlPrimer.html.

Creating a Single Web Page

If you want to create a single Web page from your research paper, the easiest but most limited method is to save your word-processed research paper in HTML (Hypertext Markup Language, the computer language that controls what Web sites look like). Different word processing programs perform this process differently, so consult your software's Help menu for specific instructions.

When the word processing software converts your document to HTML, it also converts any graphics you have included to separate graphics files. Together, your text and the graphics can be viewed in a Web browser like any other Web page.

> Note: Your research paper will look somewhat different in HTML format than in its word-processed format. In some ways, HTML is less flexible than word processing, but you can still use word processing software to make changes to your HTML-formatted paper.

Creating a Web Site with Multiple Pages

Creating a site with multiple pages is more complicated and requires careful planning and organization. A multiple-page Web site allows you to assemble a large number of shorter pages that are easier for readers to access and read (see Figure 15.2).

Research paper home page

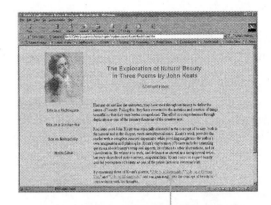

Text page

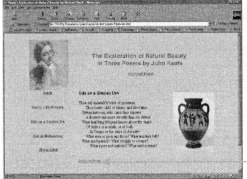

Hyperlinks for navigation

References or Works Cited page

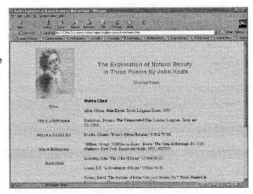

FIGURE 15.2 Three pages from a research paper Web site

Creating a Web site means creating one Web page after another; you just repeat the process and add links between the pages so readers can navigate easily from one to the next. Start with a home page that includes a title, a basic description of your project, and an index with hyperlinks to the contents of your site. Navigational elements, like links to the home page and other major pages of your site, provide a way for readers to "turn the pages" of your report.

Citing Your Sources in a Web Research Paper

Include your parenthetical citations in the text itself and create a separate Web page for references. Remember to include such a page in your plans with hyperlinks pointing to it from various places in the paper. If you are using footnotes, do not put them at the bottom of each page. Instead, create a separate page that holds all the notes, just like the References page of a traditional APA-style paper. Create each footnote number as a link to this page so readers can click on the number to go to the reference. Remember to have a link on the References page to take the reader back to the text.

15e Using Graphics in Your Electronic Research Paper

Graphics files usually take up a lot of file space, but you can save them as either JPEGs or GIFs to make them smaller. In fact, Web sites can use only graphics saved in these formats. Both formats compress redundant information in a file, making it smaller while retaining most of the image quality. You can recognize the file format by looking at the extension to the file name; GIFs have the extension .gif, and JPEGs have the extension .jpg or .jpeg.

GIF stands for Graphical Interchange Format, which develops and transfers digital images. JPEG stands for Joint Photographic Experts Group, which compresses color images to smaller files for ease of transport.

In general, JPEGs work best for photographs and GIFs work best for line drawings. To save a file as a GIF or JPEG, open it in an image-editing program like Adobe Photoshop® and save the file as one of the two types (for example, keats.jpg or keats.gif).

Programs usually have menu commands for inserting graphics; refer to your user documentation to find out how to do so. You can also borrow images from clip art or other Web sites (with proper documentation, of course). To borrow an image, go to the site with your Web browser, right-click on the image you want, and left-click on Save Image As to put it on your hard drive. You can then insert the image into your research paper.

Creating Your Own Digital Graphics

Making your own graphics file is complex but rewarding. It adds a personal creativity to your research paper. Use one of the following techniques:

- Use a graphics program, such as Macromedia Freehand® or Adobe Illustrator®. With such software you can create a graphics file and save it as a JPEG or GIF.

- Use a scanner to copy your drawings, graphs, photographs, and other matter. Programs such as Adobe Photoshop® and JASC Paintshop Pro® are useful for modifying scanned photographs.
- Create original photographs with a digital camera. Digital cameras usually save images as JPEGs, so you won't need to convert the files to a usable format.

As long as you create JPEG files or GIF files for your graphics, you can transport the entire research paper to a Web site.

15f Delivering Your Electronic Research Paper to Readers

Follow your instructor's requirements for delivering your electronic research paper or use one of the techniques in the following checklist.

CHECKLIST

Delivering Your Electronic Research Paper

- *Floppy disk.* Floppy disks are a convenient way to share information. However, they are unreliable, and papers with graphics, sound, or video may not fit on one disk.
- *Zip disk.* A Zip disk or other proprietary format will hold much larger files, but your reader/professor must own a drive that can read it.
- *CD-ROM disk.* These disks hold large amounts of data and thus work well for transmitting graphics, sound, or video files. However, you must own or have access to a CD-R (Compact Disk Recordable) or CD-RW (Compact Disk Recordable/Writable) drive. Most readers have regular CD-ROM drives that can read your disks, but you might want to confirm this beforehand.
- *E-mail.* E-mailing your file as an attachment is the fastest way to deliver your electronic research paper; however, this approach works best if you have a single file, like a word-processed research paper, rather than a collection of related files, like a Web site.
- *Website.* If you have created a Web site or Web page, you can upload your work to a Web server and readers can access your work on the Internet. Procedures for uploading Web sites vary from school to school and server to server; work closely with your instructor and Webmaster to execute this process successfully. Regardless of what method you choose, be sure to follow your instructor's directions and requirements.

■ YOUR RESEARCH PROJECT

Use your personal computer to create a slideshow of the key points for your research project. Add graphics, including pictures to highlight your examples and explanation. Save the presentation to your computers. Additionally, save the slideshow to a CD-ROM disk and submit it to your instructor.

Glossary
Rules and Techniques for Preparing a Manuscript in the Social Sciences

The alphabetical glossary that follows will answer most of your miscellaneous questions about matters of form, such as margins, pagination, dates, and numbers. For matters not addressed below, consult the index, which will direct you to appropriate pages elsewhere in this text.

Abbreviations

Employ abbreviations consistently in notes and citations. For clarity, the research style in the social sciences prefers that authors use abbreviations sparingly in the text. While some long technical terms can be abbreviated, the word must always be explained on the first use in the text or in the abstract. Abbreviations should not hinder a reader's ability to retrieve source information.

Use periods for the following abbreviations:

- Use periods and a space with initials used with personal names:
  P. B. Burrell   William Stalcup, Ph.D.
- Abbreviations that end in lowercase letters are usually followed by a period:
  assoc.   fig.   sec.   Oct.   yr.
- In abbreviations in which lowercase letters represent a word, a period usually follows each letter with no space after the period:
  a.m.   e.g.   n.p.
- Abbreviate *United States* when used as an adjective:
  U.S. Marines   U.S. Coast Guard
- Abbreviate items in the reference list:
  p. 59   Vol. 3   11th ed.
- Identify study participants with identity-concealing labels:
  G.G.1   R.O.V.   X.5

Use *no* periods for abbreviations in the following situations:

- Abbreviations and acronyms made up of capital letters use neither periods nor spaces:
  IQ   MS   AIDS   NASA
- The abbreviations for metric and United States units of measurement use no periods:
  ml   lb   kg   mm

- Form plural abbreviations and statistical symbols by adding *s* alone without italics or an apostrophe:
  IQs   CD-ROMs   *mm*s   *n*s
- State abbreviations do not use periods:
  TN   KS   Washington, DC
- Initializations do not use periods:
  FDA   UCLA   SEC   DVD

Abbreviations of scientific words

A	ampere
Å	angstrom
AC	alternating current
a.m.	ante meridiem
°C	degree Celsius
cc	cubic centimeter
Ci	curie
cm	centimeter
cps	cycles per second
dB	decibel (specify scale)
DC	direct current
deg/s	degrees per second
dl	deciliter
°F	degree Fahrenheit
g	gram
g	gravity
grt	gross registered tonnage
GWh	gigawatt-hour = 10^6 kWh
ha	hectare
hl	hectoliter
hr	hour
Hz	hertz
in.	inch
IQ	intelligence quotient
IU	international unit
J	joule
kg	kilogram
km	kilometer
kph	kilometers per hour
kW	kilowatt
L	liter
m	meter

mA	milliampere
mEq	milliequivalent
meV	million electron volts
mg	milligram
min	minute
ml	milliliter
mm	millimeter
mM	millimolar
mmHg	millimeters of mercury
mmol	millimole
mol wt	molecular weight
mph	miles per hour (convert to metric)
ms	millisecond
MW	megawatt = 10^3 kW
MΩ	megohm
N	newton
ns	nanosecond
p.m.	post meridiem
ppm	parts per million
psi	pound per square inch (convert to metric)
rpm	revolutions per minute
s	second
S	siemens
TJ	terajoule
V	volt
W	watt

Abbreviations for the Reference List

chap.	chapter
ed.	edition
Ed. (Eds.)	Editor (Editors)
3rd ed.	third edition
n.d.	no date
no.	number
p. (pp.)	page (pages)
pt.	part
qtd.	quoted
Rev. ed.	revised edition
supp.	supplement
s.v.	*sub voce (verbo)* ("under the word or heading")

Tech. Rep.	Technical Report
trans.	translator
Vol.	Volume
vols.	volumes

Abbreviations for statistical symbols

ANCOVA	Analysis of covariance
ANOVA	Analysis of variance (univariate)
d	Cohen's measure of effect size
df	degree of freedom
f	Frequency
F	Fisher's F ratio
k	Coefficient of alienation
K-R 20	Kuder-Richardson formula
M	Mean
MANOVA	Multivariate analysis of variance
Mdn	Median
MS	Mean square
n	Number in a subsample
N	Total number in a sample
ns	Nonsignificant
p	probability
P	percentage; percentile
pr	Partial correlation
Q	Quartile
SD	standard deviation
SE	standard error
SS	sum of squares
y	Ordinate
—	nil
0	negligible (generally half the smallest unit or decimal of the heading)
:	figure not available or secret
*	estimate
p	provisional figure
r	revised figure
| or —	discontinuity in series
%	percentage
% AT	percentage variation
Ø	average

MP/ØP	weighted average
AM	average annual growth
<	less than
>	greater than

Abbreviation of publishers' locations

For publishers of books, reports, brochures, and other publications that are not periodicals, give the location. In most cases, include the city and state (Grand Rapids, MI: Baker Books). Omit the state abbreviation for well-known cities such as Chicago, Tokyo, Moscow, and Jerusalem, and omit the state abbreviation if the publisher is a university that has the state within the name (Tuscaloosa: University of Alabama).

Ampersand

In the social sciences, use "&" within citations (Spenser & Wilson, 2004, p. 73) but not in the text (Spenser and Wilson found the results in error.).

Annotated Bibliography

An annotation describes the essential details of a book or article. Place it just after the facts of publication. Provide enough information to give readers a clear image of the work's purpose, contents, and special value. See pages 44–46 for a complete annotated bibliography.

Bible

Use parenthetical documentation for biblical references in the text (e.g., 2 Chron. 18.13). Do not underline the books of the Bible.

Capitalization

Capitalize some titles

For books, journals, magazines, and newspapers, capitalize the first word, the last word, and all principal words, including words that follow hyphens in compound terms (e.g., French-Speaking Islands). Do not capitalize articles, prepositions that introduce phrases, conjunctions, and the *to* in infinitives when these words occur in the middle of the title (for example, *An Almanac of the World*). For titles of articles and parts of books, capitalize as for books (e.g., "Writing the Final Draft" or "Appendix 2"). Titles on the References page require capitalization on the first word and proper nouns (including the first word of subtitles). Following is an example:

Yapko, M. D. (2003). *Tracework: An introduction to the practice of clinical hypnosis* (3rd ed). New York: Brunner-Routledge.

Capitalize after a colon

When introducing a list or series, do not capitalize:

> The test revealed three requirements for young girls: more education in science and math, more physical exercise, and a carefully monitored diet.

When introducing a complete thought or sentence, do capitalize the first word after the colon:

> The test revealed these requirements: Young girls need more education in science and math, more physical exercise, and a carefully monitored diet.

Capitalize a rule, principle, or quotation that follows a colon:

> Benjamin Franklin's maxim should be changed for the modern age: A dollar saved is a dollar earned.

See also page 133, which demonstrates the use of the colon to introduce long, indented quotations.

Capitalize some compound words

Capitalize the second part of a hyphenated compound word only when it is used in a heading with other capitalized words:

> Low-Frequency Sound Equipment

Do not use a capital letter with the second word of a hyphenated compound word:

> Short-term methods of reducing stress.

Capitalize some words in titles

For titles of books and periodical articles in reference lists, capitalize only the first word, the first word after a colon or a dash, and proper nouns:

> Klingerman, J. G., Hunter, W. E., & Whitewood, I. A. (2004). *Cocktail at the twilight of life: Modern medical advancements in sustaining the life and livelihood of HIV-AIDS patients.*

Capitalize trade names

Use capitals for trade and brand names, such as:

> Pepsi   DuPont   Dockers   Thunderbird   Nikon

Do *not* capitalize the names of laws, theories, models, or hypotheses:

> second law of thermodynamics   cognitive approach model

Capitalize proper names

Capitalize proper names used as adjectives *but not* the words used with them:

> Einstein's theory   Salk's vaccine   Pyrrhic victory

Capitalize specific departments or courses

Capitalize the specific names of departments or courses, but use lowercase when they are used in a general sense.

> Department of Psychology, *but* the psychology department
>
> Psychology 314, *but* an advanced course in psychology

Capitalize nouns used before numerals or letters

Capitalize the noun when it notes a precise place in a series:

> during Test 6   we observed Group C   see Figure 2

However, do *not* capitalize a noun that names a part of a book or table followed by a numeral:

> chapter 12   page ix   column 14

Capitalize titles of tests

Capitalize published tests but not generic test titles:

> Dental Admissions Test   mathematics exam

Capitalize numbered effects, factors, and variables

> Factors 7 & 8   Factor 23

Do *not* capitalize general groups in an experiment.

> gender effect   experimental group   weight variables

Character Sets

Most computers provide characters that are unavailable on your keyboard. These are special letters, signs, and symbols, such as _, Σ, â, and $\succ$. The software instructions will help you find and utilize these marks and icons.

Clip Art

Graphics should be used for illustrating charts and graphs, but avoid the temptation to embed clip art pictures in your document. Clip art, in general, conveys an informal, sometimes comic effect, one that is inappropriate to the serious nature of most research papers.

Copyright Law

Fair use of the materials of others is permitted without the need for specific permission as long as your purpose is noncommercial for purposes of criticism, scholarship, or research. Under those circumstances, you can quote from sources within reasonable limits. Acknowledge the source of quotations and borrowed material in your research project, including tables and figures, by giving a citation to the material in the reference list. The law is vague on specific amounts that can be borrowed, suggesting only the "substantiality of the portion used in relation to the copyrighted work as a whole." In other words, you should be safe in reproducing the work of another as long as the portion is not substantial. Your own work is protected by the U.S. Code as soon as you prepare and type the manuscript, poem, artwork, and so on.

Corrections

Because the computer can produce a printed copy quickly, you should make all proofreading corrections before printing a finished manuscript.

Covers and Binders

Most instructors prefer that you submit manuscript pages with one staple or paper clip in the upper left corner. Unless required, do not use a cover or binder. If submitting the manuscript by mail, use a strong or padded envelope. Manuscripts may be submitted electronically, but receive prior approval before e-mailing an attached submission.

Dates

See Numbers, pages A-15–A-17.

Electronic Presentations

A current trend among many instructors is to allow student researchers to submit a manuscript electronically in one of these forms:

> E-mail attachment
> floppy disk
> CD
> slide show
> Web page

Publishing your research paper electronically has a number of advantages. The tools for creating electronic documents make the task as simple as saving the file. In addition, your school probably has the resources in place for publishing your paper electronically. If not, you can complete the paper with a typical home computer. Plus, you can send your work to your readers quickly through a variety of means—e-mail, diskette, cassette, slide show, or Web site. Electronic documents can include anything that you can transfer to a digital form—text, illustrations, sound, and video—and, just as importantly, can offer hyperlinks to further information.

Figures and Tables

A table is a systematic presentation of materials, usually in columns. A figure is any nontext item that is not a table, such as a blueprint, chart, diagram, drawing, graph, photo, photostat, or map. Use graphs appropriately. A line graph serves a different purpose than a circle (pie) chart, and a bar graph plots different information than a scatter graph. Following are several samples of figures:

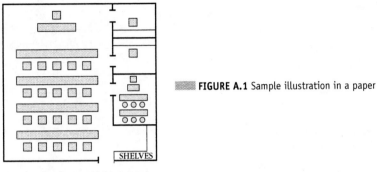

FIGURE A.1 Sample illustration in a paper

Figure 4: Audio Laboratory with Private Listening Rooms and a Small Group Room

Table 1

Response by Class on Nuclear Energy Policy

	Freshmen	Sophomores	Juniors	Seniors
1. More nuclear power	150	301	75	120
2. Less nuclear power	195	137	111	203
3. Present policy is acceptable	87	104	229	37

FIGURE A.2 Sample table in a paper

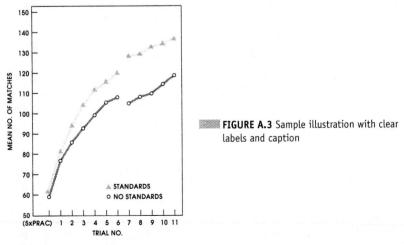

FIGURE A.3 Sample illustration with clear labels and caption

Figure 6: Mean Number of Matches by Subject with and without Standard (by Trial). Source: Locke and Bryan (289).

SUPRASEGMENTAL

STRESS

(primary)   (secondary)   (tertiary)   (weak)

PITCH

1   2   3   4 (relatively rare)
(low)   (average)   (high)   (exceptionally high)

Juncture

open

⊹⊹ at minor break, usually between words

terminal

| or ⤳ "level"

at greater break within sentence, also in apposition

level pitch

‖ or ⟋ "rising"

in "yes-no"   questions, series

pitch-rise before the pause

⟍ or ⟍ "falling"

at end of most sentences

pitch-drop, voice fades off

Figure 9: Phonemes of English. Generally this figure follows the
Trager-Smith system, used widely in American linguistics. Source:
Anna H. Live (1066).

FIGURE A.4 Sample illustration with explanatory caption

Tables are a systematic presentation of materials, usually in columns. A table is shown here:

Table 2ᵃ

Mean Sources of Six Values Held by College Students According to Sex

All Students		Men		Women	
Pol.	40.61	Pol.	43.22	Aesth.	43.86
Rel.	40.51	Theor.	43.09	Rel.	43.13
Aesth.	40.29	Econ.	42.05	Soc.	41.13
Econ.	39.45	Soc.	37.05	Econ.	36.85
Soc.	39.34	Aesth.	36.72	Theor.	36.50

ᵃCarmen J. Finley, et al. (165).

FIGURE A.5 Sample table with in-text citation source

Your figures and tables, as shown above, should conform to the following guidelines:

- Present only one kind of information in each one, and make it as simple and as brief as possible. Frills and fancy artwork distract rather than attract the reader.
- Place small figures and tables within your text; place large figures, sets of figures, or complex tables on separate pages in an appendix (see Appendix, pages 184–185).
- Place the figure or table as near to your textual discussion as possible, but it should not precede your first mention of it.

x

- In the text, explain the significance of the figure or table. Describe the figure or table so your reader can understand your observations without reference to it, but avoid giving too many numbers in your text. Refer to figures and tables by number (for example, "Figure 5" or by number and page reference ("Table 4, p. 16"). Do not use vague references (such as "the table above," "the following illustration," or "the chart below").
- Write a caption for the figure or table so your reader can understand it without reference to your discussion. Place the captain *above* the table and *below* the illustration, flush left, in full capital letters or in capitals and lowercase, but do not mix forms in the same paper. An alternative is to place the caption on the same line as the figure or table number.
- Number figures consecutively throughout the paper with Arabic numbers, preceded by "Fig." or "Figure" (for example, "Figure 4"). Place the figure number and the caption *below* the figure, as shown in Figures A.1, A.3, and A.4.
- Number tables consecutively throughout the paper with Arabic numerals, preceded by "Table" (for example, "Table 2"). Place the numbered designation one double-space flush left *above* the table.
- Insert a caption or number for each column of a table, centered above the column or, if necessary, inserted diagonally or vertically above it.
- Sources are abbreviated as in-text citations, and full documentation must appear in the References list.

Fonts

To assist with readability of the document, use a serif typeface such Times Roman (Times Roman) or Courier (`Courier`). A sans serif typeface like Ariel (Ariel) is used in figures where precise lines and columns prevail. The type size should be 12 point.

Foreign Cities

In general, spell the names of foreign cities as they are written in original sources. However, for purposes of clarity, you may substitute an English name or provide both with one in parentheses:

Köln (Cologne)   Braunschweig (Brunswick)   München (Munich)

Graphics

If they will contribute in a demonstrable way to your research study, you may create graphic designs and import them into your document. Computer software offers various methods for performing this task. See "Figures and Tables," page A-9–A-10, for basic rules.

If you create an electronic text, graphics can add exciting features that are usually absent from the traditional research paper. They tend to be one of the following types:

- *Decorative graphics* make the document look more attractive but seldom add to the paper's content. These occur when you insert a typographic symbol, such as a bulleted list or an arrow.
- *Identity graphics,* much like a corporate logo, give identity to a header on each Web page or each slide in a presentation. The logo is like a signpost for the reader.
- *Illustration graphics* provide a visual amplification of the text. For example, a photograph of Sigmund Freud might reinforce and augment a research paper on psychoanalysis.
- *Information graphics,* such as charts, graphs, or tables, provide data about your topic.

Illustration and information graphics are usually huge files, so you must compress them with a compression format, either JPEG or GIF, so named for their file name extensions: .jpg and .gif. In general, JPEGs work best for photographs and GIFs work best for line drawings.

Making your own graphics file is complex but rewarding. It adds a personal creativity to your research paper. Use one of the following techniques:

- *Use a graphics program,* such as Macromedia Freehand or Adobe Illustrator. With such software, you can create a graphics file and save it as a JPEG or GIF. Also useful are Adobe Photoshop and JASC Paintshop Pro, which are designed primarily for working with photographs.
- *Use a scanner* to copy your drawings, graphs, photographs, and other matter.
- *Create original photographs with a digital camera.* Consult your manual to learn how to create JPEGs or GIFs from your photography.
- *Create your own information graphics* in PowerPoint or Microsoft Excel.

Headers and Footers

The software of your personal computer can automatically insert a numbering or a header command to set an automatic numbering sequence. For your social sciences project, you need a shortened title and page number with five spaces between the shortened title and the page number (see page 166 for an example). Footers are seldom used.

Headings

Place the heading on a new page for every major section of your research paper (title page, opening page, abstract, notes, appendix, and references). Within the text of your material, use centered headings to reveal the manuscript's basic organization: Method, Results, and Discussion. Use side heads for subdivisions: design, tools, subjects, procedures, and so forth. See pages 179–185 for a sample research paper using these headings.

Hyphenation

Do not hyphenate words at the end of lines. If necessary, turn off your computer's automatic hyphenation command. See also "Punctuation," pages A-20–A-21, for information on compound words that require a hyphen.

Indentation

Indent paragraphs with the default tab key for consistency, usually five spaces or a half-inch. Short quotations of 40 or fewer words should be incorporated into the text of your paper and enclosed with double quotation marks (" "). Indent long quotations of 40 or more words in a double-spaced block of lines with no quotation marks (see page 133). Indent the entire block with the default tab key without the usual opening paragraph indent. If the quotation is more than one paragraph, indent the first line of second and additional paragraphs with the default tab key. Use the hanging indention for entries on the References page (see page 149).

Italics

Research writing in the social sciences requires the use of italics, and most systems and printers produce italic lettering. Otherwise, show italics by underscoring. Use italics for the following elements of your writing:

- Titles of books, periodicals, and microfilm publications
  Man without Words   *Civil War Chronicles*

- Name of a variety, species, or genus
  Characrius vociferus

- New technical terms or labels
  The term *moraine*

- A letter, word, or phrase used alone as a linguistic example
  terms of X the letter k the word *gunwale*

- Statistical symbols or algebraic variables
  $D/2 + D/3 + 3\ km = D$ $a/b = c/d$

- Scores and scales
  The F scale   Conic stand = *[20, 40]*

- Volume numbers cited in reference lists but not the page numbers
  15, 111–127

- Do *not* use italics for foreign words and phrases that are common in English.
  et al.   ad lib   per se

- Do *not* use italics for chemical, trigonometric, and nonstatistical terms.
  NHCl   cos   log

Keyboarding the Manuscript

Submit the paper on one side of heavy white bond paper in typed 12-point form using a serif typeface such as Times Roman or Courier. A sans serif font, such as Ariel, should be used in figures because it enhances the appearance of the illustration. Use your word processing program to reproduce special characters of Greek letters, symbols, and math signs in your paper.

Use no hyphens at the ends of lines. Avoid widows and orphans, which are single lines at the top or the bottom of the page; your computer should automatically help you correct this problem.

Margins

A basic 1-inch margin on all sides is recommended. These margins are usually the default setting for word processors. Place your page number 1/2-inch down from the top edge of the paper and 1 inch from the right edge. Your software has a ruler, menu, or style palette that allows you to set the header. If you develop a header, the running head may appear 1 inch from the top, in which case your first line of text may begin 1 1/2 inches from the top.

Names of Persons

Use only the last name when referring to a person in the text of your research. Use the last name with initials in the References list. However, personal communications, such as e-mail or a memo, require special treatment (see page 27).

Numbering

Pagination

Use a header to number your pages in the upper right-hand corner of the page. Depending on the software, you can create the head with the numbering or the header feature. For your social sciences project, you need a shortened title and page number with five spaces between the shortened title and the page number (see page 179 for an example). Type the heading and then double-space.

Numbering a series of items

Procedures or steps in a series are designated by Arabic numeral followed by a period.

College instructors are divided into four ranks:

1. Full professors generally have 15 or more years of experience, have the Ph.D. or other terminal degree, and have achieved distinction in teaching and scholarly publications.

2. Associate professors. . . .

3. Assistant professors. . . .

4. Instructors. . . .

Numbers

Use Arabic numerals whenever possible: for volumes, books, parts, and chapters of works; acts, scenes, and lines of plays; cantos, stanzas, and lines of poetry.

Numbers expressed in figures

- Use figures to express numbers 10 and above and words to express numbers below 10.
  15 cm long   five years old   35 years old functioning at 20%

- Use figures to express numbers below 10 when they are grouped with a comparison of numbers above 10.
  8 of 50 respondents   the 5th group out of 20   6 of 30 analyses

- When writing a technical paper, use figures for all numbers that immediately precede a unit of measurement.
  50 mg per capsule   3.3 mm in length   8 cubic meters   12 amperes

- Use figures to represent statistical or mathematical functions, including fractions, decimals, percentages, and ratios.
  0.65 grams   a ratio of 18:1   3rd quartile

- Use numerals for measurements of time, dates, ages, population, scores, exact sums of money, and specific numbers of participants.
  7.65 million viewers   AD 385 $25 each

- Use numbers that denote a specific place in a numbered series, especially in books and tables.
  Table 7   row 22   Grade 9   chapter 2

Numbers expressed in words

- Use words to express numbers below 10.
  four conditions   seven trials   three-dimensional

- Write the numbers *zero* and *one* as words for clear comprehension.
  one-upmanship   zero-sum   one-week vacation

- Refrain from beginning a sentence with a number.
  The year 1963 ended the Camelot years of the Kennedy White House.

- Common fractions should be written as words.
  one-third of the control group   three-quarters depreciation

- Maintain universally accepted usage for traditional events and occurrences.
  the Fourth of July

- Use numbers and words for large quantities and with modifiers.
  25 million people   ten 3-point shots   the first of 20 parts

- Place a zero before the decimal point when numbers are less than 1.
  0.55 mm   0.33 mmHg   0.78 s

Ordinal and cardinal numbers

Ordinal	Cardinal
fifth graders	five grades
6th and 7th years	6 years, 7 years
the twelfth column	12 columns

Inclusive numbers

Give numbers in full:

110-112   1292-1302   748-749 BC

Commas in numbers

- Place commas between the third and fourth digits from the right, the sixth, and so on (1,200 or 1,200,000). Exceptions include degrees of temperature, acoustic levels, serial numbers, page numbers, binary digits, and numbers on the right side of decimal points.
- Page and line numbers, addresses, the year, and ZIP codes do not use commas:
  page 1620   1989   12116 Nova Road   New York, NY 10012

- Add commas for year numbers of five or more figures.
  15,000 BC

- Use the number *1* in every case for numbers, not the lowercase *l* or uppercase *L,* especially if you are typing on a word processor or computer.

Numbers with abbreviations, symbols, dates, and page references

Unless they begin the sentence, use figures:

5 lbs.	$7	6:30 p.m.
56 George Avenue	3 July 2003 or July 3, 2003	page 9

Dates and times of the day

- Be consistent in using either 3 July 2003 or July 3, 2003. Use numerals for times of the day *(3:30 p.m., the 10:00 a.m. lecture),* but exceptions are made for quarter-hours, half-hours, and hours followed by *o'clock* *(half past eight, a quarter to nine, seven o'clock)*. Spell out centuries *(twenty-first century)*.

- Hyphenate century numbers when using them as adjectives *(seventeenth-century literature and fourteenth- and fifteenth-century wars)*.
- Decades can be written out *(the eighties)* or expressed in figures *(1960s* or *the '90s)*. The abbreviation BC follows the year, but AD proceeds the year *(240 BC, AD 456)*. Some writers now use *BCE,* "*before the common era,*" and the abbreviation *CE,* "*common era,*" and both follow the year *(43 BCE or 1498 CE)*.

Numbers in documentation

Use numbers with in-text citations and reference entries according to the following examples:

(2 Sam. 2.1-8)
(Candler, 2004, pp. 42–46)
2 vols.
Rpt. as vols. 13 and 14
MS CCCC 210
102nd Cong., 1st sess. S. 2411
16 mm., 29 min., color
Monograph 1962-M2
Memory and Cognition, 3, 562–590

Paper

Print on one side of heavy white bond paper. Use the best quality paper available; avoid erasable paper and onionskin. Most instructors request that you bind the pages of your manuscript with one staple or paper clip in the top left corner. Do not enclose the manuscript within a cover or binder unless your instructor asks you to do so.

Percentages

Use numerals with appropriate symbols (3%, $5.60) to represent percentiles, ratios, and percentages:

the 9th percentile   a ratio of 14:1   less than 2%

Proofreader Marks

Be familiar with the most common proofreading symbols so you can correct your own copy or mark your copy for a typist or keyboarder. The most common proofreading symbols are shown next:

Common Proofreading Symbols

ι error in spelling (mi*s*take) with correction in margin

lc lowercase (mis*T*ake)

⊃ close up (mis take)

I delete and close up (miss take)

⊢⊣ delete and close up more than one letter (the ~~mistakes and~~ errors continue)

∧ insert (mi*s*take)

∿ ⓣⓗ transpose elements (th*ei*)

⊂⊃ material to be corrected or moved, with instructions in the margin, or material to be spelled out, (corp.)

caps or ≡ capitalize (Huck finn and Tom Sawyer)

¶ begin a paragraph

No¶ do not begin a paragraph

∧ insert

℮ delete (a mistakes)

add space

⊙ add a period

‸ add a comma

‸ add a semicolon

∨ add an apostrophe or single closing quotation mark

∨ add a single opening quotation mark

∜ ∜ add double quotation marks

ⓑⓕ change to boldface

stet let stand as it is; ignore marks

Punctuation

Consistency is the key to punctuation. Proofreading your paper for punctuation errors will improve the clarity and accuracy of your writing. Conform to the following guidelines.

Apostrophe

To form the possessive of singular nouns, add an apostrophe and *s (the typist's ledger)*. Add only the apostrophe with plural nouns ending in *s (several typists' ledgers)*. Use the apostrophe and *s* with singular proper nouns of people and places even if the noun ends in an *s (Ryerson's hypothesis, Binion's theory, Arkansas's social climate,* but *the Rawlingses' family dysfunction)*. To form the possessive of nouns in a series, add a single apostrophe and an *s* if the ownership is shared *(Barker and Millen's text on the restoration theory of sleep)*.

A-18

Exceptions are the names of *Jesus* and *Moses (Jesus' scriptures, Moses' words)* and Hellenized names of more than one syllable ending in *es (Euripides' dramas)*. Use apostrophes to form the plurals of letters *(a's* and *b's)* but not to form the plural of numbers or abbreviations *(ACTs in the 18s and 19s, the 1980s, sevens, three MDs)*.

Brackets

Use brackets to enclose phonetic transcription, mathematical formulas, and interpolations to a quotation. An interpolation is the insertion of your words into the text of another person.

> Jergin (2004) said, "The cluster of skin sores and lesions [herpes viruses] produced a serious infection that demanded immediate treatment" (p. 89).

Use brackets to enclose parenthetical material that is already inside parentheses:

> (Results for the experimental group [$\underline{n}$ = 5] are listed in Table 3.)

Brackets are also used to present fractions:

> $\underline{a}$ = [(1 + $\underline{b}$)/$\underline{x}$]$^{1/2}$

In general, use parentheses first ( ), then brackets [( )], and finally braces {[( )]}.

Colons

Use colons to introduce a list of examples or to introduce elaboration on what was said in the first clause. Insert one space only after the colon. Capitalize the beginning of the information after the colon if it is a complete sentence.

> Jimmerson reminds us of the critical effects associated with pesticides introduced into a habitat: Man is ultimately responsible for his own actions and the loss of original species.

See also pages A-5–A-6.

Commas

Use commas between items listed in a series of three or more, including before the *and* and *or* that precedes the last item. For example:

> Creeglaw (2004), Tiller (2003), and Wellman (2004) agree with Merchison (2001) on this point.

Never use a comma and a dash together. The comma follows the parenthesis if your text requires the comma:

> How should we order our lives, asks Thompson (2003), when we
> face "hostility from every quarter"?

The comma goes inside single quotation marks as well as double quotation marks:

> Such irony is discovered in Smith's article (1995), "The touches
> of irony in Carl Jung's 'collective unconscious,'" but it is not
> mentioned in most textual discussions.

Dashes

Use dashes to set off special parts of the text that require emphasis. On a computer, use the character set, which will give you an unbroken line. Otherwise, type two hyphens with no blank space before or after, as shown here:

> The modes of treatment most common in therapy--psychoanalytic,
> directive, and nondirective--set different roles for the patient and the
> therapist.

Exclamation marks

Exclamation marks make an emotional ending to a sentence. They should be avoided in research writing. A forceful declarative sentence is preferable.

Hyphens

Use hyphens to divide the syllables of words, but never at the end of a line. Instead, leave the lines short, if necessary, rather than divide a word. Disengage any automatic hyphenation. If you must use hyphenation for publishing the work with full justification of the lines, always double-check word division by consulting a dictionary. Do not hyphenate proper names.

- Use a hyphen for a compound word that illustrates or modifies the subject:
  same-age learners   high-anxiety testers

- Use hyphens for descriptive phrases:
  four-by-four rubric   to-be-announced procedures

- Use a hyphen for compound words that use a number:
  fifth-year high school students   five-step program

Do *not* use hyphens for compound words ending in *-ly*, chemical terms, foreign expressions, fractions, single-letter modifiers, or the comparative and superlative of adjectives:

arbitrarily selected specimens   macrobiotic acid producers
two-thirds of the control group   Type A contributors
less motivated students

Parentheses

Use parentheses to enclose words and numbers in your text in the following situations:

- Reference citations:
  (Barak & Fisher, 2002, p. 145)

- Independent matter:
  The more recent findings (see Figure 6) show . . . .

- Headings for a series:
  The tests were (a) . . . (b) . . . and (c) . . . .

- First use of an abbreviation:
  The test proved reaction time (RT) to be . . . .

- Expressing mathematical groupings or statistical values:
  $(r - 8)/(s - 5)$ $(t = 0.10)$

Avoid nesting one set of parentheses within another set by using brackets:

The test (a study of reaction time [RT] in seconds) proved invalid.

Periods

Use a period to signal the end of complete sentences of the text, endnotes, footnotes, and all bibliography entries. Use one space after a period; however, when periods are used between numbers to indicate related parts *(2.4* for *act 2, scene 4),* use no space. The period normally follows the parenthesis. (The period is placed within the parenthesis only when the parenthetical statement is a complete sentence, as in this instance.)

Quotation marks

Enclose all quotations used as part of your text, except for long indented quotations, where the indentation signals the use of a quotation. Quotations require proper handling to maintain the style of the original; they also require precise documentation. Use quotation marks for titles of articles, essays, short stories, short poems, songs, chapters of books, unpublished works, and episodes of radio and television programs.

Use quotation marks for words and phrases that you purposely misuse, misspell, or use in a special sense; thereafter, do not enclose the word in quotation marks.

> The "patrons" turned out to be criminals searching for a way to launder the stolen money.

Use italics, not quotation marks, to highlight linguistic examples, such as a letter, word, phrase, or sentence:

> Avoid confusion about the usage of *their, they're,* and *there.*

> The term *psychosexual maturity* was first advanced by Sigmund Freud.

Semicolons

Use semicolons to join two distinct independent clauses:

> Carlson reminds us of crucial differences in behavior profiles that no scientist should forget; every individual subject comes from a different educational and socio-educational background.

Roman Numerals

Use Arabic numerals in the text of your document:

Vol. 5   Ch. 17   Plate 21

Retain roman numerals if they are a part of the established terminology:

Elizabeth II   Act IV   Type III reaction

Running Heads

Repeat a shortened title in the upper right corner of every page five spaces in front of the page number (see the sample paper, page 179).

Slang

Avoid the use of slang. When using it in a language study, enclose in double quotation marks any words to which you direct attention. Words used as words, however, require italics (see "Titles within Titles," page A-23).

Spacing Lines of the Text

As a general rule, double-space everything: the body of the paper, all indented quotations, and all reference entries. Use double spacing within all headings and separate the headings from the text with double spacing. Separate the text from indented quotes and from tables and figures by double-spacing, but before and after a displayed equation you may use triple- or quadruple-spacing. Avoid single spacing and 1.5 spacing.

Spelling

Spell accurately. Always use the computer to check spelling if the software is available. When in doubt, consult a dictionary. If the dictionary says a word may be spelled in two ways, be consistent in the form employed, as with *theater* and *theatre,* unless the variant form occurs in quoted materials. Use American (as opposed to British) spelling throughout.

Statistical and Mathematical Copy

Use the simplest form of equation that can be made by ordinary mathematical calculation. If an equation cannot be reproduced entirely by keyboard, type what you can and fill in the rest with ink. As a general rule, keep equations on one line rather than two:

$$(a + b)/(x + y)$$

Use triple or quadruple line spacing above and below an equation.

Theses and Dissertations

The author of a thesis or dissertation must satisfy the requirements of the college's graduate program. Therefore, even though you may use the style advocated here, you must also abide by certain additional rules with regard to paper, typing, margins, and introductory matter such as title page, approval page, acknowledgment page, table of contents, abstract, and other matters. Use both the graduate school guidelines and this book to maintain the appropriate style and format.

Titles within Titles

For a title to a book that includes another title indicated by quotation marks, retain the quotation marks.

> *Views of Elling's "Primordial Sea"*

For the title of an article within quotation marks that includes a title to a book, retain the italic lettering.

> "*Leadership* as a Study of Political Survival"

For a title of an article within quotation marks that includes another title indicated by quotation marks, enclose the shorter title within single quotation marks.

> "Personal Excellence Found in Reading 'Emotional Intelligence'"

For an italicized title to a book that incorporates another title that normally receives italics, do not italicize the shorter title nor place it within quotation marks.

> *Using* Modern Man in Search of a Soul *in the Classroom*

A Listing of Reference Works for Your General Topic

We have tried to make this list as user-friendly as possible to enable you to select rather quickly a few basic references from one of six general categories. Three of four items from a list are more than sufficient to launch your investigation. Each category has two lists:

1. Library reference books and electronic databases mean a trip to the library, but the academic databases can be accessed anywhere by logging into your library's network—from your dorm room, a computer lab, or the library itself.
2. Reputable Internet sources accessed by a browser, such as Google, Lycos, AltaVista, and others.

Remember, too, that the library offers an electronic catalog of all its books as well as access to general interest databases, such as:

InfoTrac
FirstSearch
NewsBank
Lexis-Nexis Academic
netLibrary
Online Books Page
Oxford Reference Online

Here are the sections with the page number that begins the classification.

1. Historic Issues: Events, People, and Artifacts, page A-25.
2. Issues of Health, Fitness, and Athletics, page A-26.
3. Social and Political Issues, page A-28.
4. Environmental Issues, Genetics, and the Earth Sciences, page A-31.
5. Issues in Communication and Information Technology, page A-33.
6. Issues in Religion, Psychology, and Philosophy, page A-35.

By no means are the lists definitive, but one of them should serve as your launching pad for the beginning of the project. These works carry you deeper and deeper toward specific material you can collect for your summaries, paraphrases, and quotations.

If you are interested in social issues of the past, famous people, and ancient artifacts, you need sources in history, biography, art history, architecture, anthropology, and so on. Listed below are important reference works in the library and on the Internet that can launch your investigation.

At the library, investigate these books and academic databases:

Abstracts in Anthropology. Farmingdale, CT: Baywood, 1970–date. This reference book gives brief descriptions of thousands of articles on the cultural development of human history.

America: History and Life. This database gives you access to thousands of articles in history and the life of the nation.

American National Biography. 24 vols. New York: Oxford, 1999. This set of books is the place to start for a study of most historical figures in American history.

Anthropological Literature. Pleasantville, NY: Redgrave, 1979–date. This reference book contains an excellent index to scholarly articles in all aspects of anthropological research.

Dictionary of American History. 3rd ed. 10 vols. New York: Scribner's, 2003. This set of books is a well-documented, scholarly source on the people, places, and events in U.S. history; it includes brief bibliographies of recommended sources.

Encyclopaedia Britannica. This database to the famous encyclopedia provides an ideal platform from which to launch your investigation.

Encyclopedia of American Architecture. Eds. R. T. Packard and B. Korab. 2nd ed. New York: McGraw, 1995. The history of architecture shown here is a history of the nation's development.

Goldentree Bibliographies in History. This site contains a series of books published in different years by different publishers on specific periods in American history (e.g., *Manifest Destiny and the Coming of the Civil War, 1840–1861*).

Historical Abstracts. Santa Barbara, CA: ABC-CLIO, 1955–date. This set of printed abstracts provides a quick overview of historical issues and events worldwide.

Illustrated Encyclopedia of Mankind. 22 vols. Freeport, NY: Marshall Cavendish, 1989. This massive work has been a standard in the field for some time.

JSTOR. This database provides electronic images of historical documents and significant articles on a wide range of historical topics.

Lexis-Nexis Primary Sources in U.S. History. This far-ranging academic database gives, for example, excellent sources into American women's studies.

Recently Published Articles. Washington, DC: American Historical Association, 1976-date. These printed volumes provide an effective index to articles in *American Historical Review, Journal of American History, Journal of the West,* and many others.

World History FullTEXT. As the title indicates, this database provides full-text versions to documents and articles in world history.

Annual Reviews: Anthropology at http://arjournals.annualreviews.org/loi/anthro?cookieSet=1> This Web site provides a search engine for locating reviews of books and articles on hundreds of topics.

Anthropology Internet Resources at http://www.wcsu.edu/socialsci/antres.html Western Connecticut State University maintains this excellent academic site.

Archiving Early America http://earlyamerica.com This Internet site displays eighteenth-century documents in their original form for reading and downloading, such as the Bill of Rights and the speeches of Washington, Paine, Jefferson, and others.

History Best Information on the Net (BIOTN) http://library.sau.edu/bestinfo/Majors/History/hisindex.htm This Internet site covers American history, ancient and medieval history, church and Christian history, and European history, with sections devoted to historical documents, images, maps, and events.

Issues of Health, Fitness, and Athletics

If you have an interest in the social and psychological aspects of sports medicine, diet, good health, nutrition, and similar topics, you should begin your investigation with some of the reference works listed below, which you will find in the library or on the Internet.

Atlas of Human Anatomy. 3rd ed. Frank H. Netter. Teterboro, NJ: ICON, 2003. This reference work contains wonderful illustrations of the human body, extensively labeled.

Black's Medical Dictionary. 39th ed. Lanham, MD: Barnes & Noble, 1999. This reference work houses a standard resource in medicine.

Consumer Health and Nutrition Index. Phoenix, AZ: Oryx, 1985-date. This reference work contains an index, published quarterly, to sources for consumers and scholars.

Cumulated Index Medicus. Bethesda, MD: U.S. Department of Health and Human Services, 1959-date. This reference work is an essential starting point for most papers in medical science.

Cumulated Index to Nursing and Allied Health Literature. Glendale, CA: CINAHL, 1956-date. This reference work offers nursing students an index to *Cancer Nurse, Journal of Practical Nursing, Journal of Nursing Education,* and many more journals; may be listed as *CINAHL* on the library's network; look there also for *PubMed* and *Health and Wellness.*

Encyclopedia of the Human Body. Richard Walker. New York: DK, 2002. This reference work includes both bibliographical references and a useful index for students.

Encyclopedia of Human Nutrition. 3 vols. San Diego, CA: Academic, 1999. This reference work offers a good starting point for a paper on nutrition issues.

Food Science and Technology Abstracts. Reading, UK: International Food Information Service, 1928–date. This reference work offers an index to not only journal sources but also books and conference proceedings.

Health and Wellness. This health sciences and health care database lists citations and summaries of most articles and the entire text of some articles in journals, magazines, newspapers, pamphlets, and reference books.

Index Medicus. Bethesda, MD. U.S. National Library of Medicine, 1960–date. This reference work is a premier source of journal articles in the field of medicine; available as both book and electronic form.

Miller-Keane Encyclopedia and Dictionary of Medicine, Nursing, and Allied Health. 6th ed. Philadelphia: Saunders, 2003. This reference work offers practical applications as well as explanations of concepts and terminology. The reference is now offered in an electronic version also.

Physical Education Index. Cape Giradeau, MO: BenOak, 1978–date. This reference work indexes most topics in athletics, sports medicine, and athletics.

PubMed. The public access gateway to MEDLINE, the National Library of Medicine's bibliographic database, covers the fields of medicine, nursing, dentistry, veterinary medicine, the health care system, and the preclinical sciences.

Wiley InterScience. This reference work provides citations, abstracts, and full-text articles from over 300 journals in business, chemistry, computer science, earth science, education, engineering, finance, law, life and medical Sciences, management, mathematics, physics, psychology, and statistics.

On the Internet, investigate these sites:

Food Safety Web Site http://www.ces.ncsu.edu/depts/foodsci/agentinfo Sponsored by the North Carolina Cooperative Extension Service, this site offers consumers and students information on food safety and links to other useful sites.

Global Health Network http://www.pitt.edu/~super1/index.htm This site allows users with access to documents in public health as provided by scholars at the World Health Organization, NASA, the Pan-American Health Organization, and others; links to agencies, organizations, and health networks.

Healthfinder http://www.healthfinder.gov This site provides access to "reliable consumer health and human services information" online, including full-text publications, databases, Web sites, and libraries; contains links to over 550 sites and some 500 full-text documents.

Medweb: Medical Libraries http://www.medweb.emory.edu/MedWeb/ This site connects users with medical libraries and their storehouses of information. It also gives links to other health-related Web sites; sponsored by Emory University.

National Institutes of Health http://www.nih.gov This site leads the nation in medical research resources and provides substantive information on topics from cancer and diabetes to malpractice and medical ethics as well as links to online journals for the most recent news in medical science.

Outside Online http://outsideonline.com/index.html This site is devoted to outdoor sports such as biking, skiing, backpacking, and camping, with reviews of current sports and equipment.

PubMed http://www.ncbi.nlm.nih.gov/PubMed This site offers numerous citations to journals and other periodicals, including many full-text articles.

SPORTQuest http://www.sportquest.com This site offers a searchable directory of links to thousands of selected sites dealing with 80 sports and related topics; some of the information is accessible only through paid subscriptions. The site also offers links to free information on the Web about individual sports and their teams, history, rules, and events.

Tufts University Nutrition Navigator http://navigator.tufts.edu This site contains a rating guide to nutrition Web sites, divided for categories of users such as women, men, or professionals.

USDA Food and Nutrition Center http://www.nal.usda.gov/fnic This site connects readers to the vast nutrition-related resources of the National Agricultural Library.

Social and Political Issues

If you have an interest in social work at nursing homes, current events such as political conflicts of liberals and conservatives, congressional legislation on student loans, education, and the SAT examinations, gender issues, and similar topics, you should begin your investigation with some of the reference works listed below, which are in the library or on the Internet.

At the library, investigate these books and academic databases:

ABC: Pol Sci. Santa Barbara, CA: ABC-CLIO, 1969–date. This reference work indexes the tables of contents of about 300 international journals in the original language.

CIAO (Columbia International Affairs Online). This database covers theory and research in international affairs from documents published between 1991 and the present.

Columbia Gazetteer. This online database is a comprehensive encyclopedia of geographical places and features political, physical, and special places like national parks, monuments, and shopping malls.

CQ Researcher. This reference database contains documents covering hundreds of hot-topic issues such as abortion, child abuse, election reform, and civil liberties.

The Concise Encyclopedia of Democracy. Eds. Stephen A. Flanders et al. Washington, DC: Congressional Quarterly, 2000. This reference work gives a comprehensive survey of key issues and topics in current events that have affected democracy during recent centuries.

Education Abstracts. New York: Wilson, 1994. This reference work provides short descriptions of hundreds of articles.

Education Index. New York: Wilson, 1929–date. This reference work indexes articles in such journals as *Childhood Education, Comparative Education, Education Digest, Journal of Educational Psychology,* and many more.

Encyclopedia of Sociology. Ed. Edgar F. Borgatta et al. 2nd ed. 5 vols. Detroit: Macmillan, 2000. This encyclopedia offers a starting point for research, giving you terms, issues, and theories to motivate your own ideas.

ERIC. The Educational Resources Information Center (ERIC) is the premier national bibliographic database of education literature.

Facts on File World Political Almanac: From 1945 to the Present. Chris Cook and Whitney Walker. New York: Checkmark Books/Facts on File, 2001. This reference work examines current world political situations, issues, and statistics.

GPO. This reference work indexes the resources of the U.S. Government Printing Office; it corresponds to the print version, *Monthly Catalog of the Government Printing Office,* and has search engine and links to more than 400,000 records.

Index to Legal Periodicals and Books. New York: Wilson, 1908–date. This reference work offers perspectives on laws that govern various social and legal issues.

International Political Science Abstracts. Oslo: International Political Science Association, 1951–date. This reference work provides comprehensive, worldwide coverage of more than 600 periodicals, with abstracts in English.

JSTOR. This database provides electronic images of historical documents and significant articles on a wide range of historical topics.

NewsBank. NewsBank provides searchable full-text articles appearing in local publications.

Political Handbook of the World. Eds. Arthur S. Banks et al. Binghamton, NY: CSA, 1928–date. This handbook examines governments and intergovernmental organizations, with notes on major political developments.

Project MUSE. This database includes current issues of nearly 200 journals covering the fields of literature and criticism, history, the visual and performing arts, cultural studies, education, political science, gender studies, economics, and others.

Public Affairs Information Service Bulletin (PAIS). New York: Public Affairs Information Service, 1915–date. This reference work is an annual bulletin with bibliographies useful in all areas of the social sciences, including politics.

Social Sciences Index. New York: Wilson, 1974–date. This reference work provides a vital index to all aspects of sociology, social work, education, political science, geography, and other fields.

Social Work Research and Abstracts. New York: NASW, 1964–date. This invaluable reference work offers research in any area of social work.

Sociological Abstracts. San Diego, CA: Sociological Abstracts, 1953–date. This reference work contains the key source for skimming sociology articles before going in search of the full article.

ViVa. This work provides a current bibliography of articles about women's and gender history, including related topics such as prostitution, witchcraft, housework, sexuality, birth control, infanticide, the family, gynecology, and masculinity.

Westlaw. This database contains federal and state court cases and statutes (laws).

Women's Issues. 3 vols. Ed. M. McFadden. Englewood Cliffs, NJ: Salem/Magills, 1997. This reference work provides a comprehensive survey of the major movements and specific issues for a good historical perspective on women.

Women's Studies Index. Boston: Hall, 1989–date. This reference work offers an annual index considered by many librarians the best source for immediate information on women's issues.

Women's Studies Abstracts. Rush, NY: Rush, 1972–date. This reference work offers a quick overview of hundreds of articles and books on women's issues.

On the Internet, investigate these sites:

Bureau of the Census http://www.census.gov This site provides census data on geography, housing, and the population and allows user to examine specific information about targeted counties.

Chronicle of Education http://chronicle.merit.edu This site contains "Academe This Week" from *The Chronicle of Education,* a weekly print magazine about education on the undergraduate and graduate levels; subscription is necessary for full access.

FedStats: One-Stop Shopping for Federal Statistics http://www.fedstats.gov This site provides access to official U.S. government statistical data and serves as a gateway to government agencies' Web pages, where specific data are found.

FedWorld http://www.fedworld.gov/ Sponsored by the Department of Commerce; this site offers federal government information to scholars and citizens alike, as well as job searchers.

Feminist Theory Web Site http://www.cddc.vt.edu/feminism/ This site provides "research materials and information for students, activists, and scholars interested in women's conditions and struggles around the world." It consists of three parts with source information: various fields within feminist theory, different national/ethnic feminisms, and individual feminists.

Gallup Organization http://www.gallup.com One of the oldest, most trusted public opinion polling groups in the country; this site provides data from opinion polls, indexed by subject, as well as information on polling methods.

Internet Legal Resources Guide http://www.ilrg.com/ Designed for both legal professionals and laypersons, this site offers a categorized index of more than 4,000 select Web sites and thousands of locally stored Web pages, legal forms, and downloadable files.

Library of Congress http://www.lcweb.loc.gov This site provides the Library of Congress catalog online for books by author, subject, and title; it also has links to historical collections and research tools.

Online Educational Resources http://quest.arc.nasa.gov/ This site provides an extensive list of educational articles and documents on everything from SAT scores to day care programs.

Political Science Resources on the Web http://www.lib.umich.edu/govdocs/polisci.html This site contains a vast data file on government information—local, state, federal, foreign, and international; it is a good site for political theory and international relations, with links to dissertations, periodicals, reference sources, university courses, and other social science information.

Praxis http://caster.ssw.upenn.edu/~restes/praxis.html This site has a massive collection of articles on socioeconomic topics, with links to other social science resources.

Thomas http://thomas.loc.gov This site gives you access to congressional legislation and documents indexed by topic, by bill number if you have it, and by title. It also allows you to search the *Congressional Record,* the Constitution, and other government documents. It links you to the House, Senate, Government Printing Office, and General Accounting Office.

United States Congress http://www.congress.org This site is designed to give citizens access to their elected officials through information bulletins and letters or e-mails.

White House Web http://www.whitehouse.gov This site provides a graphical tour, messages from the president and vice president, and accounts of life at the White House. Visitors to this site can leave a message for the president in the guest book.

Women's Studies Librarian http://www.library.wisc.edu/libraries/WomensStudies This site provides information on important contributions by women in science, health, and technology, with links to their activities in literature, government, and business.

Environmental Issues, Genetics, and the Earth Sciences

If you have an interest in cloning, abortion, population growth, poverty in underdeveloped countries, and similar topics, you should begin your investigation with some of the reference works listed following, which you can find in the library and on the Internet.

Bibliography and Index of Geology. Alexandria, VA: American Geological Institute, 1933–date. Monthly, with annual indexes, this reference work indexes excellent scholarly articles in geology.

BioOne. This database provides access to scientific research, focusing especially on the biological, ecological, and environmental sciences.

Ecological Abstracts. Norwich, UK: Geo Abstracts, 1974–date. This reference work allows users to examine the brief abstract before finding and reading the complete article.

Environment Abstracts Annual. New York: Bowker, 1970–date. This reference work provides abstracts to the major articles in the field.

The Environmental Index. Ann Arbor, MI: UMI, 1992–date. This reference work indexes numerous journals in the field, including *Environment, Environmental Ethics, Journal of Applied Ecology,* and others.

Geographical Abstracts. Norwich, UK: Geo Abstracts, 1972–date. This reference work provides a quick overview of articles whose full text you can seek later.

GeoRef. The GeoRef database includes the American Geological Institute's geoscience archive of over 1.9 million records of North American geology since 1785 and other areas of the world since 1933.

Grzimek's Animal Life Encyclopedia. 2nd ed. 17 vols. Bernhard Grzimek. Detroit: Thomson/Gale, 2003. This reference work is an extensive resource for the student, with bibliographies leading to additional resources.

Publications of the Geological Survey. Washington, DC: GPO, 1985–date. This index to the Government Printing Office is updated with regular supplements.

World Resources. Oxford: Oxford UP, 1986–date. This reference work contains chapters on conditions and trends in the environment worldwide. Also provides statistical tables.

On the Internet, investigate these sites:

The Academy of Natural Sciences http://www.acnatsci.org/library/link.html This site links researchers to hundreds of articles and resource materials on issues and topics in the natural sciences.

Discovery Channel Online http://www.discovery.com This site offers an online version of television's Discovery Channel; it features a keyword search engine.

Envirolink http://envirolink.org This site's search engine allows access to environmental articles, photographs, action alerts, organizations, and additional Web-based sources.

ICE Biblionet http://ice.ucdavis.edu/biblio/biology.html#biology Sponsored by the Information Center for the Environment (ICE) at the University of California, Davis, this site offers many links to sources.

The Virtual Library of Ecology and Biodiversity http://conbio.net/VL/welcome.cfm Sponsored by the Center for Conservation Biology, this site consists primarily of an index of links to other Web sites in categories such as endangered species, global sustainability, and pollution.

West's Geology Directory http://www.soton.ac.uk/~imw This site indexes over 200 Web pages devoted to geology. Its massive directory has direct links to geological field guides and bibliographies.

Issues in Communication and Information Technology

If you have an interest in talk radio, television programming for children, bias in print journalism, developing computer software, the glut of cell phones, and similar topics, you should begin your investigation with some of the reference works listed below, which you can find in the library or on the Internet.

At the library, investigate these books and academic databases:

Computer Abstracts. London: Technical Information, 1957–date. This work provides short descriptions of important articles in the field.

Computer Literature Index. Phoenix, AZ: ACR, 1971–date. This index identifies articles on computer science in a timely fashion with periodic updates.

Digital Communication: Fundamentals of and Applications. Bernard Sklar. New York: Prentice-Hall, 2001. This book serves as a beginner's guide to the new digital age.

Encyclopedia of Computer Science. Eds. Anthony Ralston, Edwin D. Riley, and David Hemmendinger. Rev. 4th ed. New York: Grove, 2000. This reference work gives a thorough list of computer concepts and theories.

Encyclopedia of Computer Science and Technology. Ed. J. Belzer. 22 vols. New York: Dekker, 1975–1991. Supplement 1991–date. This reference work provides a comprehensive source for launching a computer investigation.

Information Technology Research, Innovation, and E-Government. Washington, DC: National Press Academy, 2002. Focuses on the use of the Internet in government administration.

The Elements of Style. William Strunk, Jr., and E. B. White. Boston: Allyn & Bacon, 1999. A classic book that teaches and exhorts writers to avoid needless words, urges the use of the active voice, and calls for simplicity in style.

On Writing Well. 25th anniv. ed. William K. Zinsser. New York: HarperResource, 2001. This book is a well-written text on the art of writing, especially on the best elements of nonfiction prose.

Style: Ten Lessons in Clarity and Grace. 7th ed. Joseph M. Williams. New York: Longman, 2003. This book offers an excellent discussion of good writing style and the means to attain it.

On the Internet, investigate these sites:

AJR Newslink http://newslink.org/menu.html This site provides links to newspapers (including campus publications), television stations, and radio stations worldwide; not all links on the site are active, but it still merits attention by students.

American Communications Association: Communication Studies Center http://www.uark.edu/~aca/acastudiescenter.html The parent site of the site listed next; it provides resources in business communication, communication education technologies, gender and communication, language and linguistics, and mass media and culture.

Communication Institute for Online Scholarship http://www.cios.org/ Though the site requires either a library subscription or individual membership, it is a good source of resources in the field of communications; perhaps your local or college library subscribes already.

Computer Science http://library.albany.edu/subject/csci.htm A good starting point for the student, this site provides numerous links to resources in the discipline.

The First Amendment Center http://www.firstamendmentcenter.org/default.aspx This site features comprehensive research coverage of key First Amendment issues and topics, a unique First Amendment Library, and guest analyses by respected legal specialists.

Information Technology Association of America http://www.itaa.org/index.cfm This site contains information and resources encompassing computers, software, telecommunications products and services, Internet and online services, systems integration, and professional services companies.

Internet Resources for Technical Communicators http://www.soltys.ca/techcomm.html This site offers links to Internet resources for technical writers or communicators.

Journalism and Mass Communication Resources on the Web http://www.lib.iastate.edu/collections/eresourc/journalism.html This site takes users to resources and Web sites on associations, book reviews, bibliographies, libraries, media, information science programs, and departments of communication in various universities.

Newspapers.com http://www.newspapers.com/ This site provides a comprehensive portal site for U.S. city and campus newspapers.

Technical Communication Online http://www.techcomm-online.org/ This site is the official Web site for the *Journal of the Society for Technical Communication,* with searchable articles and other information for researchers as well as links to related sites.

Virtual Computer Library http://www.utexas.edu/computer/vcl/ This site gives access to academic computing centers at the major universities as well as an index to books, articles, and bibliographies.

Writing Research Papers http://www.ablongman.com/lester This site accompanies the 11th edition of another textbook by the same authors with cross-reference icons throughout the text to carry the Web user to a wealth of information on research and research writing.

Issues in Religion, Psychology, and Philosophy

If you have an interest in human values, moral self-discipline, the ethics of religious wars, the power of religious cults, the behavior of children with single parents, the effect of the environment on personality, and similar topics, you should begin your investigation with some of the reference works listed below, which you will find in the library or on the Internet.

At the library, investigate these books and academic databases:

Cambridge Dictionary of Philosophy. 2nd ed. Ed. R. Audi. New York: Cambridge, 1999. This reference work is an excellent base from which to launch your investigation into philosophical issues.

Encyclopedia of Psychology. 8 vols. Ed. Alan E. Kazdin. New York: Oxford, 2000. This is the most comprehensive basic reference work in the field; published under the auspices of the American Psychological Association.

Index of Articles on Jewish Studies. Jerusalem: Jewish National and University Library Press, 1969–date. This reference work indexes the major religious journals on Jewish issues.

Mental Measurements Yearbook (MMY) This database contains information on all English-language standardized tests covering educational skills, personality, vocational aptitude, psychology, and related areas.

Philosopher's Index: A Retrospective Index. Bowling Green, OH: Bowling Green University, 1967–date. This reference work indexes philosophy articles in journals such as *American Philosophical Quarterly, Humanist, Journal of the History of Ideas, Journal of Philosophy,* and many more.

PsycINFO. This database includes citations and summaries of journal articles, book chapters, and books, covering psychological aspects in medicine, psychiatry, nursing, sociology, education, and related fields.

Psychological Abstracts. Washington, DC: APA, 1927–date. This reference work provides brief abstracts to articles in such psychology journals as *American Journal of Psychology, Behavioral Science, Psychological Review,* and many more. On the library's network, look for *PsycINFO.*

Routledge Encyclopedia of Philosophy. 10 vols. Ed. E. Craig. New York: Routledge, 1999. This work contains the most comprehensive, authoritative, and up-to-date reference work in the field; a condensed version is available in some libraries.

On the Internet, investigate these sites:

The American Philosophical Association http://www.amphilsoc.org/ This site provides articles, bibliographies, software, a bulletin board, gopher server, and links to philosophy sites containing college courses, journals, texts, and newsletters.

Episteme Links: Philosophy Resources on the Internet http://www.epistemelinks.com/ This site offers links to sites containing philosophical topics, traditions, and periods as well as biographies, full texts, and related sites on individual philosophers, movements, and works.

PsychREF: Resources in Psychology on the Internet http://maple.lemoyne.edu/~hevern/psychref.html This database is an index to resources for research in psychology, academic skill development, and academic advisement issues such as graduate school or career planning.

Credits

Chapter 3, Figure 3.1, page 31
Population and Demographics: Clarksville-Montgomery County, Tennessee from www.clarksville.tn.us. Used by permission.

Chapter 4, Figure 4.1, page 51
From PsycINFO. Reprinted with permission of the American Psychological Association, publisher of the PsycINFO Database, all rights reserved.

Chapter 5, Figure 5.4, page 67
Reproduced with permission of Yahoo! Inc. Copyright © 2005 by Yahoo! Inc. YAHOO! and the YAHOO! logo are trademarks of Yahoo! Inc.

Chapter 5, Figure 5.5, page 73
Homepage of the *Larchmont Chronicle,* www.larchmontchronicle.com. Used by permission.

Chapter 5
Microsoft product screen shots reprinted with permission from Microsoft Corporation.

Chapter 5, Figure 5.6, page 78
Book search results for "Fad Dieting" from Barnes & Noble, http://www.bn.com. Used by permission.

Chapter 6, pages 85–86
Used with permission from *Reclaiming Children and Youth,* edited by Nicholas J. Long and Larry K. Brendtro, 12:3 (Fall 2003), "From Streaming Mad to Staying Cool" by Eva L. Feindler and Karen E. Starr. For subscription information and to order back issues, contact: Compassion Publishing, Ltd., 3315 North 124th Street, Suite J, Brookfield, WI 53005; phone 262-317-3430 or 1-800-285-7910; fax 262-783-2360; or e-mail: contact@compassionpublishing.com

Chapter 6, page 87
Myriam Mongrain and Lisa C. Vettese, *Personality & Social Psychology Bulletin,* Vol. 29, Issue 4, April 2003, page 545. Copyright 2003 Sage Publications. Reprinted by permission of Sage Publications, Inc.

Chapter 6, pages 87–88
Author's Abstract from "Gender differences in adolescents' behavior during conflict resolution tasks with best friends" by K. A. Black in *Adolescence* 35.139 (Fall 2000). Used by permission.

Chapter 7, page 96
From *The Lessons of Terror* by Caleb Carr, copyright © 2002 by Caleb Carr. Used by permission of Random House, Inc.

Chapter 10, page 144
First three lines from "Morning Song" from Ariel by Sylvia Plath. Copyright © 1961 by Ted Hughes. Reprinted by permission of HarperCollins Publishers and Faber and Faber.

Appendix A, Figure A.3, page A-9
Line graph from "Cognitive Aspects of Psychomotor Performance" by Edwin A. Locke and Judith F. Bryan in the *Journal of Applied Psychology,* Vol. 50, 1966. Used by permission of the author.

Appendix A, Figure A.4, page A-10
Anna H. Live, "Phonemes of Language" from "Pattern in English" from *The Journal of General Education,* Vol. 18, Issue 2, p. 94. Copyright © 1966 by The Pennsylvania State University. Reproduced by permission of the publisher.

Index